THE BOOK OF
CONTAINER
GARDENING

2

2

2

3

3

4

2

3

4

3

3

4

4

5

6

4

5

6

7

6

7

8

7

8

9

11

10

Range of average
annual minimum
temperatures

1	Below -50° F
2	-50° to -40°
3	-40° to -30°
4	-30° to -20°
5	-20° to -10°
6	-10° to 0°
7	0° to 10°
8	10° to 20°
9	20° to 30°
10	30° to 40°
11	Above 40°

THE BOOK OF

CONTAINER GARDENING

MALCOLM HILLIER

Photography by
MATTHEW WARD

SIMON AND SCHUSTER

A DORLING KINDERSLEY BOOK

SIMON AND SCHUSTER
Simon & Schuster Building
Rockefeller Center
1230 Avenue of the Americas
New York, NY 10020

First published in Great Britain
in 1991 by Dorling Kindersley
Publishers Limited
9 Henrietta Street,
London WC2E 8PS

ART EDITOR
Kevin Ryan
PROJECT EDITOR
Mary-Clare Jerram
EDITOR
Susan Thompson
SENIOR ART EDITOR
David Robinson
MANAGING EDITOR
Jane Laing
PRODUCTION MANAGER
Maryann Rogers

Computer page make-up by
The Cooling Brown Partnership
in Great Britain
Text film output by Manuscript
in Great Britain
Color reproduction by Columbia
in Singapore
Printed and bound by
Imago in China

10 9 8 7 6
Library of Congress Cataloging in
Publication Data
Hillier, Malcolm
The book of container gardening/
Malcolm Hillier.
"A Dorling Kindersley book"--T.p.
verso.
Includes index.
ISBN 0-671-72253-0
1. Container gardening. I. Title.
SB418.H55 1991
635.9'86--dc20   90-48624
CIP

CONTENTS

INTRODUCTION

Plants have been grown in decorative and utilitarian containers for thousands of years. From early mosaics and writings, we know that the ancient Egyptians, Greeks, and Romans grew aromatic plants, such as myrtle, box, and bay in clay pots. They were aware that it was a practical and efficient growing technique, especially in areas where the soil was poor or shallow.

✻ In southern Spain, during the early part of the second millennium, the Moors created wonderfully decorative, enclosed, and intimate gardens using many containers. Two famous gardens laid out in the middle of the fourteenth century, at the Alhambra and the Generalife in Granada, survive to this day. They have now been restored and, although they are not completely accurate reproductions of the originals, they still contain the essence of their early design and planting.

—— MEDIEVAL GARDENS ——

In Britain, early illustrated manuscripts of the twelfth, thirteenth, and fourteenth centuries show pots of plants growing in palaces and monastic gardens. However, it was not until the fifteenth and sixteenth centuries that there was a great blossoming of creative gardening. Inspired by the Italians, these designs frequently featured planted containers, often made from stone and lead. In northern Europe, tub-grown citrus fruit trees, emulating the plantings of the Mediterranean countries, were wheeled outside from the shelter of their orangeries during the warmer summer weather to decorate formal paved terraces.

—— THE LAST TWO CENTURIES ——

The same inspiration fired the Victorians with enthusiasm. Production of all types of containers, small as well as large, proliferated during the nineteenth century. They manufactured copies of classical urns in cast iron, as well as the traditional materials: stone, lead, and terracotta. They made elaborate, garlanded and swagged pots for standing on terraces beside well-manicured lawns, and in summer planted them with tender exotics that had been grown in the greenhouse.

✻ The Edwardians, too, cherished a great love of gardens. Conservatories were the rage, and pots of plants, such as begonias, bellflowers, fuchsias, plumbagos, and schizanthus, were moved from them, into the house and garden to provide color and emphasis.

✻ Nowadays, containers are widely used in almost all gardens. Even people without a garden can have a window box or hanging basket on an outside wall. Pots and tubs are invaluable in gardens where growing space is at a premium, but they are also useful for decorating paved terraces, roof gardens, and balconies or verandas.

PANSY BASKET
A small rustic basket of pansies, planted to make a charming feature in a Victorian garden in England. It might have been displayed on a table or bench.

MOORISH INFLUENCE
Decorative containers of plants were used extensively at the fourteenth-century Alhambra gardens, established by the Moors in Granada, Spain.

—— CORRECT CONDITIONS ——

Growing plants is one of life's greatest pleasures. It is so simple, either to start them off from seed or to buy them once they are over their teething problems and tantrums, and raise them, watching the response to a little loving care. I cannot pretend that all plants are easy to grow, but the great majority ask for little more than to be planted in the correct potting mixture, to be given enough water – as well as a little nourishment – from time to time, and to be placed in the right situation. They are rarely overly fussy and soon adapt to conditions which, while they may not be absolutely ideal, are not diametrically opposed to their likes and dislikes. These requirements are factors that I will look at in the following chapters, so that you can assess which plants you may like to grow together and where, in the places available, they will give you their very best display.

Growing plants in containers is a very controlled method of raising them. Each plant, or group of plants, can be given exactly the right type of soil and amounts of water and fertilizer. The site chosen for the container's placement must be taken into account when selecting the plants. Will they have sun or shade, a harsh or a sheltered exposure, or very cold or mild temperatures? Such factors can make or break a display in a very short time. The majority of plants like to grow and flower in sunny or partially sunny positions. A smaller number enjoy the shade, and only a few plants are happy in exposed places.

The elements are harsher on plants in containers, than on their counterparts grown in richly cultivated garden beds or borders. Heat and winds dry out pots and plants in containers quickly, rain does not easily reach their limited soil area, and extreme cold can freeze the pot and root ball solid. However, you can control the watering, and make sure that you place plants that are adversely affected by winds in sheltered positions. If you live in a cold area, avoid growing the more tender plants, or, if you are determined to, take measures to protect them from frost. You can wrap vulnerable specimens in burlap or a good layer of leaves or hay or, if space permits, sink the container into the ground for the winter. The best solution, particularly for tender plants like marguerites and standard fuchsias, is to take them into a greenhouse, conservatory, or a light, unheated room.

—— A DESERVING SITE ——

Container plantings have the benefit of being raised above ground level, which gives them greater importance and visual impact, but you still need to make sure that the plants are being seen and enjoyed to their best advantage, without making them inaccessible for day-to-day maintenance. One of the most enjoyable summer pastimes is eating outside, so grow pots of scented plants close to the garden table: lavender, flowering tobacco plants, lilies, night-scented

NATURAL STONE CONTAINER
The crevices in a wall can be treated like a container garden, and planted with species that require only a little soil. Here, aubrieta and grape hyacinths grow.

stock, scented-leaved geraniums, or climbers such as trachelospermum, angel's trumpets, summer-flowering jasmine, or honeysuckle.

❦ Always consider the ultimate size of the plant in relation to its chosen site. If your windows are small, for example, it is inadvisable to grow large plants in your window boxes, for they will block the light. Conversely, if you place a planting in front of a fence or wall, select something that will grow tall and wide against it. Anything too small will be lost against a large expanse.

—— TYPES OF CONTAINERS ——

The size of the container needs careful consideration. It must neither swamp the plant, nor make it top heavy and put it at the mercy of the winds. And it must be large enough to allow room for proper root development, especially if you intend to grow the larger shrubs and trees.

❦ Containers that have a natural affinity with their surroundings are usually the most attractive. Clay, wood, and stone are my first choices, followed by the materials that simulate them: reconstituted stone, fiberglass, and good plastic. Choose pots that relate to nearby architectural details. Containers in terracotta, natural wood, and stone look good against traditional building materials, while simulated reconstituted stone, white or colored plastic, and fiberglass suit the more austere situations where the background is glass or a painted wall, or the paving is a new material.

❦ In addition to the less usual containers, such as strawberry pots and herb pots, improvised containers can be most effective. Old chimney pots, galvanized buckets, and large painted tins, crates, stone and ceramic sinks, fish kettles, crocks, old saucepans, large shells, a wheelbarrow, metal or plastic bins, or hollowed-out tree trunks can all be used to great effect, at minimal cost.

❦ Containers always work well grouped together. Plant large shrubs or trees in the big containers placed at the back of the collection, and perhaps fill the lower containers in front with annuals, bulbs, and low-growing perennials. There are no rules about grouping containers, although I find that it is generally better not to have too many different types of containers in the same area.

—— WEATHERING EFFECTS ——

Most containers look better when they are well weathered. Left in the sun, patches of white will appear on terracotta, as the salts in the clay leach

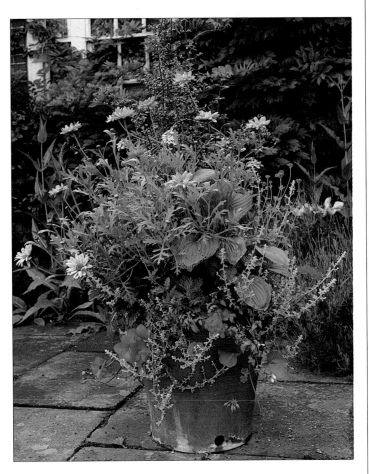

STONE AND TERRACOTTA
A weathered pot on a terrace bursts with hosta leaves, the silver foliage of a licorice plant, and the flowers of chrysanthemums, verbenas, and geraniums. Notice how the terracotta blends with the stone slabs.

out. In shade, moss and lichen will start to grow on the sides of the pot and its color will change, sometimes deepening to a dark rust and sometimes lightening to peach and sandy hues. You can speed up the aging process by painting live yoghurt, soot, and manure on to porous containers; make sure that you coat their top rim as well as their sides.

—— TEMPORARY OR PERMANENT ——

Some container plantings are relatively permanent; the plants can stay in the same pot for many years. Other arrangements can be more temporary, perhaps planted to look attractive for just one or two seasons. As temporary plantings pass their best, provided they are not too heavy, you can move them to less prominent situations. Alternatively, dismantle them and replace the plants with others for the future. A third alternative is to add seasonal color to the more permanent plantings, if there is enough space in the container.

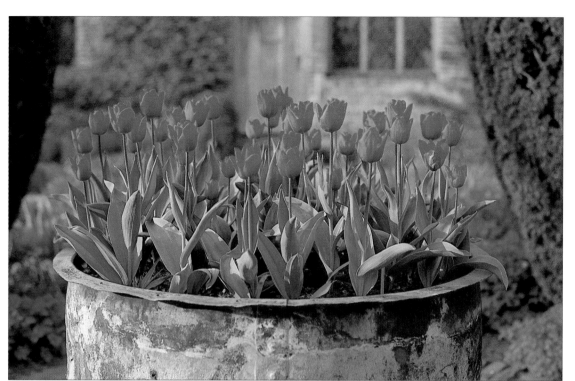

SPRING COLOR
Scarlet tulips (LEFT) grow in an ancient copper pot, corroded by the weather to a stunning, rich, bluey green hue. When the flowers have finished, transplant the bulbs to a border in the garden, and fill the container with colorful bedding annuals for a display during the summer months and into the early autumn.

LEAFY FOIL
A rich planting of fuchsias, geraniums, and lobelias, crammed into an old wooden cart (BELOW). Evergreens, such as the ivy and golden euonymus seen here, are invaluable, providing a leafy foil to the more seasonal flowering annuals.

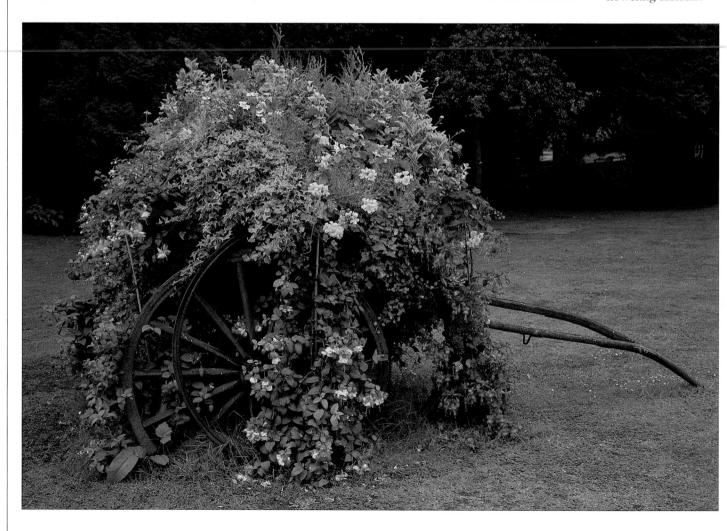

Permanent plantings can consist of shrubs, trees, or perennials, either grown as single specimens, or as a grouping of several of the same type of plant in one container. Temporary seasonal plantings consist of annuals, biennials, and bulbs that look attractive in mixed selections, as well as planted on their own. Before container-grown shrubs or trees have grown too large, and produced root sytems that take up most of the container, they can be underplanted with seasonal color or more permanent trailing plants.

Most annuals grow better in the right container than in the open ground, whereas containerized shrubs, trees, and climbers, although they will grow well, tend not to reach the same size that they would if planted in open ground.

FLOWERS, FOLIAGE, AND FRAGRANCE

The flowering capabilities of shrubs and perennials grown in containers are not as great as for those grown in the open, and so it is wise to consider the benefits of the foliage as well as flowers. If the position receives sun or half-sun, you can consider many wonderful plants with attractive leaves, ranging in color from leaf green through gold, lime, and yellow, to gray, silver, and white, and rust, copper, pink, purple, and plum. The choice for a shady place is slightly more limited, but there are still interesting combinations of plant form, leaf shape or texture, and flowers.

Fragrance is an essential part of the garden. Until quite recently the perfume of flowers, which was so valued in the seventeenth, eighteenth, and nineteenth centuries, had been rather neglected. During this century, the emphasis has been on breeding flowers for their shape, size, and color. Scent has not been a major consideration. Now, perfume is again becoming important, with plant catalogs describing fragrance in glowing terms. Great steps have been made in developing new roses

FLOWERS EVERY SUMMER
The agapanthus filling the wooden tubs lining this sunny wooden deck will flower year after year, provided the winter is not too cold. They thrive when grown in containers, because their roots favor cramped conditions.

that have all the characteristics of the old roses: flower shape, color, and perfume plus the advantage of a long flowering season. Plenty of the smaller-growing roses – the varieties most suitable for container culture – have delicious rich scents.

SEASONAL CHANGES

In most regions, summer is the best season for sumptuous displays, but in hot southern or western areas, spring, autumn, or winter may be far better. The peak season of any garden coincides with the most pleasant weather, maximizing our appreciation of the forms, color combinations, and scents of the plantings. The most popular summer plants have not won their place by chance. They are the ones that flower over a long period. Many summer plantings continue through the autumn, especially if the weather is neither too cold nor windy. Chrysanthemums and asters epitomize autumn with their vibrant display of rich pinks, reds, and oranges.

Where it is cold and gray in winter, rich evergreens can give endless pleasure, enhancing the view from the warmth of your house. Spring too, can be brought close to the windows, with bulbs and other early-flowering plants, either in window boxes or in pots near the house. Our aim should always be to stimulate the senses as much as possible. Container gardening provides you with the chance to create plantings of all shapes and sizes, using trees, shrubs, annuals, perennials, and bulbs, all of which are glorious for their combinations of flower, leaf, and fragrance.

PLANTING DESIGNS

COMBINING PLANTS THAT ENJOY each other's company and growing them in containers, gives great pleasure. The color of flowers and leaves, their shapes and perfumes, are exciting elements with which to play. Pale or bright, tamed or wild, let the plants be an inspiration for your container designs.

HOT COLORS
*Cascading geraniums, bedding dahlias, and modiolastrum make
a vibrant summer planting.*

WINDOW BOXES

O N A COLD winter's morning, I love looking out of the kitchen window at the rich, golden-green plants sitting in the window boxes, just beyond the pane of glass. It is a spot that never catches the sun, but it is quite bright and the plants always look happy. Nearly everyone can have a window box or two, even if they live high above the ground with no garden at the front or back. Of course, window boxes need not be used only in window recesses. They can look most effective resting on the ground against a wall or a fence, or edging a balcony so that trailing plants can cascade down the side of the building.

——— CLOSE FIT ———

Window boxes on sills look best if they almost fit the window recess. Boxes are manufactured in a range of sizes, so that it is usually possible to find one that is a suitable size for your sill. They are also made in a great range of materials: plastic, fiberglass, composition wood, and terracotta. Some of the plastic ones are not very strong. In the middle, they tend to bulge outward with the weight of soil, although clips are available from stores to help keep the box in shape. They are the cheapest, and they are mostly available in white, black, and green. Stronger plastic window boxes are sold in various forms, but I find that the plainer ones look best. Fiberglass is a more expensive material, but it is rigid and will last for many years. Plain designs and models made to resemble lead or painted wood are available.

⚔ Wooden boxes always look good because of their natural affinity to plant material, but they will eventually rot, even if well-treated with wood preservatives and painted every year. You

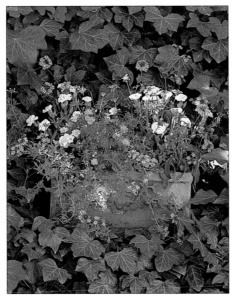

INFORMAL IVY SETTING
A small terracotta box (ABOVE) decorated with angels' heads, and filled with pinks, swan river daisies, and verbenas sits comfortably on the ledge of an ivy-covered wall.

FRENCH-STYLE WINDOW BOX
A mass of ivy-leaved geraniums (LEFT), tumble out of a window box in France. To achieve this effect, the geraniums should be planted 7-8in (18-20cm) apart.

can get around this problem by using a well-made plastic box that fits your sill, with a little room to spare at each side, and then making a wooden cover for it. You drop the newly planted plastic box into the completed wooden cover. When choosing a color for your wooden cover, it is best to let the plants be the masters of the box: extremely brightly colored or over-decorated boxes can detract from the natural beauty of the flowers and foliage in your planting.

——— TERRACOTTA OPTION ———

Because of the beautiful natural quality of terracotta, I find that window boxes made in this material always tend to look most effective. Before buying anything, measure your window sill to ensure a good fit. Bear in mind that in exposed situations soft terracotta can easily flake and crack, so in cold areas it may be best to avoid using it, except during the warm summer and early autumn months, before the damaging frosts arrive.

——— SAFE AND SECURE ———

Window boxes can be extremely heavy, especially when they have been watered, so you must fix them securely in place. On sills that slope gently forward, prop up the front of the box, slightly, to keep it level, and secure metal brackets either to the sides of the window recess or on the sill itself to prevent the window box from slipping forward.

⚔ Window box arrangements in sunny spots need plenty of water in hot summer weather, so prevent excess water from running down the side of the building by placing a tray under the box. Plastic trays are available from most garden centers. Remember not to leave the container sitting in water.

PERFUME AND PETUNIAS

I T IS ALL TOO EASY to plant the same old favorite annuals every year, knowing that they will do well, flower for several months a year, and provide plenty of color. For greater interest, I try to use my favorites in combination with some lesser-known plants.

❦ Here, petunias – immensely hard-working plants producing masses of flowers – are associated with the sweetly scented, rich purple heads of heliotrope, spikes of cream and purple salvias, and variegated pink and silver-leaved trails of wandering jew – plants that all thrive when grown together. Remember that petunias should be planted in new soil each season to ensure that they will not suffer from petunia wilt passed on from the previous year. Otherwise they need little attention, except for watering and a weekly dose of liquid fertilizer.

PRACTICAL MATTERS

SOIL
Plant in a well-drained potting mixture of medium nutritional value.
SITE
Place in a sunny position.
WATERING
Keep well-watered but not soggy. Give liquid fertilizer once a week.
PLANTS
Grow four petunias, three heliotropes, three salvias, and three wandering jews in a 30in- (75cm-) long, terracotta window box.

∽ PLANTING A WINDOW BOX ∽

1 *Thoroughly clean the window box with warm water and a mild detergent. Cover the base with clean pebbles or pottery chips.*

2 *Half fill the terracotta window box with a well-drained potting mixture of medium nutritional value. If the potting mixture has dried out, dampen it before you start planting.*

3 *Experiment with the positioning of the plants while they are still in their pots until you are happy with the effect, placing the taller plants at the rear, and the trailing ones at the sides and toward the front. Turn the plants out of their pots, loosen the roots at the base of each root ball, then firm the plants into place with more potting mixture. When the planting is completed, the soil level should be about ¾in (2cm) below the top of the planter, to facilitate watering.*

Plant Positions

The heliotrope (RIGHT) tends to become straggly, so it is best planted at the back of the window box. Initially, pinch out the growing tips to encourage bushy growth. Position the petunias and wandering jews toward the front, with the upright salvias in between. Plant in early summer. This arrangement will flower for only one season.

• Heliotrope
(*Heliotropium arborescens*)
The scent of the flowers is reminiscent of cooked cherries, hence its common name of 'cherry pie'.

• Petunia (*Petunia* x *hybrida*)
The white-striped flowers come in a wide range of cheerful colors.

• Salvia
(*Salvia splendens*)
Spikes of flowers appear in summer, autumn, and all year in frost-free zones

Victorian Theme

The rich plum, purple, and white coloring of the petunias, heliotrope, salvias, and trailing wandering jew, growing in an old window box, gives the arrangement a slightly Victorian feel.

• Wandering jew (*Tradescantia fluminensis* 'Variegata')
A good trailing plant for a window box of summer annuals.

SUN LOVERS FOR A WINDOW SILL

I LIKE PLANTINGS that make a positive statement. This does not necessarily mean that the colors should always be brilliant, nor that the leaf and flower shapes of the various species should be strikingly different. It suggests that the arrangement should have a sense of structure about it, which makes it look both inevitable and interesting.

✱ In this summer window box, yellow gazanias spill down over the edge of the container, below mounds of delicate foliage and large gold and cream zinnia flowers, leaving the sides exposed in an unexpected way. Notice how well all the colors work together: although the scheme is predominantly gold and yellow, silver gazania leaves and white and yellow, golden feverfew flowers were introduced for contrast. I do not believe in adhering to rules relating to color and form because, if you do, the plantings tend to become boring and predictable. Give free rein to your imagination. Successful arrangements combine common sense with a touch of daring.

Zinnia (*Zinnia elegans*)
For optimum flowering, deadhead regularly.

Golden marjoram (*Origanum vulgare* 'Aureum')
A delicious herb that looks good, too.

Golden feverfew (*Chrysanthemum parthenium* 'Aureum')
Cut back regularly to encourage bushy flowering stems.

Summer Sunshine

✱ Mixing flowering annuals with plants that have interesting foliage can give even the most stalwart of old faithfuls a new look. Here, zinnias and trailing gazanias are combined with the striking foliage of golden marjoram and golden feverfew to create a planting that instantly spells summer. The gazanias and zinnias both need sun for their flowers to open; the flowers of golden marjoram, however, are best removed to promote its fine display of leaves.

Gazania (*Gazania rigens*)
A beautiful combination of silver leaves and yellow flowers.

PRACTICAL MATTERS

SOIL
Plant in a well-drained potting mixture of medium nutritional value.

SITE
Place in a sunny position.

WATERING
Take care not to overwater. Feed once a week.

PLANTS
Grow two gazanias, four zinnias, two golden marjorams, and two golden feverfews in a 30in- (75cm-) long, yellow-painted wooden window box.

Blue Backdrop
❦ Planted boxes need not always sit on window sills. This box is set against the base of an old unused door. The door's deep blue coloring gives the yellows and golds of the summer flowers tremendous strength.

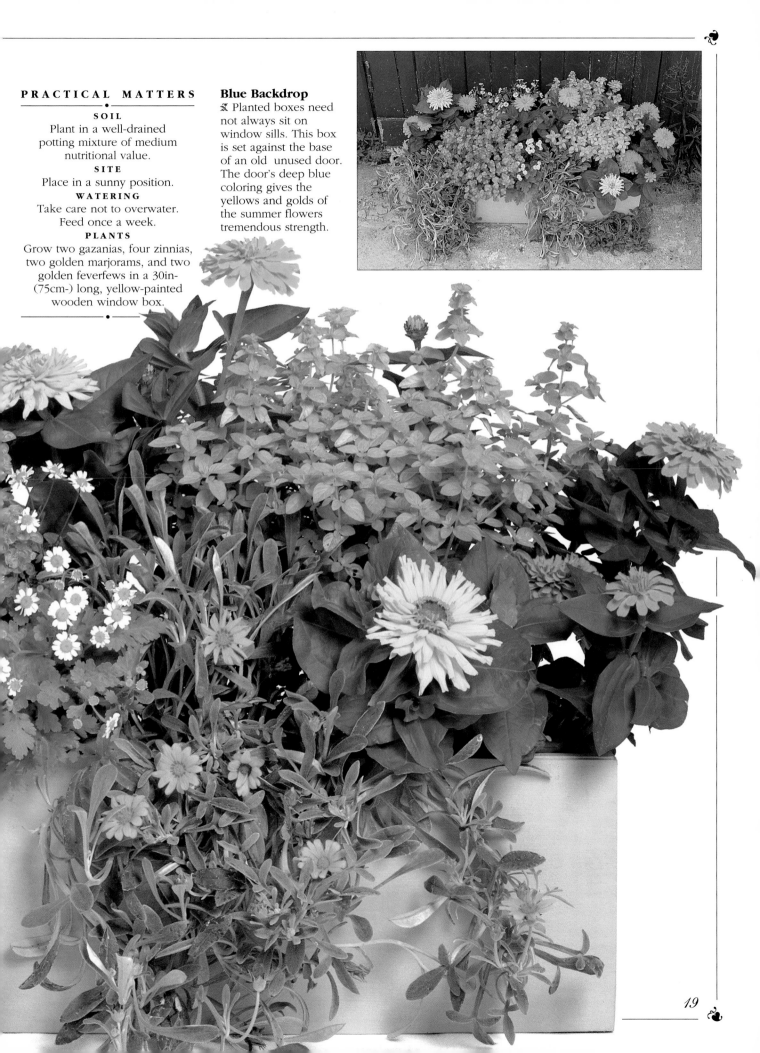

SHIMMERING FLOWERS AND FOLIAGE

SILVER FOLIAGE AND WHITE FLOWERS combine to create a delicate shimmering effect in a simple, white plastic window box. This summery scheme is best placed on a low window sill that sees plenty of sun, and is also situated well away from the road – pollution does not suit silver-leaved plants and quickly covers white flowers with a dirty sheen. The zonal geraniums and the marguerites need deadheading to encourage a continuous display.

� Other white-flowered plants could replace the geraniums: white varieties of bellflowers, petunias, pansies, impatiens, and flowering tobacco plants all give a spectacular summer show. Choose a combination that gives interesting contrasts.

Santolina (*Santolina neapolitana* 'Sulphurea')
Pale yellow flowers appear above the silver aromatic leaves in mid summer.

Dusty miller (*Senecio maritima*)
Treated as an annual, its fine silvery foliage grows very quickly and may need an occasional trim.

White and Silver

The plain, white plastic window box sets off the various leaf shapes and textures provided by the silver plants in this bright arrangement, and yet at the same time reflects the pure white of the geraniums and marguerites. Notice how the pale yellow santolina flowers add just a hint of color variation.

Zonal geranium
(*Pelargonium* 'Modesty')
A pretty, pure white form of one of the most reliable of annuals.

Marguerite
(*Chrysanthemum frutescens*)
A small-flowered variety, ideal for growing in a window box.

PRACTICAL MATTERS

SOIL
Plant in a well-drained potting mixture of medium nutritional value.

SITE
Place in a sunny position.

WATERING
Water well, but do not allow to become soggy at any time.

PLANTS
Grow three zonal geraniums, two marguerites, two dusty millers, two southernwoods, one santolina, and four plecostachys in an 32in- (80cm-) long, white plastic window box.

Southernwood
(*Artemisia abrotanum*)
A semi-evergreen shrub with strongly fragrant foliage.

Plecostachys
(*Plecostachys serpyllifolium*)
The delicate silver foliage of this small-leaved tender perennial cascades over the window box.

THE LAST OF SUMMER

WHILE WE TEND TO THINK of annuals in terms of the flowers they produce and their flowering time, many species and varieties also have leaves that can be used to great effect. Three of the varieties in this planting boast attractive foliage, although the variegated nasturtiums with their wonderful green leaves splashed with cream have taken over the front of the arrangement.

🌿 Coleus, seen toward the back, is grown solely for its leaves, which come in a startling array of colors. Begonias have the bonus of both decorative flowers and foliage. Their strongly veined, heart-shaped leaves make a bold statement in any planting, and their flowers appear for months. Begonias and nasturtiums flower particularly well in autumn when many other annuals start to taper off.

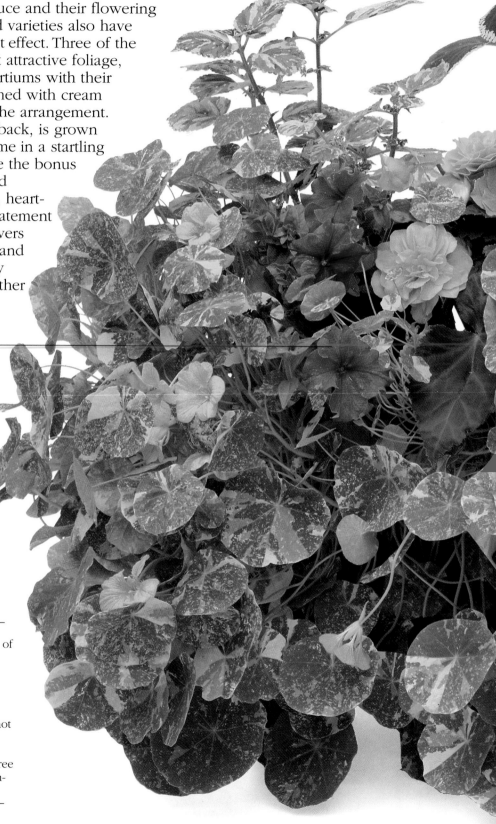

Petunia (*Petunia x hybrida*)
The red flowers are not blemished by bad weather.

Rampant Growers
🌿 All the annuals in this planting – especially the nasturtiums – are vigorous growers, so do not put them in an interesting or decorative window box. At the height of the display the flowers and foliage will conceal the sides.

PRACTICAL MATTERS

SOIL
Plant in a well-drained potting mixture of medium nutritional value.

SITE
Place in a sunny site that is not too exposed to wind.

WATERING
Water to keep the soil just moist, but not soggy. Do not overfeed.

PLANTS
Grow five nasturtiums, three coleus, three begonias, and three petunias in a 28in- (70cm-) long, plastic window box.

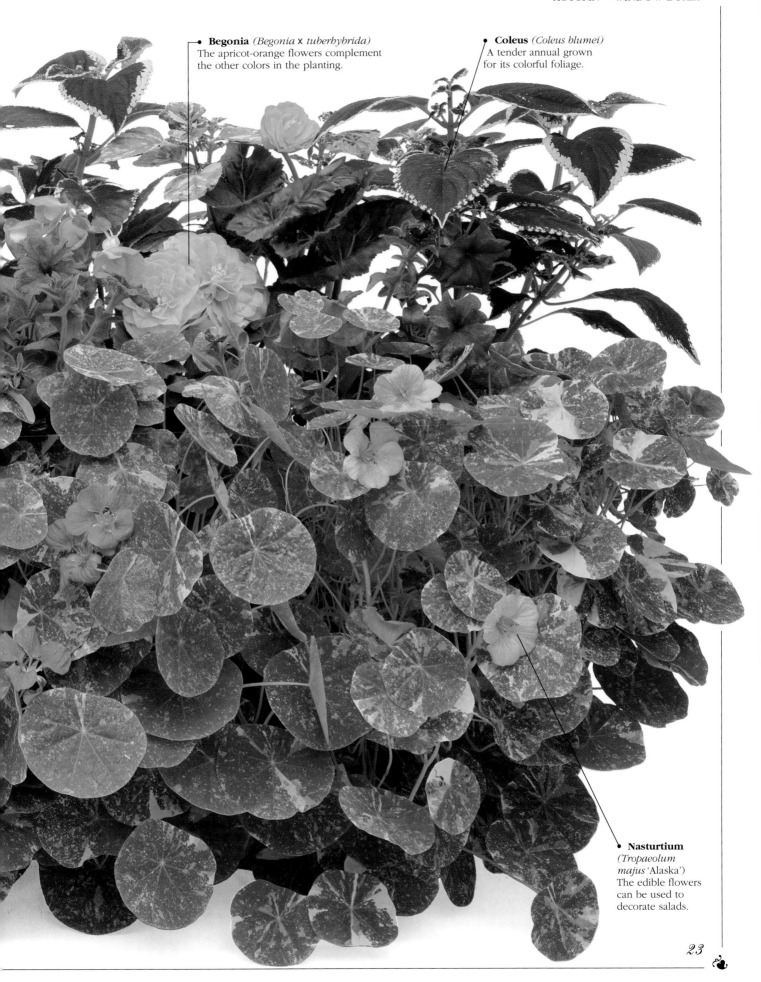

• **Begonia** (*Begonia* x *tuberhybrida*)
The apricot-orange flowers complement
the other colors in the planting.

• **Coleus** (*Coleus blumei*)
A tender annual grown
for its colorful foliage.

• **Nasturtium**
(*Tropaeolum
majus* 'Alaska')
The edible flowers
can be used to
decorate salads.

HAZE OF HEATHERS

WITH THE ENORMOUS RANGE of varieties available, it is possible to have heathers in flower every month of the year. They do have very specific growing needs – acid soil and moist conditions – but by growing them in a container, you can easily meet these requirements, encouraging the plants to perform well. *Calluna vulgaris*, the species in this white window box, has had many varieties developed from it, with flowers that vary from pink, through purple and lilac, to white. The spires of flowers appear from late summer until early winter, depending on the variety, and are excellent in combination with conifers, which enjoy the same conditions.

✗ When the heathers have finished flowering, cut off the flower heads. With its mixed foliage, this planting will continue to look attractive throughout the winter. Otherwise, replace the heathers with varieties of *Erica* x *darleyensis,* which have pretty pink, cream, or red flowers during the winter months.

• **Heather** (*Calluna vulgaris*)
A hardy evergreen, flowering from late summer to early winter.

Moorland Flowers
✗ The misty colors of the heathers (RIGHT) are backed by silver-gray clouds of cypress foliage. To make the flowers last, give the heathers a daily water spray to simulate the conditions of their native moorland.

PRACTICAL MATTERS
•
SOIL
Plant in an ericaceous (acid) potting mixture, peat, and sharp sand (proportions 3:2:1).
SITE
Place in a sunny position, which is sheltered from cold winds.
WATERING
Water to keep the plants moist during mild weather, and give a liquid fertilizer once a month.
PLANTS
Grow five Lawson's cypress, five heathers, and four ivies in a 30in- (75cm-) long, plastic window box.
•

● Lawson's cypress
(*Chamaecyparis
lawsoniana* 'Nana Glauca')
A slow-growing conifer.

● Ivy (*Hedera helix* 'Elegance')
A trailing silver-edged variety.

Clipped Hedge

✄ Clip the conifers in this window box
(ABOVE) to make a miniature hedge at the
back of the arrangement. This is best done
from mid summer to autumn, when the
new growth is established. Thereafter, give
them an occasional clip, perhaps twice a
year, to keep them trim and neat.

ARRAY OF EVERGREENS

A SURPRISINGLY WIDE SELECTION of evergreen plants have interestingly shaped or attractively colored foliage, which makes them useful for year-round container plantings, and winter arrangements in particular. Extremely harsh winters can be a problem for plants in containers, but a small selection can withstand the icy winter onslaught. Those with interesting foliage include abelia, cotoneaster, Cornish heath, euonymus, holly, calico bush, privet, box, ivy, lavender, andromeda, periwinkle, and many conifers: false cypress, juniper, spruce, yew, and Eastern hemlock, to name just a few possibilities.

✗ For an amusing winter arrangement, plant decorative cabbages and evergreen skimmia in autumn (SEE PAGES 164-5). Their bright colorful leaves will bring pleasure through the winter months. Like edible cabbages, the decorative forms eventually bolt, so you will have to pull them out in spring.

✗ Containers, too, can suffer in very low temperatures: terracotta and glazed ceramic pots often break in cold weather. Some are frost-proofed when they are made, so if you live in a frost-prone area, check before you buy.

PRACTICAL MATTERS

SOIL
Plant in a slightly acid potting mixture.
SITE
Place in a sheltered, sunny or semi-shady position.
WATERING
Water occasionally. Do not water when temperatures fall below freezing.
PLANTS
Grow three skimmias, five dusty millers, and four winter cherries in a 32in-(80cm-) long, wooden window box.

Winter Buds and Berries
✗ A white, wooden window box makes an excellent foil for this mix of dark greens, silvers, and orange. In temperate climates the planting will give a bright display from late autumn to early summer, with the skimmias producing pink buds throughout the winter and white flowers in the summer. This planting is not suitable for very cold or very hot regions.

• **Winter cherry**
(Solanum capsicastrum)
An invaluable plant for winter color in containers.

Arborvitae •
(*Thuja orientalis*
'Aurea Nana')
If left to mature, these
compact golden balls
of leaves will eventually
become conical.

Mexican orange •
(*Choisya ternata* 'Sundance')
The leaves stay golden all year.
Scented flowers open
in late spring.

• **Juniper** (*Juniperus conferta*)
A low spreading conifer, ideal for
growing at the front of a window box.

• **Euonymus** (*Euonymus
fortunei* 'Emerald 'n' Gold')
The glowing gold and green
foliage is tinged pink in winter.

• **Skimmia** (*Skimmia
japonica* 'Rubella')
For a good crop of berries,
most female skimmias need
a male pollinator nearby.

• **Dusty miller**
(*Senecio maritima*)
Usually grown as
annuals, these silver-
leaved plants often
survive mild winters.

Golden Glow

⚹ A honey-colored, reconstituted stone
window box supports a variety of golden
and green-leaved shrubs. Particular care
over the positioning of the plants creates an
arresting overall shape. This arrangement
looks attractive throughout the year.

PRACTICAL MATTERS
———— • ————
SOIL
Plant in a potting mixture of medium
nutritional value.
SITE
Suitable for any position.
WATERING
Water once every two weeks in winter,
unless temperatures fall below freezing. In
summer, keep moist and feed once a month.
PLANTS
Grow two arborvitae, two Mexican oranges,
three euonymus, and one juniper in a 38in-
(105cm-) long, reconstituted
stone window box.
———— • ————

TERRACOTTA BAROQUE

WITH ITS DECORATIVE, pale blue swirls and owl-like feet, this fascinating window box suggests a planting with an unusual color scheme. Although many colors would work well in it, these apricots, pinks, maroons, and rusts are especially effective. The apricot hyacinths pick up the color of the container and blend surprisingly well with the pinks. The maroon and rust auriculas accentuate the pink of the tulips, and the touch of yellow heightens the effect of the other colors, bringing the whole scheme to life.

—— SPRING SCENTS ——

This is an arrangement that appeals to the nose as well as delights the eye. Hyacinths have a perfume that seems to epitomize spring, although it can be almost too strong. Auriculas release a sweet fresh scent, slightly reminiscent of early irises. More delicate but quite pervasive is the smell of the polyanthus, and even the tulips have a light, sweet peppery perfume.

—— TENDER CARE ——

All primulas are excellent for growing in containers, although the auriculas must be protected from rain and frost to flower perfectly. The shelter of a window recess provides an ideal site. Care will be rewarded, for few garden flowers have such extraordinary yet beautiful color combinations.

PRACTICAL MATTERS

SOIL
Plant in a lightweight potting mixture of medium nutritional value.

SITE
Place in a sunny or semi-shady position, sheltered from excessive rain.

WATERING
Keep barely moist, but not dry.

PLANTS
Grow seven hyacinths, six auriculas, ten tulips, and three polyanthus in a 27in- (68cm-) long, handmade, terracotta window box.

Hyacinth
(*Hyacinthus orientalis* 'Orange Boven')
Like most hyacinths, this variety has a delicious scent.

Polyanthus
(*Primula vulgaris* hybrids)
Sadly, these do not grow well in hot weather.

Clay Swirls
The box is best placed at eye-level so that it can be seen to its maximum advantage. Hyacinths, tulips, auriculas, and polyanthus vie for attention in this decorative, handmade window box. I avoided using any trailing plants, such as periwinkle or ivy, as they would cover the front of the container and conceal its striking pattern.

Tulip *(Tulipa* 'Peach Blossom')
A pretty double variety which
flowers in early spring.

Auricula
(Primula auricula)
These alpine
primulas are
available in an
extraordinary
range of
colors.

Ornamental terracotta
The color wash slip on this
highly ornate window box
helps soften the harsh color
of new terracotta.

FAVORED HELLEBORES

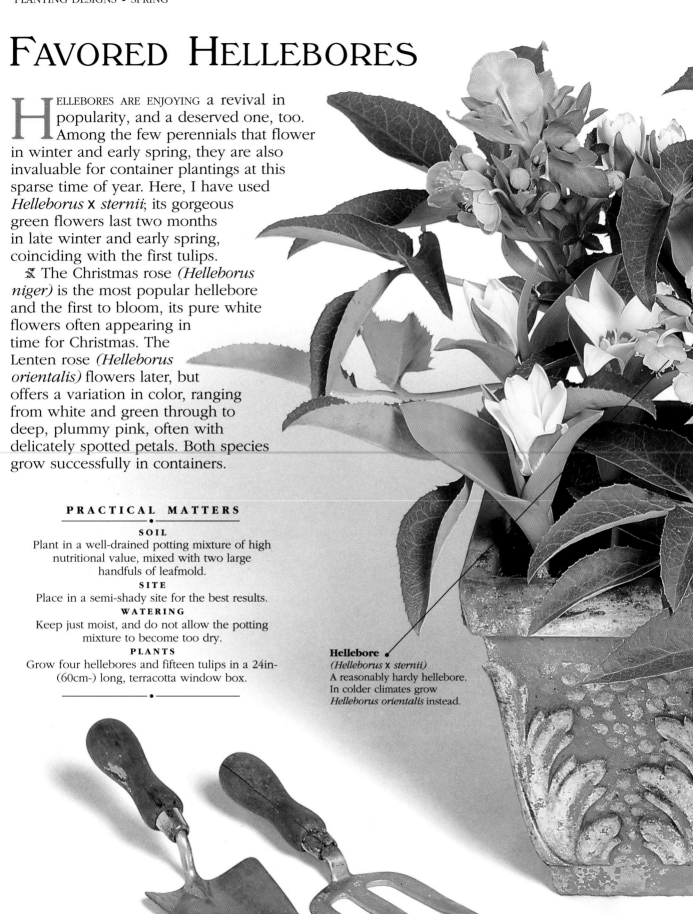

HELLEBORES ARE ENJOYING a revival in popularity, and a deserved one, too. Among the few perennials that flower in winter and early spring, they are also invaluable for container plantings at this sparse time of year. Here, I have used *Helleborus* x *sternii*; its gorgeous green flowers last two months in late winter and early spring, coinciding with the first tulips.

❧ The Christmas rose *(Helleborus niger)* is the most popular hellebore and the first to bloom, its pure white flowers often appearing in time for Christmas. The Lenten rose *(Helleborus orientalis)* flowers later, but offers a variation in color, ranging from white and green through to deep, plummy pink, often with delicately spotted petals. Both species grow successfully in containers.

PRACTICAL MATTERS

SOIL
Plant in a well-drained potting mixture of high nutritional value, mixed with two large handfuls of leafmold.

SITE
Place in a semi-shady site for the best results.

WATERING
Keep just moist, and do not allow the potting mixture to become too dry.

PLANTS
Grow four hellebores and fifteen tulips in a 24in- (60cm-) long, terracotta window box.

Hellebore
(Helleborus x *sternii)*
A reasonably hardy hellebore. In colder climates grow *Helleborus orientalis* instead.

Waterlily tulip
(*Tulipa* 'Ancilla')
A low-growing
kaufmanniana
hybrid, favored
for early spring
plantings.

China-like Flowers
◁ A simple, yet effective,
early spring planting of
hellebores and tulips
growing in a decorative,
terracotta window box.
The striped tulips are an
interesting foil to the
hellebores. Position the
window box where you
can appreciate the delicacy
of the hellebores' almost
china-like flowers.

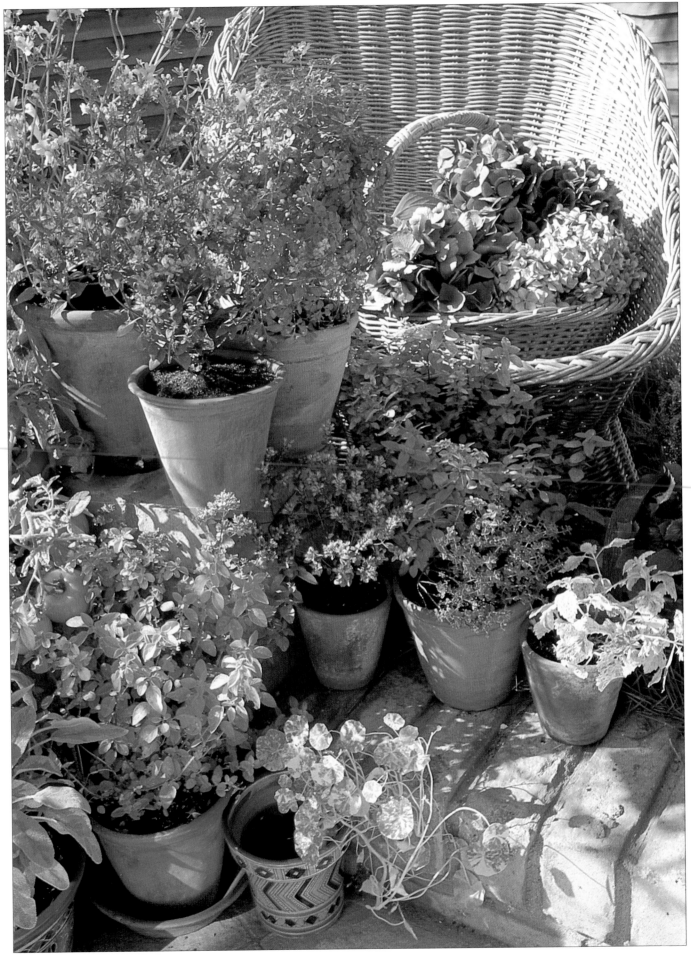

POTS

THE TRADITIONAL flower pot, with sides that slope outward slightly, has been used in gardens since Roman times. Until recently, this type of pot was always made out of terracotta, a once-fired, porous red clay, which is very attractive but can crack and flake with weathering in very cold temperatures. Sometimes, elements are added to the clay before it is fired to make it frost-proof. If you live in a cold area where frosts are likely, make sure that the terracotta you buy has been treated this way.

�器 Decorative, glazed ceramic pots, often from the Far East, Italy, and Spain, are now widely available. They come in a beautiful range of colors, but tend to be even less frost-proof, for glaze can easily crack. However, many are frost-resistant so always check before you buy.

�器 As terracotta is a highly porous material, it absorbs a lot of moisture from the potting mixture; the moisture then evaporates into the air. Because of this, plants in terracotta pots require more frequent watering than plants in plastic pots. It is also advisable to soak terracotta pots thoroughly before planting them because it is essential that new plants have a plentiful supply of water to start them off.

—— PATINA OF AGE ——

Over the last thirty years, plastic pots have become widely used. They are cheaper than terracotta, frost-proof, and, because they are not porous, absorb less moisture from the soil. But this means that they do not take on a patina of age, and it is this patina which, I think, makes terracotta pots so beautiful and so much more interesting to plant. If I use terracotta, I usually

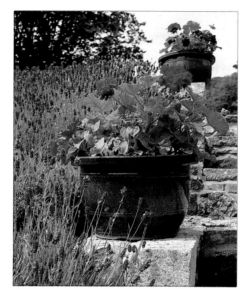

CHINESE CERAMICS
Set against a sea of lavender, blue-glazed Chinese pots of zonal geraniums (ABOVE) stand grandly on the plinths bordering a flight of brick and stone steps.

PAINT EFFECTS
Sun-loving herbs (LEFT) grow in a selection of color-washed terracotta pots, an effect achieved by applying a dilute water-based paint to the outsides of the pots.

paint the outside of the pot with a coat of live yoghurt to speed up the weathering process. Placed in a shady position, it soon becomes covered with moss; if it is in a sunny spot, gray-white patches develop. Pots made of stone or reconstituted stone can also be weathered in this way.

�器 For a change from the traditional color of terracotta, which tends to be on the harsh side, you can give pots a color-wash (LEFT), by applying a wash of dilute water-based paint. I find that the blue-green colors and terracotta-pinks are the most effective – try to avoid yellows as they do not work as well as the other colors.

—— POT COLLECTION ——

Small pots can often make more of an impact on a terrace or patio if they are arranged in a group. They also look stunning on an old, wire-work plant stand (SEE PAGE 127). They need not be exactly the same design or size. Indeed, the grouping usually looks more effective if it consists of different-sized and shaped pots. You can also have fun mixing and matching the different materials from which they are made. Stone, reconstituted stone, and terracotta all look fine side-by-side. More unusual is a mixture of glazed ceramic pots, well-designed plastic, or fiberglass containers in sympathetic colors, and metal pots with subtle sheens; they can also complement each other, giving a sophisticated look.

✱ I find that pots are also useful in herbaceous borders. Filled with flowering plants or colorful foliage, pots can add interest to a patch that lacks color at a particular time of year. They can also help to introduce a little height to an area with low-growing plants or a newly planted plot.

JUST TULIPS

SIMPLE SPRING BULBS, such as tulips, hyacinths, crocuses, and narcissi, are easy to grow in pots, as well as in any other sort of container. They are not demanding and the cold rarely affects them. Only high winds and torrential rain, when the tulips are in bloom, can mar their brilliant display.

Tulips have been highly valued for many centuries by gardeners, encouraging the bulb hybridizers to develop more and more forms. Bulb growers specify whether the bulbs are early, mid, or late season, but it is always a little hit or miss. To ensure that all the flowers in an arrangement come out at once, it is best to grow only one variety in each pot, unless you know the varieties well.

—— LAYERED PLANTING PLAN ——

Plant the bulbs in mid to late autumn, as soon as you get them home from the garden center. Do not allow them to dry out. Provided they are in good condition, you can plant them up until early winter. Expect them to flower four to five months after planting. To get best results, plant fresh bulbs each autumn and move the old bulbs into the garden.

For a dense tulip planting and magnificent show, plant the bulbs in two layers. This way you will pack twice as many bulbs in, and therefore have twice as many flowers later, giving a spectacular display. Here, I have risked growing two different varieties together: a dramatic yellow and red striped parrot tulip with an attractive, deep-red fringed form. I have grown both these forms in the past and I know that they should flower simultaneously.

⌁ PLANTING A POT OF BULBS ⌁

1 *Place clean pebbles or pottery chips over the drainage holes, and add charcoal to keep the soil sweet. Next, firm in a slightly alkaline potting mixture to about 8in (20cm) from the top of the container. Place the 'Flaming Parrot' bulbs on this, 1in (2cm) apart.*

2 *Sprinkle more of the potting mixture over the bulbs until they are nearly covered. Place a layer of 'Redwing' tulip bulbs above the gaps between the bulbs in the first layer. Fill with potting mixture to 1in (2cm) below the top of the pot to facilitate watering. Water lightly.*

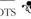

Perfect Partners

☙ Tulips come in an enormous range of flower shapes and colors, presenting the enterprizing gardener with endless opportunities to create eye-catching combinations. With their yellow and red coloring, but varied flower form and difference in height, 'Flaming Parrot' and 'Redwing' make excellent companions. Both are late-flowering hybrids.

PRACTICAL MATTERS

SOIL
Plant in a well-drained, slightly alkaline potting mixture.
SITE
Place in a sunny or shady position.
WATERING
Keep the potting mixture just moist, but do not water in extremely cold conditions.
PLANTS
Grow twelve 'Redwing' tulip bulbs and fifteen 'Flaming Parrot' bulbs in a 12in- (30cm-) diameter ceramic pot.

• **Parrot tulip** (*Tulipa* 'Flaming Parrot')
The parrot tulips are distinguished by their frilly-edged petals. All flower in late spring.

• **Tulip** (*Tulipa* 'Redwing')
A deep red, incurved flower with fringed edges to its petals.

Pink Tulip Picture

☙ 'Picture,' distinguished by its pale pink, waxy flowers, is an especially attractive tulip for an old, weathered terracotta pot. I planted twenty bulbs in this pot, which measures 12in (30cm) in diameter, and then covered the potting mixture with moss.

TOWERS FOR FLOWERS

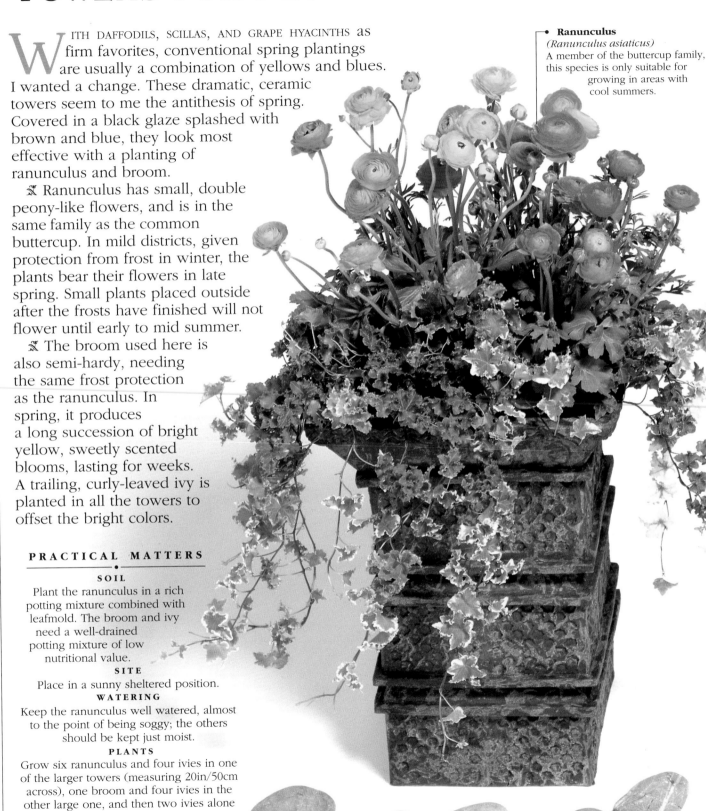

WITH DAFFODILS, SCILLAS, AND GRAPE HYACINTHS as firm favorites, conventional spring plantings are usually a combination of yellows and blues. I wanted a change. These dramatic, ceramic towers seem to me the antithesis of spring. Covered in a black glaze splashed with brown and blue, they look most effective with a planting of ranunculus and broom.

Ranunculus has small, double peony-like flowers, and is in the same family as the common buttercup. In mild districts, given protection from frost in winter, the plants bear their flowers in late spring. Small plants placed outside after the frosts have finished will not flower until early to mid summer.

The broom used here is also semi-hardy, needing the same frost protection as the ranunculus. In spring, it produces a long succession of bright yellow, sweetly scented blooms, lasting for weeks. A trailing, curly-leaved ivy is planted in all the towers to offset the bright colors.

• **Ranunculus**
(Ranunculus asiaticus)
A member of the buttercup family, this species is only suitable for growing in areas with cool summers.

PRACTICAL MATTERS

SOIL
Plant the ranunculus in a rich potting mixture combined with leafmold. The broom and ivy need a well-drained potting mixture of low nutritional value.

SITE
Place in a sunny sheltered position.

WATERING
Keep the ranunculus well watered, almost to the point of being soggy; the others should be kept just moist.

PLANTS
Grow six ranunculus and four ivies in one of the larger towers (measuring 20in/50cm across), one broom and four ivies in the other large one, and then two ivies alone in the smaller tower (measuring 12in/30cm).

Ivy *(Hedera helix* 'Parsley Crested') Distinguished by a mass of light green, frilly leaves.

Pebbled Setting
⚜ A sunny combination of ranunculus, broom, and ivy that looks cheerful even in dull weather. Place this arrangement on a pebbled area, or stone or gray brick pavings. An ivy-clad wall would provide the perfect background.

Broom *(Cytisus canariensis)* The sweet perfume of this broom from the Canary Islands carries well on the air.

Ceramic towers
Handmade pots with a matt black, brown, and blue glaze make striking containers for plants.

ELEGANT COMPANIONS

Only a handful of spring bulbs grow to a good size. They include Solomon's seal (BELOW), which flowers in late spring and early summer and likes a shady or semi-shady site, and the crown imperials (RIGHT). Grown in three colors – yellow, orange, or deep red – the crown imperials are at their best in mid to late spring in a semi-shady or sunny spot. While the crown imperials are very imposing, the Solomon's seal is cool, quiet, and elegant. Both bear their flowers well above ground level, so they look best if they are underplanted with a mound of low-growing plants in complementary colors that flower at the same time. Pansies and forget-me-nots fulfil this role well, but English daisies or aubretia are viable alternatives. The crown imperials and the Solomon's seal flower in their pots for several years. After flowering, let the soil dry out and the foliage die down.

— WEATHERED TERRACOTTA —

Both these arrangements are planted in swagged terracotta pots. To hasten the weathering process, I painted yoghurt on the pot holding the crown imperials. The yoghurt attracted moss and lichen, which look especially effective on pots with raised patterns.

PRACTICAL MATTERS
•
SOIL
Plant in a well-drained potting mixture of high nutritional value.
SITE
Place in a semi-shady site.
WATERING
Keep just moist in winter and spring. Do not water in frosty weather.
PLANTS
Grow two clumps of Solomon's seal, and five forget-me-nots in a 15in- (38cm-) diameter, swagged terracotta pot.
•

Solomon's seal
(*Polygonatum* x *hybridum*)
The white, hanging trumpet-shaped flowers are flushed green.

Forget-me-not
(*Myosotis* 'Blue Ball')
The clear blue flowers fade to pink. A variety best grown as a biennial.

Dappled Shade
The graceful arching stems of the Solomon's seal rise sedately from a froth of blue forget-me-nots, its white flowers nodding above. One of my favorite combinations, this planting looks special in the dappled shade of a tree that has just come into leaf.

Crown imperial
(Fritillaria imperialis 'Lutea')
Plant the bulbs in autumn
for blooms in mid spring.

Pansy *(Viola* x
wittrockiana
Universal Series)
A beautiful apricot strain
flowering from early spring
to mid summer.

PRACTICAL MATTERS

SOIL
Plant in a well-drained potting mixture
of medium nutritional value.

SITE
Place in a sunny or
semi-shady position.

WATERING
Water to keep the soil just moist. After
flowering, let the soil dry out.

PLANTS
Grow eight crown imperial bulbs and
six pansies in a 17in- (42cm-)
diameter terracotta pot.

Regal Golds
❧ The combination of
yellow crown imperials
and orange pansies
works well in the
weathered terracotta
pot. Unfortunately,
crown imperials have a
rank odor, so place the
pot where it can be
seen, but not smelled.

FLAMBOYANT AZALEAS

AZALEAS AND OTHER RHODODENDRONS are extremely easy to grow in containers. In their native habitats they are woodland plants, so they perform best in acid soil and in dappled shade; they do not like very hot, dry summer weather. Ideally, you should grow them by themselves, or with another permanent planting so that you avoid disturbing their roots too frequently.

—— SPRING FLOWERS ——

Most azaleas flower for just a few weeks in late spring, but they are especially useful for filling an awkward gap in the gardening calendar, after the bulb season has finished but before the summer flowers begin. Their flowers, which often smother the plant, cover an enormous range of colors. Remove them once they have died so that the plant will put its energy into new growth, instead of producing seed. Feed when they have finished flowering, but only until mid summer, otherwise too much late soft growth will develop.

—— WINTER WATERING ——

All rhododendrons are shallow-rooted, so they dry out easily. It is important to make sure that the potting mixture is always just moist, even during the winter. Rain reaches the roots of deciduous azaleas during the winter, because they have no leaves to shelter the soil, but evergreen rhododendrons will still need to be watered regularly.

PRACTICAL MATTERS

SOIL
Plant in a well-drained, acid potting mixture, with added leafmold.
SITE
Place in a semi-shady site.
WATERING
Keep the soil just moist throughout the year. After flowering, feed weekly until mid summer.
PLANTS
Grow one azalea and four ferns in each 17in- (42cm-) diameter terracotta pot.

• **Azalea** (*Rhododendron* 'Fedora')
An evergreen variety with phlox-pink blossoms.

Hot Clashing Colors

⚞ Azalea flowers cover an enormous range of colors. I find the more violent shades work well together. These three grow with a ruff of ferns that favor exactly the same site, soil, and watering conditions. As each azalea grows larger, you can transfer the entire root ball, together with the ferns, into a larger pot.

• **Azalea** *(Rhododendron 'Vuyk's Scarlet')*
Brilliant red flowers smother this evergreen variety at the height of its flowering season.

Azalea *(Rhododendron 'Konigen Emma')* •
One of the Mollis hybrids, grown for its colorful autumn foliage as well as the spring flowers.

• **Fern** *(Polystichum setiferum)*
A species that stays evergreen throughout the winter months.

SPRING NARCISSI

Double daffodil
(*Narcissus* 'Tahiti')
A robust form, with
double flowers and
a slight scent.

Pots look most effective filled to overflowing with spring bulbs. Narcissi are among the easiest to grow. I find that it is best to plant just one variety in each pot – you can still contrast the various flower forms and colors by filling several pots, each displaying a different flower.

I can never resist growing at least one pot of a fragrant variety: the paperwhite and pheasant eye narcissi have a sweet scent but, to me, the perfume of the jonquils is the most delicious. Plant the bulbs in autumn, layering them (SEE PAGE 34) for maximum visual impact.

Shades of Spring
The sky-blues of these frost-proof ceramic pots, planted with the clear yellows of four varieties of narcissus, epitomize the colors of a spring day.
Experiment with different varieties, choosing from the enormous range of colors: pink, apricot, and white, as well as yellow and orange.

Large-cupped daffodil
(*Narcissus* 'Salmon Trout')
As the flowers age, the perianths turn pink.

Cyclamineus daffodil
(*Narcissus* 'Tête-à-Tête')
A small form with reflexed petals and a good perfume.

PRACTICAL MATTERS

SOIL
Plant in a well-drained potting mixture of medium to rich nutritional value.

SITE
Anywhere, but avoid high heat and bright sunlight to prolong flowering.

WATERING
Keep just moist, but never allow to become soggy.

PLANTS
Grow 24 bulbs in each 10-14in- (25-35cm-) diameter pot, and cover the potting mixture with moss.

Double daffodil
(*Narcissus* 'Yellow Cheerfulness')
A scented variety.

ROSES ALL SUMMER

THE BEAUTY OF THE ROSE is indisputable: it has a sumptuous look that epitomizes summer. However, the plant on which the flowers grow is not such a beauty. For much of the year the rose bush is a gangly awkward plant with unattractive stems covered by vicious thorns, and leaves that are prone to disease.

By growing roses in containers, you can bring them into the limelight when they are at their best, and keep them out of sight when they are not. Only the smaller roses do well in containers: polyanthas, cluster-flowered varieties, and miniatures. The larger varieties will never produce an abundance of blooms.

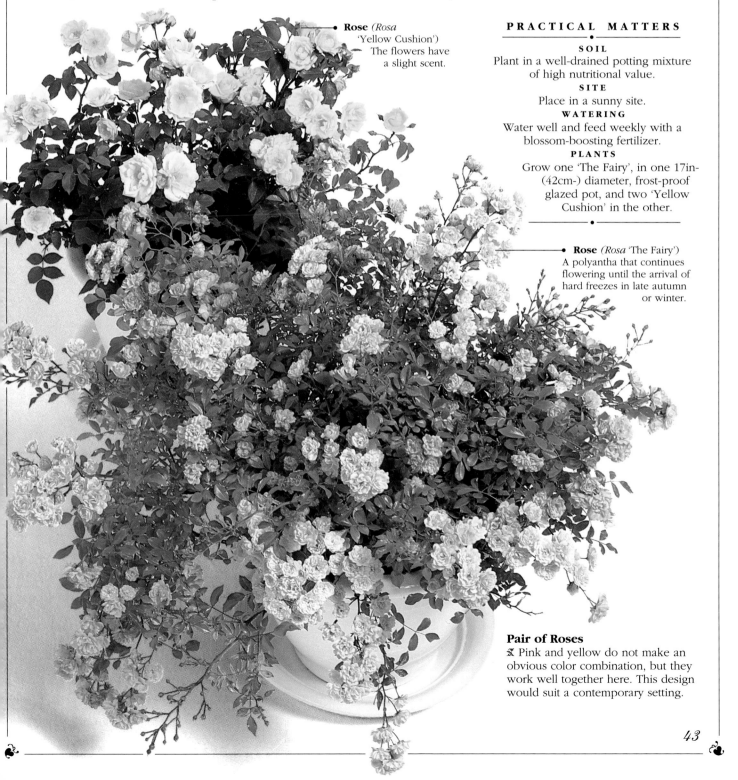

Rose (*Rosa* 'Yellow Cushion') The flowers have a slight scent.

Rose (*Rosa* 'The Fairy') A polyantha that continues flowering until the arrival of hard freezes in late autumn or winter.

PRACTICAL MATTERS

SOIL
Plant in a well-drained potting mixture of high nutritional value.

SITE
Place in a sunny site.

WATERING
Water well and feed weekly with a blossom-boosting fertilizer.

PLANTS
Grow one 'The Fairy', in one 17in- (42cm-) diameter, frost-proof glazed pot, and two 'Yellow Cushion' in the other.

Pair of Roses
✗ Pink and yellow do not make an obvious color combination, but they work well together here. This design would suit a contemporary setting.

PINK GERANIUMS

GERANIUMS ARE THE MOST REWARDING plants to grow. They flower abundantly, require little attention, and do extremely well in containers. In a sunny or semi-shady position with plenty of light, they grow quickly into substantial plants, producing plentiful flushes of flowers from early summer until the first frosts. They frequently survive light frosts and go on producing flowers well into the winter. However, the combination of late cold spells and damp usually kills them. This is no bad thing, because they tend to get woody and unshapely in their second flowering season, and usually produce fewer flowers. It is, therefore, best to grow new plants every year, either from seed sown in late winter (for flowering that summer), or from cuttings taken in late summer, for flowering the following summer. Both methods are relatively easy. (For details on the different propagation techniques, SEE PAGES 182-3.)

Different types and varieties of geranium grow well together in the same container, provided they are equally vigorous. Some of the smaller-growing varieties can become swamped by the larger, more robust forms, so it is advisable to avoid combining them.

∽ PLANTING A POT ∽

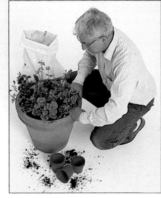

1 *Place pebbles or pottery chips in the base of the pot, then firm in the potting mixture to 4in (10cm) below the rim. With the plants still in pots, arrange geraniums in the center, and verbenas around the edge to trail over the side of the pot.*

2 *Tap the plants out of their pots (before planting, water them to soak the roots) and gently loosen the base. Firm into position, adding potting mixture so that its final level is 1½in (4cm) below the pot rim. Remove dead leaves, and water.*

Zonal geranium *(Pelargonium 'Fraicher Beauty')* The perfectly formed, pale pink flowers are double.

Martha Washington geranium *(Pelargonium 'Langley Smith')* A small-flowered variety with white petals marked carmine-pink.

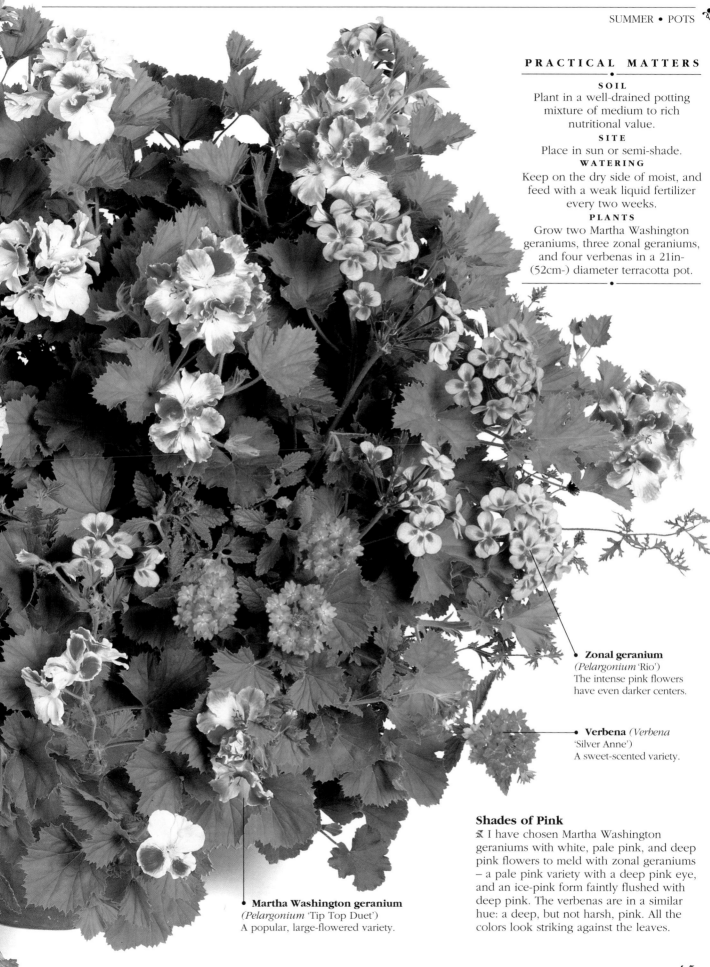

PRACTICAL MATTERS

SOIL
Plant in a well-drained potting mixture of medium to rich nutritional value.

SITE
Place in sun or semi-shade.

WATERING
Keep on the dry side of moist, and feed with a weak liquid fertilizer every two weeks.

PLANTS
Grow two Martha Washington geraniums, three zonal geraniums, and four verbenas in a 21in-(52cm-) diameter terracotta pot.

Zonal geranium
(Pelargonium 'Rio')
The intense pink flowers have even darker centers.

Verbena *(Verbena* 'Silver Anne')
A sweet-scented variety.

Shades of Pink
✗ I have chosen Martha Washington geraniums with white, pale pink, and deep pink flowers to meld with zonal geraniums – a pale pink variety with a deep pink eye, and an ice-pink form faintly flushed with deep pink. The verbenas are in a similar hue: a deep, but not harsh, pink. All the colors look striking against the leaves.

Martha Washington geranium
(Pelargonium 'Tip Top Duet')
A popular, large-flowered variety.

TENDER FLOWERING SHRUBS

THESE TWO SHRUBS – a plumbago and an abutilon – give a
continuous display of flowers throughout the summer and
autumn. Both are tender, however, so you must treat them as
annuals, unless you are gardening in a frost-free climate, or have a
cool conservatory in which to overwinter them.
They grow extremely fast and will give a good
show of flowers during the summer in
which they are planted. The
plumbago shown here
produces a succession of pure
sky-blue flowers from early
summer until early winter. In
ideal conditions, it will reach 10ft
(3m) high. The abutilon has similar
attributes: it carries a profusion
of yellow bell-shaped flowers
flushed with peach for several
months and grows large
in just one season. It is
also frost-tender.

Plumbago
(*Plumbago auriculata*)
A tender fast-growing
climber with trusses
of blue flowers.

Tender Care
✗ This plumbago is
supported by three bamboo
stakes. As it grows, tie in the
main stem and a few of the side
shoots, but do not cut it back or it
will not flower. If overwintering,
prune plumbago hard to promote
new flowering growth in the
spring. The gypsophila is planted
in the side cups of the
upturned chimney pot.

PRACTICAL MATTERS

SOIL
Plant in a well-drained potting
mixture of high nutritional value.
SITE
Place in a sheltered, sunny site.
WATERING
Water well. Feed once a week.
PLANTS
Grow one plumbago and five
gypsophila in a 15in- (38cm-)
diameter chimney pot.

Gypsophila
(*Gypsophila repens*
'Dorothy Teacher')
Produces delicate
powder puffs of
little flowers.

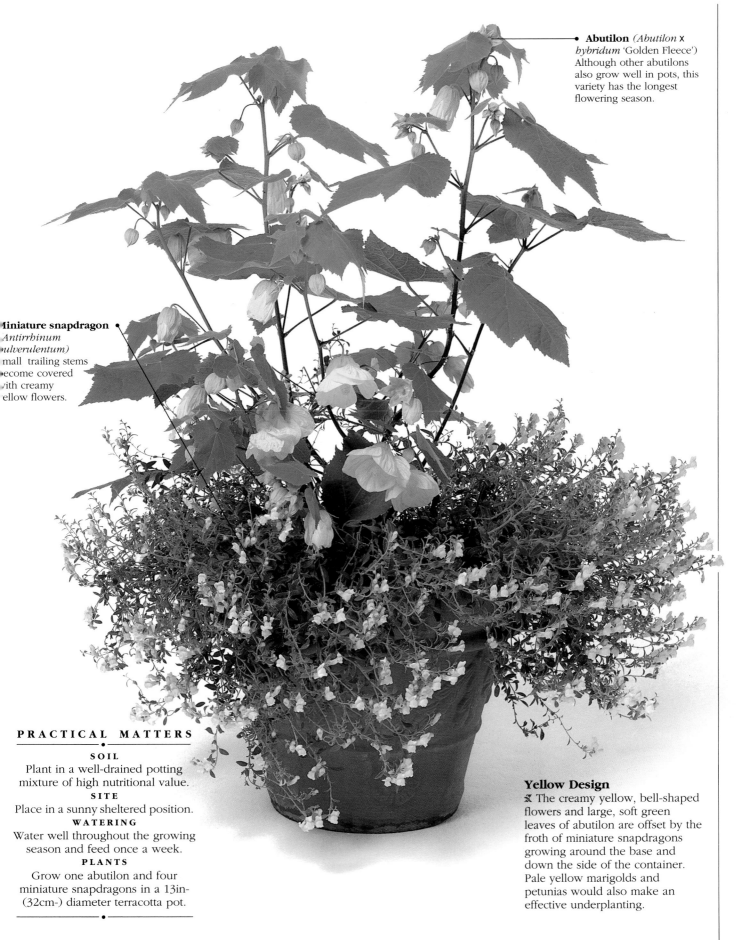

Abutilon (*Abutilon* x *hybridum* 'Golden Fleece')
Although other abutilons also grow well in pots, this variety has the longest flowering season.

Miniature snapdragon
(*Antirrhinum pulverulentum*)
Small trailing stems become covered with creamy yellow flowers.

PRACTICAL MATTERS

SOIL
Plant in a well-drained potting mixture of high nutritional value.
SITE
Place in a sunny sheltered position.
WATERING
Water well throughout the growing season and feed once a week.
PLANTS
Grow one abutilon and four miniature snapdragons in a 13in- (32cm-) diameter terracotta pot.

Yellow Design
✿ The creamy yellow, bell-shaped flowers and large, soft green leaves of abutilon are offset by the froth of miniature snapdragons growing around the base and down the side of the container. Pale yellow marigolds and petunias would also make an effective underplanting.

VARIEGATED GERANIUMS

GERANIUMS, SOMETIMES CALLED PELARGONIUMS, are rewarding plants to grow in containers. They put on a continuous show of flowers from the beginning of summer until the first frosts of autumn or early winter – in warmer dryer climates they often continue to flower through the winter. As a bonus, many of the varieties have beautifully patterned leaves, which are sometimes scented.

—— GERANIUM VARIETIES ——

Four types of geranium are grown in gardens: zonal, ivy-leaved, scented-leaved, and Martha Washington. The most common are the zonal geraniums, distinguished by their rounded fleshy leaves with a variegated band. Their heads of small single or double flowers vary in color from red and orange, through pink and mauve, to white. The ivy-leaved varieties have single or double flowers, small ivy-like leaves, and a trailing habit, which makes them ideal for hanging baskets. Martha Washington geraniums are grown for their large showy flowers although, unfortunately, they are easily damaged by wet weather. The scented-leaved geraniums are valued for their foliage. Their insignificant flowers are best removed to encourage the growth of the leaves, noted for their lemon, apple, rose, pine, or mint fragrances.

✿ Geraniums perform best in a sunny site. When the young plants are 6in (15cm) tall, remove the leading growing tip to make them bush out well. Deadhead regularly to encourage flowering.

Zonal geranium *(Pelargonium* 'Dolly Varden')
Handsome green, purple, and cream leaves with scarlet flowers.

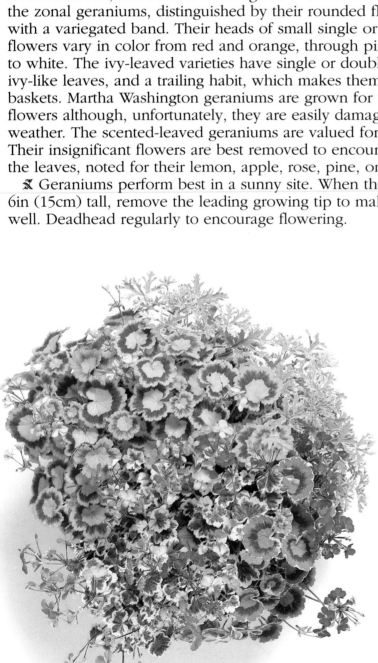

Patterned Foliage
✿ Four geraniums, chosen for their striking leaf patterns as well as their flowers, grow in this handmade terracotta pot. The three zonal varieties have a distinct band on their leaves. The scented-leaved variety at the front is grown for its aromatic cream-edged leaves.

Scented-leaved geranium
(Pelargonium 'Lady Plymouth')
When bruised, the pretty leaves of this variety exude a delicious, sharp lemon scent.

Strategic Planning
✿ Plant 'Lady Plymouth,' the scented geranium, at the front of the planting so that passers-by gently bruise the foliage and release its scent. The other three geraniums all have a bushy habit, which introduces height and bulk to this luxuriant arrangement.

Zonal geranium
(*Pelargonium* 'Frank Headley')
Pink flowers appear above the
cream-edged green leaves.

Zonal geranium
(*Pelargonium* 'Mrs Quilter')
The lime-green leaves with
chestnut patterning and the
salmon-pink flowers make
a stunning combination.

PRACTICAL MATTERS

SOIL
Plant in a well-drained potting mixture of
medium nutritional value.

SITE
Flowering is most prolific in a sunny site,
although the plants still grow well in a
semi-shady position.

WATERING
In hot sunny weather water daily, but do
not allow the roots to become soggy –
they rot easily. Feed lightly once a week.

PLANTS
Grow three zonal geraniums and one
scented-leaved geranium in a 12in-
(30cm-) diameter terracotta pot.

LILIES AND BELLFLOWERS

LILIES ARE REWARDING PLANTS to grow in pots. They produce an abundance of spectacular flowers that last for several weeks in summer, yet their demands – a sunny or semi-shady site and a rich potting mixture – are not difficult to meet. For summer flowers, plant the lily bulbs in late autumn, or during the winter in areas where hard freezes are rare. Once their flowering shoots appear in late spring, introduce some lower-growing annuals or perennials between and around them, so that their trumpet-shaped blooms eventually rise from a mound of flowers that complements both their color and their elegant form.

Lily *(Lilium 'Connecticut King')* This variety carries gorgeous, upward-facing blooms on its 36in- (1m-) high stems in the early summer.

Bellflower *(Campanula carpatica)* A clump-forming perennial with long-lasting flowers in summer.

A Fitting Base
✄ A deep blue, glazed Chinese pot provides an elegant base for the mound of bellflowers and the regal stems of lily blooms, which soar high above them.

PRACTICAL MATTERS

SOIL
Grow in a very well-drained potting mixture, enriched with compost and leafmold.

SITE
Place in a sunny or semi-shady site.

WATERING
Keep the potting mixture moist, but not soggy, and give a weekly liquid fertilizer during the growing season.

PLANTS
Grow ten lilies and five bellflowers in a 16in- (40cm-) diameter pot.

PALACE PURPLE

OO OFTEN, WE NEGLECT THE PLANTS that have interesting leaf shapes and colors, in favor of those that produce attractive flowers. Here, as a change from flowering summer annuals, I have planted a group of showy foliage perennials. Easy to grow in semi-shade, they will look good right through summer and autumn for years to come. *Hosta montana* 'Aureo-marginata', and *Leucothoe fontanesiana* 'Rainbow', also perennials with wonderful leaves, are other possibilities for this long-lasting and colorful melange.

PRACTICAL MATTERS

SOIL
Plant in a well-drained potting mixture of high nutritional value.
SITE
Place in a semi-shady or shady site.
WATERING
Water all the plants well, especially the houttuynia.
PLANTS
Grow one heuchera, one houttuynia, and one piggy-back plant in a 19in- (48cm-) diameter terracotta pot.

Aura of Elegance
The deep purple coloring of the heuchera leaves is accentuated by the speckled golds of the piggy-back plant and the multicolored houttuynia leaves.

Houttuynia (*Houttuynia cordata* 'Chamaeleon') The pretty colored leaves have a pungent orange scent.

Heuchera (*Heuchera* 'Palace Purple') The purple foliage is sometimes used in cut flower arrangements.

Piggy-back plant (*Tolmiea menziesii*) A perennial that is easy to propagate, as new plants grow from the leaf-stem joints.

CASCADING DIASCIAS

SINGLE SPECIES PLANTINGS can work well in containers, especially when the chosen plant is as beautiful as the diascia. A perennial with terminal clusters of shell-like flowers which have two spurs, it comes in a range of soft pinks. Although rarely grown, it is an undemanding plant and produces a profusion of flowers over a long period in summer, and even into the early autumn. Position it in a sunny spot, where it can be seen to full advantage. It is not that hardy, so only leave it outside over winter in gardens that escape hard frost.

✄ Usually the plants that grow into a full, bushy mounded shape make the best single species arrangements. Among the favorite annuals, geraniums, petunias, nasturtiums, verbenas, and zinnias all stand out well on their own, either in one color or in a glorious wild mixture.

PRACTICAL MATTERS

SOIL
Plant in a well-drained potting mixture of medium nutritional value.

SITE
Place in a sunny position.

WATERING
The potting mixture should be kept moist, but avoid overwatering. Feed once a week.

PLANTS
Grow two diascias in this 11in-(27cm-) diameter terracotta pot.

Trails of Pink
✄ The pretty salmon-pink flowers of diascia are borne in profusion along trailing semi-upright stems in summer and early autumn, almost concealing the terracotta pot from which the plants grow. They should not be allowed to dry out during the summer.

Diascia •
(Diascia rigescens)
This is one of the hardiest species.

STRIKING BEGONIAS

For many years, I had an aversion to begonias; indeed I still find that the very large-flowered, show varieties with day-glo colors are sometimes difficult to live with. Now, I probably over-extol them. Many begonias are subtle in their appeal, and some have beautiful leaves. The foliage of the rex varieties, used here, comes in a range of subdued, yet exquisite, colors and is often elaborately spotted or striped. They are tender perennials and are well suited to container culture.

PRACTICAL MATTERS

SOIL
Plant in a rich, well-drained potting mixture.

SITE
Place in a damp shady site.

WATERING
Water well in the growing and flowering season. Feed once a week.

PLANTS
Plant two rex begonias and four 'Billie Langdon' in a 16in- (40cm-) diameter pot and three 'Norah Bedson' in a 10in- (25cm-) diameter, glazed ceramic pot.

Subdued Scheme
✗ Two deep blue, Chinese glazed pots set off the pure white flowers and highly decorative leaves of these begonias. Plant the tubers of 'Billie Langdon' in spring. The other two varieties are usually grown indoors, but can be placed outdoors in summer.

• **Rhizomatous begonia** (*Begonia* 'Norah Bedson') In winter, when the plant is indoors, do not water too much if the light level is low.

• **Tuberous begonia** (*Begonia* x *tuberhybrida* 'Billie Langdon') Grown for its plentiful, pure white flowers.

• **Rex begonia** (*Begonia rex* 'Merry Christmas') The exotic-looking leaves are evergreen.

53

SUMMER SHADE LOVERS

O NLY A FEW shade- and semi-shade-loving plants produce masses
of beautiful flowers over a long period in summer. Tuberous
begonias are some of the showiest. They are not hardy, but
you can overwinter them easily. Before the first frosts, take the pots
inside and stop watering the plants so they dry off. Remove the
browned foliage, gently brush off the soil and store in almost-dry
peat, giving them a very small amount of water, occasionally, to stop
the tubers from shrivelling. Keep in a dry, cool, but frost-free place.
Plant the tubers out the following spring.

Here, I have mixed begonias with fuchsias and flowering tobacco
plants, also shade lovers. Fuchsias must also be overwintered in a cool
but frost-free place. Flowering tobacco plants, which are annuals, have
the advantage of being scented, especially in the evenings.

Tuberous begonias
(*Begonia* x
tuberhybrida)
The large showy flowers come
in a range of reds, pinks,
oranges,
yellows and
white.

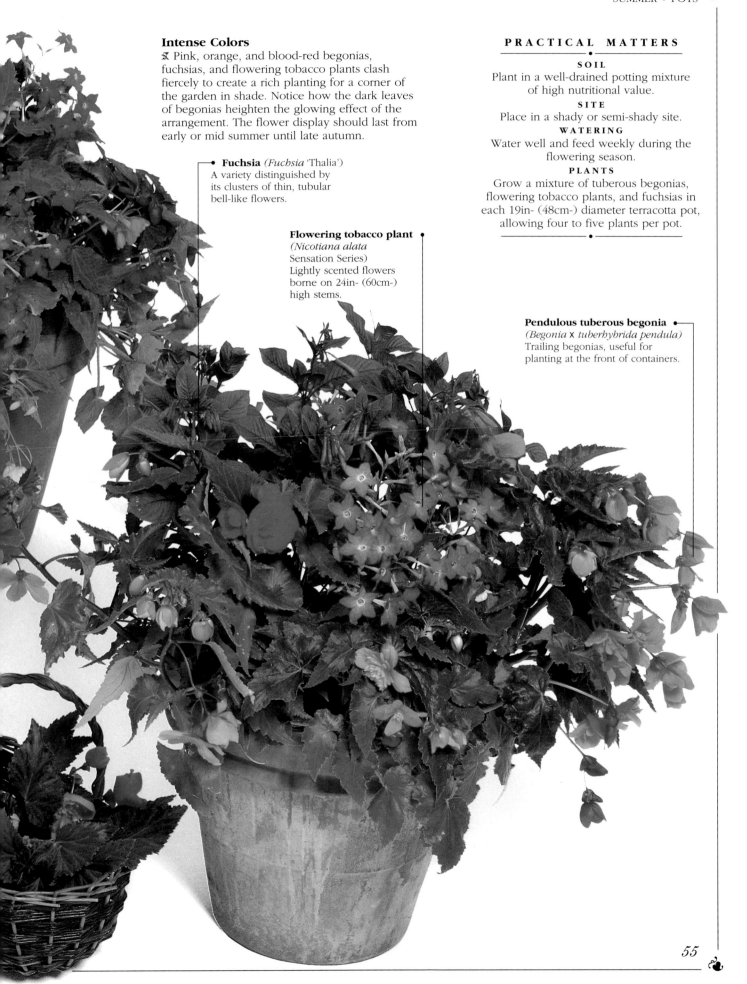

Intense Colors

✄ Pink, orange, and blood-red begonias, fuchsias, and flowering tobacco plants clash fiercely to create a rich planting for a corner of the garden in shade. Notice how the dark leaves of begonias heighten the glowing effect of the arrangement. The flower display should last from early or mid summer until late autumn.

• **Fuchsia** *(Fuchsia* 'Thalia') A variety distinguished by its clusters of thin, tubular bell-like flowers.

Flowering tobacco plant • *(Nicotiana alata* Sensation Series) Lightly scented flowers borne on 24in- (60cm-) high stems.

Pendulous tuberous begonia • *(Begonia* x *tuberhybrida pendula)* Trailing begonias, useful for planting at the front of containers.

PRACTICAL MATTERS

SOIL
Plant in a well-drained potting mixture of high nutritional value.

SITE
Place in a shady or semi-shady site.

WATERING
Water well and feed weekly during the flowering season.

PLANTS
Grow a mixture of tuberous begonias, flowering tobacco plants, and fuchsias in each 19in- (48cm-) diameter terracotta pot, allowing four to five plants per pot.

QUARTET OF GLAZED POTS

POTS OF VARYING heights and diameters, each holding just one plant species, can make a most effective grouping. I tend to choose containers that are strongly linked, either by the material from which they are made, or by the color of their outer surfaces. Add interest to the group by selecting plants with different growth habits – upright, mounding, trailing or mat-forming – but make sure that they have one feature to relate them visually to one another.

The containers should also suit the position that you have in mind for them. This group of rich brown, glazed pots would work well if placed on brick or wood, or maybe standing on some informal steps. The glazed terracotta pots seen here are available from most garden centers. Always check whether the pots are frost-proof. Glazed terracotta pots do not last as long as unglazed pots, so check their durability in extreme cold.

Houttuynia (*Houttuynia cordata* 'Chamaeleon')
When crushed, the colorful leaves of this perennial plant give off a pungent, citrus-like smell.

Dwarf aster
(*Aster novi-belgii*, dwarf form)
An aster bearing masses of rich pink flowers in autumn.

PRACTICAL MATTERS
•
SOIL
Plant in a potting mixture of high nutritional value.
SITE
All these plants require a sunny position, except houttuynia, which enjoys a little dappled shade.
WATERING
The houttuynia requires very moist conditions. For the other plants keep the potting mixture moist, but not soggy. Feed once a week.
PLANTS
One plant is grown in each 9in- (23cm-) diameter pot, with the exception of the asters, when three plants are grown.
———— • ————

Hebe *(Hebe* 'Lindsayi')
An attractive neat hebe, with
evergreen leaves and a long
flowering season.

Ceratostigma
(Ceratostigma
plumbaginoides)
A perennial with flowers
and foliage that both look
their best in late summer
and early autumn.

Autumn Hues
✄ The colors found in the flowers
and foliage of these autumn plants
help unify this grouping. Notice
how the pale pink spikes of the
hebe and the richer hues of the
dwarf asters pick out the splashes
of color found in the houttuynia's
foliage. While the ceratostigma
produces its intense blue flowers
in autumn, its leaves also turn a
rich red, reflecting the other warm
hues around them. Glazed clay
pots are ideal for setting off the
autumn flower and foliage colors.

DECORATIVE BERRIES

FEW PLANTS PRODUCE such a dramatic range of colored berries as pernettya and its hybrids. Set off by the small, glossy evergreen leaves, the fruits vary from dark plum-red, through bright red, to pink, and finally white. Only the female plants carry berries, although it is necessary to have a male plant nearby for pollination. In this arrangement, a male shrub has been introduced among the more decorative females, but you could grow one in a nearby border. As pernettya is evergreen and hardy, you could keep it in this glazed ceramic pot permanently to enjoy its glossy foliage in winter, and then its tiny white flowers in the spring and early summer.

PRACTICAL MATTERS

SOIL
Plant in a slightly acid potting mixture.

SITE
Place in a sunny site.

WATERING
Keep the soil moist through the growing season. Feed once a fortnight.

PLANTS
Grow four pernettyas in a 16in- (40cm-) diameter, glazed ceramic pot.

Pernettya *(Pernettya mucronata* 'Edward Ball') A male plant.

Pernettya *(Pernettya mucronata* 'Bell's Seedling') A female plant bearing bright red fruits.

Pernettya *(Pernettya mucronata* 'Mulberry Wine') A female plant that bears dusky pink fruits.

Pernettya *(Pernettya mucronata* 'Alba') A female variety grown for its white fruits.

Green Harmony
⚜ This large, rich green, glazed and frost-proofed pot has a strong affinity with the color of the pernettyas' small, spiky leaves, yet at the same time it provides a perfect foil for the shining red, white, and pink berries that appear in the autumn.

CHRYSANTHEMUM TREE

WITH THEIR STRONG resemblance to miniature trees, plants grown as standards look most attractive in terracotta pots.

✿ The best plants to train into flowering, mop-headed standards are spray chrysanthemums, fuchsias, and geraniums. Take cuttings in autumn and overwinter them under glass. Remove side shoots as the plant grows, and support the main stem with a stake, approximately 36in (1m) long. When the main stem reaches 30in (75cm) high, leave the side shoots to grow; when the stem reaches 36in (1m), pinch out the growing tip, then allow the side shoots to bush out.

✿ Evergreen shrubs can also be trained in this way, but they are slower growing: a standard box or bay tree might take four years to develop a 36in- (1m-) high stem. Although lacking in significant flowers, all make elegant evergreen displays when clipped to shape.

Flowering Standard

✿ The coloring in the blooms of this standard chrysanthemum is echoed by the foliage and flowers of the stonecrops that grow around its stem.

PRACTICAL MATTERS

SOIL

Plant in a loam-based potting mixture of medium nutritional value.

SITE

Overwinter in a light frost-free situation, then move to a sunny position in late spring when danger of frost has passed.

WATERING

Avoid overwatering. Feed once a week.

PLANTS

Grow one standard chrysanthemum and six stonecrops in a 16in- (40cm-) diameter terracotta pot.

Chrysanthemum
(*Chrysanthemum* 'Dawn Mist')
A perennial, bearing sprays of single, white, daisy-like flowers tinged pink.

Stonecrop (*Sedum sieboldii*
'Folius medio-variegatus')
A trailing succulent that has tiny, pink star-like flowers in mid autumn.

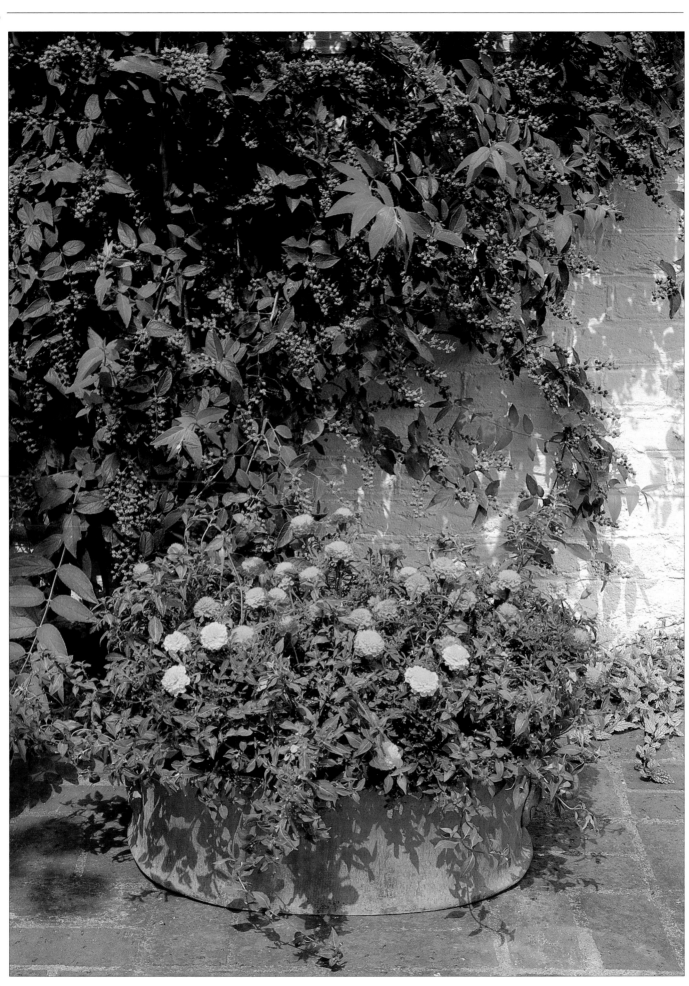

Low Bowls

Low bowls are comfortable-looking containers for plants. Unpretentious, and often hardly visible below the planting, they should carry a mound of plants just a little above the ground. They are at their most attractive when they can be seen from above, or at least from a fairly high angle. If the bowl is very shallow, there will be only a little room for the roots, limiting the type of plants you can grow. In very shallow bowls, only succulents, such as houseleeks, will grow well. If you want to grow low annuals and trailing perennials, use bowls that are at least 6in (15cm) deep.

KITCHENWARE

Many containers used in the home can easily become low bowls in the garden, although if they started life as watertight vessels you will need to drill holes in them to provide adequate drainage. Bowls made of glazed ceramic are easily damaged by frost, so save them for summer and early autumn plantings, and use hardier containers for year-round displays.

✻ Antique, copper wash basins and copper milk or cream pitchers are no longer easy to find, but they make the most beautiful plant containers. You can leave them outside over winter, and, as they weather, the copper becomes oxidized and changes to a wonderful greeny blue hue. This weathering process can be hurried along by painting the outside surface of the vessel either with vinegar or some cheap wine.

MIX AND MATCH

A group of bowls can make a simple but effective display at the base of a flowerbed, provided the plants behind them are not too tall. Plants that make mounded shapes or those that are trailers

LAVENDER HUES
Blue marguerites, pansies, pale blue lobelias, and morning glory (ABOVE) combine in a planting scheme intended to complement the lavender backdrop.

COPPER COLORING
An antique, copper cream pitcher (LEFT) is planted with marigolds and cigar flowers, which were chosen to reflect the color of the container and the brick paving.

tend to look best in low bowls. Echo colors found in the flowerbed in the designs for the bowls. I like to see very simple plantings in bowls – a planting of one type of ivy, sweet alyssum, or lobelia. You could also try begonias, pansies, perennial candytuft, pinks, or bellflowers.

✻ If you want to mix plants, I find that the bowl should be more than 12in (30cm) across, but even then, I think it is best to restrict the color range. If you want to introduce more than one color, use more than one bowl, but still stick to colors that relate to each other and plants that have similar forms.

SEASONAL SCHEMES

In a sunny or semi-shady position during the summer, a bowl of cranesbill *(Geranium endressii)*, with its non-stop display of pretty, little pink flowers, a bowl of lilac-colored pansies, and a larger bowl of Californian bluebells are breath-taking. On shady paving, against a backdrop of green foliage, you could grow bowls of the yellow-flowering, gold-leaved creeping Jenny, cranesbill *(Geranium nodosum)*, with its delicate, cup-shaped pink flowers, and the piggy-back plant.

✻ For spring in semi-shade or shade, try planting bowls of miniature tulips, maybe one bowl of red 'Plaisir', one of creamy white 'Concerto', and another one of 'Toronto' with its bright red flowers, brown-yellow base, and bronze anthers.

✻ In winter, bowls of different ivies look effective standing on a garden table or arranged in a line along the top of a low wall. The golden-variegated forms, and the yellow-leaved variety, 'Buttercup,' are especially attractive, introducing some light relief among the dark glossy evergreens, which tend to dominate those gardens in cold regions during the winter months.

FLOWERING BERGENIAS

BERGENIAS ARE HANDSOME AND HARDY, low evergreen perennials with large leaves that look attractive in the depths of winter in mild climates. During warm spells they may flower in mid winter, although the main display is from late winter to early spring. They are extremely easy to grow, requiring little attention apart from judicious watering. Leucothoes have beautiful evergreen foliage that is often green, but sometimes tinged red in winter.

PRACTICAL MATTERS

SOIL
Plant in well-drained, acid potting mixture.

SITE
A sheltered semi-shady position is best.

WATERING
Keep well watered. Remember that the large leaves form a barrier to rain.

PLANTS
Grow three bergenias and two leucothoe in a 17in- (42cm-) diameter, reconstituted stone bowl.

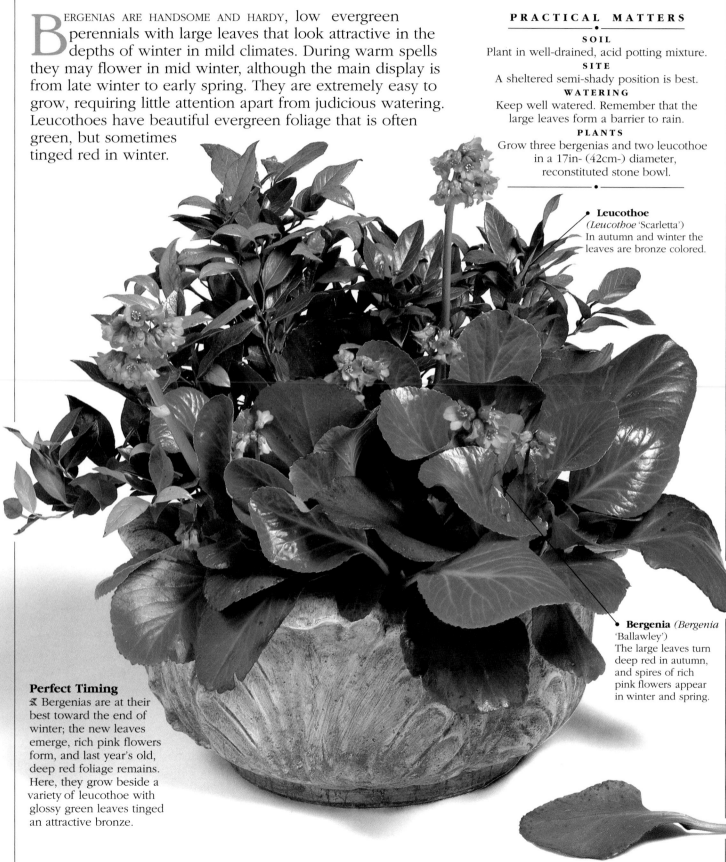

Leucothoe
(*Leucothoe* 'Scarletta')
In autumn and winter the leaves are bronze colored.

Bergenia (*Bergenia* 'Ballawley')
The large leaves turn deep red in autumn, and spires of rich pink flowers appear in winter and spring.

Perfect Timing
✿ Bergenias are at their best toward the end of winter; the new leaves emerge, rich pink flowers form, and last year's old, deep red foliage remains. Here, they grow beside a variety of leucothoe with glossy green leaves tinged an attractive bronze.

SPRING BLUES

BLUE AND WHITE is a beautiful spring color combination: clean and fresh, it is a scheme that echoes the intense blue skies of early spring. It seemed appropriate to plant this arrangement of grape hyacinths, periwinkle, and Siberian squills in a blue ceramic bowl. Grape hyacinths have a delicious scent, which is sweet and buttery. If taken indoors, they fill an entire room with their fragrance. The grape hyacinths are posed behind a trailing lesser periwinkle, covered with flowers in late winter and early spring. To the right, a clump of Siberian squills grows.

PRACTICAL MATTERS

SOIL
Plant in a well-drained, lightweight potting mixture of medium nutritional value.

SITE
Ideally set in semi-shade.

WATERING
Through the winter, keep the potting mixture just moist.

PLANTS
Grow one periwinkle, twenty-five grape hyacinth bulbs, and ten Siberian squills in a 18in- (45cm-) diameter, frost-proof ceramic bowl.

Grape hyacinth
(*Muscari azureum*)
A variety producing sky-blue scented flowers.

Grape hyacinth
(*Muscari botryoides* 'Album')
A white-flowered variety.

Close-at-hand
✗ Set this bowl of blue and white spring flowers on a garden table close to the house, so it can easily be seen and frequently visited for a quick whiff of the grape hyacinth's delicious, sweet butter scent.

Variegated foliage
A lesser periwinkle with variegated leaves is also available. Try growing it with white grape hyacinths instead of the blue variety.

Lesser periwinkle
(*Vinca minor*)
An evergreen perennial that spreads rapidly and produces a succession of flowers over a long period.

Siberian squill
(*Scilla siberica*)
Delicate, clear blue, bell-like flowers appear on short stems after the leaves have emerged.

CHINESE BOWL OF SUN ROSES

AS MID SUMMER approaches, it is difficult to keep up with the profusion of flowers in the garden. While most of the flowering plants can be grown in the larger containers, only those with a shallow root run – annuals and some low-growing shrubs – are suitable for planting in bowls. Halimiocistus, an evergreen shrub producing silky, saucer-shaped flowers for many weeks in summer, has been chosen for this glazed Chinese bowl. To perform well, it needs sun and a very well-drained soil, as it hates to be soggy at the roots. It will not tolerate too much cold, especially when combined with damp conditions.

❧ Other summer-flowering plants that do well in low bowls include rock roses, fuchsias, morning glory, heathers, hebes, lavender, and potentillas.

❧ Bowls filled with plants that have outward-facing or pendent flowers, such as fuchsias and ceanothus, are most effectively displayed above ground level, perhaps on a low wall or garden table. Those with flowers that face upward – rock roses, potentillas, and morning glory – are best on the ground.

• **Halimiocistus** (*Halimiocistus wintonensis* 'Merrist Wood Cream') An evergreen shrub that reaches 24in (60cm) high and flowers in early and mid summer.

PRACTICAL MATTERS

SOIL
Plant in a very well-drained potting mixture of medium nutritional value, and gravel (proportions 4:1).

SITE
Place in a sunny site. In cold areas, provide frost and wind protection.

WATERING
Do not overwater or allow to become soggy. Feed once every two weeks.

PLANTS
Grow three halimiocistus in a 15in-(38cm-) long, oval, glazed ceramic bowl.

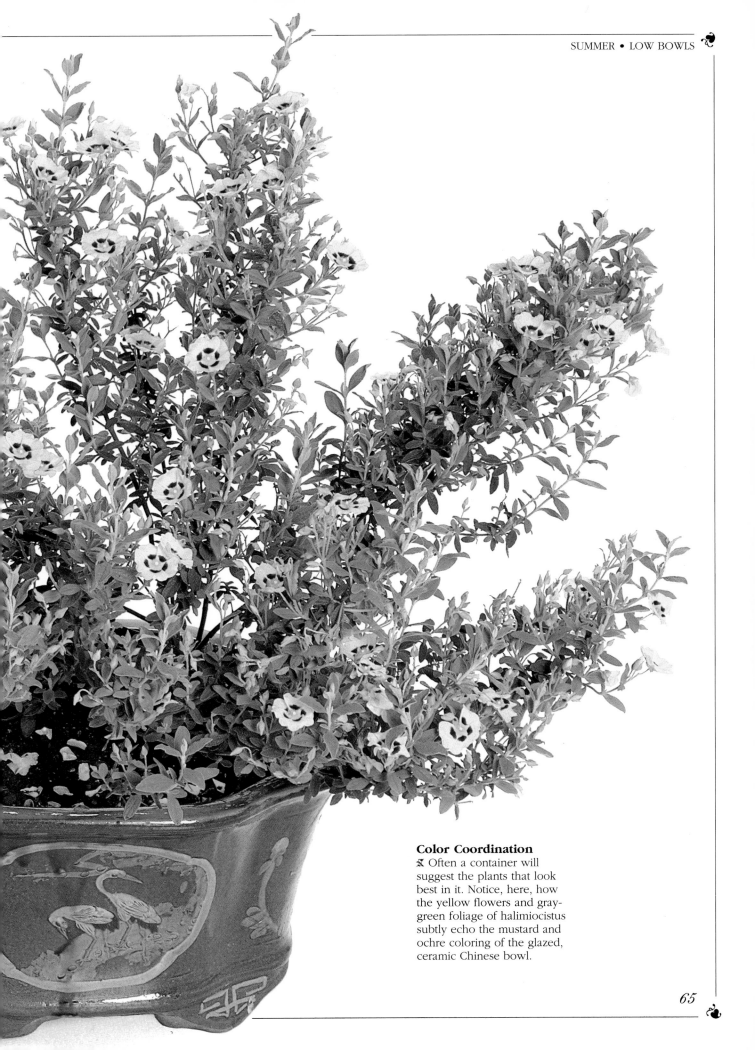

Color Coordination

✕ Often a container will suggest the plants that look best in it. Notice, here, how the yellow flowers and gray-green foliage of halimiocistus subtly echo the mustard and ochre coloring of the glazed, ceramic Chinese bowl.

PINK AND MAUVE TRIO

With a few exceptions, summer bedding annuals do not tend to grow very tall, and so make ideal subjects for low bowls, especially the plants that sprawl or form a dome. I have used semi-shade-loving impatiens in several plantings because they are versatile, have a very long flowering period, attractive leaves, and an ease of growth that is matched by few other plants. They will grow in any situation, even strong sun, although they then will need extra water to compensate for the drying effect of such a condition. If there is any problem, it is that they may take over in a mixed planting, so cut them back as soon as they start to overpower smaller plants, such as the ageratum used here.

A wealth of other annuals would be just as successful in this bowl. Among the sun lovers, there are geraniums – either upright or trailing ivy-leaved varieties – low-growing dahlias, petunias, lobelias, snapdragons, chrysanthemums, sweet alyssum, marigolds, verbenas, and nasturtiums. For low bowls in semi-shade or shade, try begonias (which are as versatile as impatiens), dwarf flowering tobacco plants, fuchsias, and pansies.

Verbena (*Verbena tenera* var. *maonettii*)
Sadly, this pretty variety has no scent.

Ageratum (*Ageratum* 'Bengali')
The small, delicate flowers contrast with the bolder blossoms of the impatiens.

PRACTICAL MATTERS

SOIL
Plant in a well-drained, rich potting mixture.

SITE
Place in a semi-shady site.

WATERING
Keep just moist and feed once a week.

PLANTS
Grow four impatiens, three ageratum, and three verbenas in a 17in- (42cm-) diameter terracotta bowl.

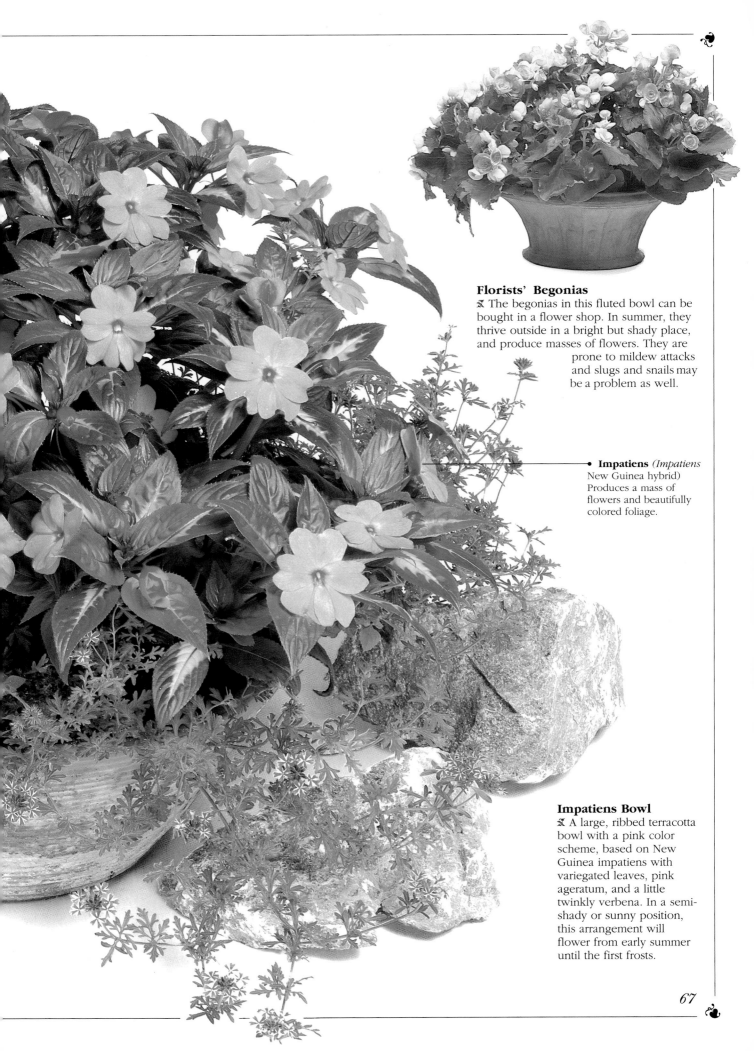

Florists' Begonias

✄ The begonias in this fluted bowl can be bought in a flower shop. In summer, they thrive outside in a bright but shady place, and produce masses of flowers. They are prone to mildew attacks and slugs and snails may be a problem as well.

• **Impatiens** *(Impatiens New Guinea hybrid)* Produces a mass of flowers and beautifully colored foliage.

Impatiens Bowl

✄ A large, ribbed terracotta bowl with a pink color scheme, based on New Guinea impatiens with variegated leaves, pink ageratum, and a little twinkly verbena. In a semi-shady or sunny position, this arrangement will flower from early summer until the first frosts.

URNS AND JARS

URNS ARE THE MOST BEAUTIFUL of all containers. By definition, they can be any large jar or vessel that is rounded in shape, but they are usually grand containers with open, flaring or bulbous top sections, balanced on feet or base columns. Originally, they were made to hold the ashes of the dead and they had a lid: the word urn comes from the Latin *urere*, meaning to burn, and the Greek for a jar, *hurhke*.

GARDEN ORNAMENTS

Urns have been used as garden ornaments for centuries. They became especially popular in seventeenth- and eighteenth-century Italy. Made from stone, lead, or terracotta, they were usually extremely decorative with swagging, fluting, and elaborately carved handles. The Victorians produced quantities of urns: many of the cast iron ones can still be found, but for a high, often extortionate, price.

⚡ It has to be said that antique urns sometimes look best used like a piece of sculpture, as an unplanted garden ornament. The many reproductions of classical urns made in reconstituted stone, fiberglass, and terracotta, however, are better looking when planted.

⚡ Although most urns tend to be tall compared with their base section, they do not look good holding tall plants. This is especially true of the classical type of urn, with a bulbous top and narrowing stem flaring down to a square base, which sits on a short or tall column that is either cylindrical or straight edged. These urns tend to look best when their planting reflects the height of the container part of the urn, and has a good mass of sideways growth. Since the urn is already

ANTIQUE URN
Pink-flowering diascias and the delicate, silver-leaved plecostachys brim over the edges of a magnificent lead urn (ABOVE), strategically placed to the side of a gravel path.

BORDER SITUATION
A terracotta urn filled with yellow daisies and black-eyed Susan (LEFT) stands discreetly in a mixed border, adding height and color in mid-summer.

on a stem, a plant with an exposed, upright trunk looks uncomfortable. Choose plants that make a fountain shape, appearing to emanate from the center of the urn's base.

STRATEGIC SITING

Like very large pots and troughs, urns can be extremely weighty, and it is impractical to move them around too often. So think about the site carefully. Place them in important positions on your best lines of sight, maybe on an axis leading from a major house window, or at the end of a long path. A pair of small urns looks good on either side of a path as it leaves a terrace, or flanking a flight of steps; a single urn is exciting at the crossing of two paths, especially if there is a vista leading to it. Otherwise, urns can be placed against tall walls or dark green hedges, and beside any doorways and arches. Positioning an urn informally in a border is a beautiful way of bringing interest to an area that lacks color at a particular time of year. Urns can also look splendid planted in the center of a formal pond. If access is difficult, plant them with something like ivy, perhaps, that requires only minimum attention.

EXOTIC OIL JARS

Oil jars from the Mediterranean or large Chinese jars also make stunning containers, although you will need to drill drainage holes in them. Also, find out if they will stand your climate in winter. The Greek and part-glazed jars from the south of France are barely frost-proof. They work well with trailing plants tumbling out of them. Without drainage holes, you can fill them with water and grow delicate, small-leaved aquatic plants in them.

FOUNTAIN OF FLOWERS

GETTING THE PROPORTIONS for plantings in urns right is not easy. Surprisingly, tall plants often appear most uncomfortable, whereas low plantings work better. A simple arrangement, such as a single planting of ivy, can look wonderful spilling like flowing water over the lip of an urn. This well-proportioned stone urn is magnificent filled with plants that spray out of it like a fountain. The broom makes a great show in late spring, but its roots soon leave little room for the addition of other plants. If you want color in the summer, transplant the broom after it has flowered and replace it with summer annuals.

Broom (*Cytisus* 'Cornish Cream') In late spring, the slender stems are wreathed with scented flowers.

Peony-flowered tulip (*Tulipa* 'Carnival de Nice') The striped, double globular flowers are produced late in the season.

Spring Urn
Cream and yellow, with touches of red, make a cheerful combination for late spring. Plant the ivy, broom, and tulip bulbs in late autumn. As the broom has very delicate stems and foliage, it does not impede the tulips' growth.

Ivy (*Hedera helix* 'Telecurl') Plant ivy around the edge, to soften the sides without concealing its graceful outline.

PRACTICAL MATTERS

SOIL
Plant in a potting mixture of medium nutritional value.
SITE
Place in a sunny site.
WATERING
Keep the potting mixture moist, but not soggy.
PLANTS
Grow two brooms, ten tulip bulbs, and five ivies in a stone urn, the bowl of which measures 17in (42cm) across and 14in (35cm) deep.

Lantana (*Lantana camara*)
Varieties range from red and pink through orange, yellow, and white.

Golden feverfew (*Chrysanthemum parthenium* 'Aureum')
The delicate leaves and flowers have an astringent aroma.

Swedish ivy (*Plectranthus coleoides* 'Variegatus')
A foliage plant that is ideal for containers.

Plecostachys (*Plecostachys serpyllifolia*)
The tiny silver leaves tumble over the sides of the jar.

CHINESE JAR

CHINESE JARS OR URNS make fabulous containers. I felt the colors of this jar called for a yellow and cream planting. Lantana is a good choice as it is a quick-growing annual that is covered in flowers all summer. Feverfew, with its froth of white flowers and delicate leaves, seeds itself all over my garden, so I often use it in my summer container plantings. The silver trailing plecostachys and variegated Swedish ivy complete the picture. All but the feverfew are tender, so bring the arrangement in for winter.

PRACTICAL MATTERS

SOIL
Plant in a potting mixture of medium to rich nutritional value.
SITE
Place in a sunny site.
WATERING
Water well in hot sunny weather. Feed every two weeks.
PLANTS
Grow one lantana, two Swedish ivies, four plecostachys, and two golden feverfew in a Chinese jar, measuring 18x21in (45x52cm).

Tall Order
Rising from a mass of bushy and trailing, variegated and silver-leaved plants, the tall lantana complements the shape of the Chinese jar. Remove any lantana seed heads to encourage more flowers.

STATELY SPLENDOR

WIDE URNS LOOK THEIR BEST when filled by plants with a spreading habit. The curving shape of the base of this urn suggests that the plants also should have an outward-curving form. The bowl of the urn is quite shallow and larger plants would not grow happily in it, which is just as well because they would look uncomfortable.

If a wide urn is placed on a wall or high column so that it is primarily seen from below, it is best planted with trailers such as evergreen ivies, periwinkles, or flowering ivy-leaved geraniums, petunias, fuchsias, or hanging begonias.

A REFRESHING CHANGE

It is always fun to have a change from the old faithfuls, so here I have created an arrangement with pentas, lantana, and the prostrate weigela 'Looymansii Aurea.' Pale pink, orange, and pale yellow with lime-green makes a stylish combination. The planting will be in flower for many weeks, and then will have attractive foliage from spring through the summer. Pentas and lantana are tender, and therefore need to be grown as annuals in colder areas, but the gold-leaved weigela is hardy.

Another interesting arrangement for this urn could be an all-white display, which always looks elegant. You could use 'Mont Blanc' lavatera, the variegated ivy-leaved geranium, 'Elegante,' and 'Daybreak' gazanias. In spring, try a mass planting of 'Greuze' tulips, or one of the scented narcissi, and surround it with 'La Grave' periwinkle.

Soft-colored Stone

A soft, sand-colored, reconstituted stone urn with a summer planting of some lesser-known species: lantana, pentas, and a gold-leaved weigela. Planted to be seen from almost any angle, it would look good standing on a square stone column at the end of a straight path, or on a wall stanchion or pillar on a terrace.

PRACTICAL MATTERS
SOIL
Plant in a well-drained, rich potting mixture.
SITE
Place in a site that has sun for part of the day.
WATERING
Keep well watered and feed every two weeks.
PLANTS
Grow five lantana, three pentas, and three weigela in a 30in- (75cm-) diameter, reconstituted stone urn.

Pentas *(Pentas lanceolata)*
Produces clusters of pink,
lilac, red, or white flowers
in summer and autumn.

Lantana *(Lantana camara)*
Pinch off the tips of young
lantana plants to promote a full
bushy habit.

Weigela *(Weigela*
'Looymansii Aurea')
To maintain vigor, prune out a
few old branches to ground
level after flowering.

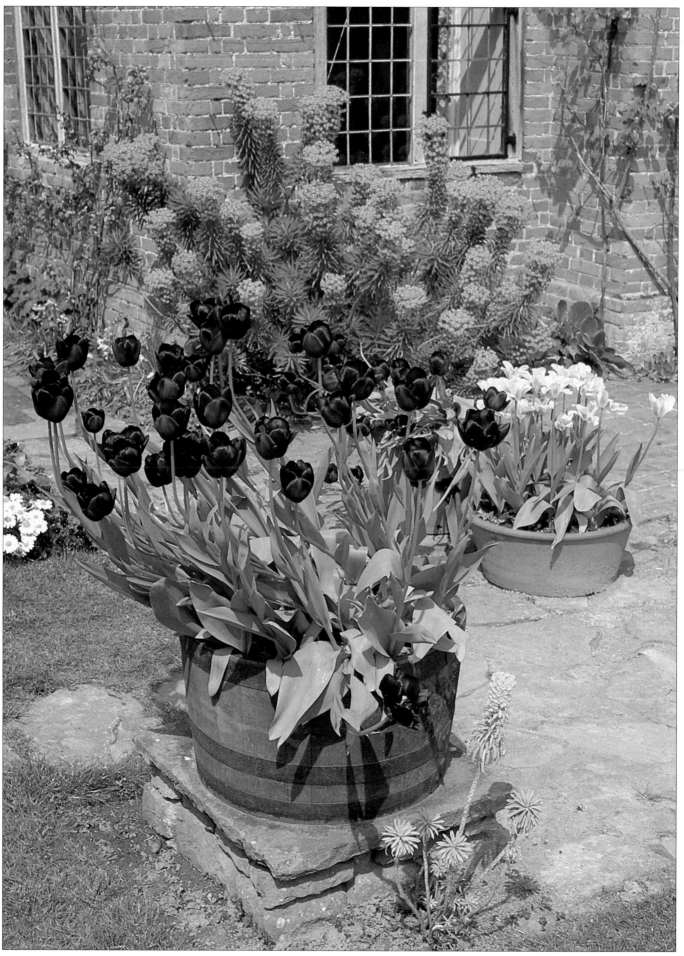

BARRELS AND TUBS

IN SOME INSTANCES, you may find that you require an especially large container – perhaps to grow shrubs, small trees, or simply a large planting. Garden centers now have a wide range on sale, including ceramic and terracotta tubs, fiberglass planters, and old beer barrels. There is also scope for improvisation. Crocks and various other containers from the kitchen can be used for growing plants, if you drill holes in their bases.

FIBERGLASS

As fiberglass can easily be molded to any shape, and colored in any shade, it is widely used to make simple plant tubs or replicas of wooden Versailles planters, elaborate lead containers, and other antique containers that are hard to find and extremely expensive. If done well, fiberglass imitations can look most convincing. They are moderately hard wearing, they are light to move around, and they require little maintenance.

BEER BARRELS

Originally, the familiar wooden barrel with iron bands was used for maturing and storing beer. Cut in half, it makes an excellent container for plants, and will last outside for several years, until the metal bands rust away. It is important to keep the wood of this type of barrel moist; if allowed to dry out, the wood contracts, causing the metal bands to fall off, and the barrel to collapse. Usually, moisture from the soil is adequate to prevent this from happening. It is always worth checking barrels bought from garden centers because if they have been stored empty for some time, the wood may have dried

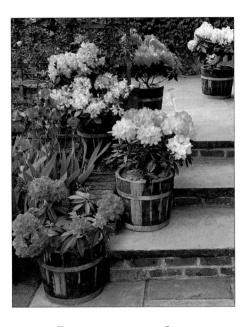

RHODODENDRONS ON STEPS
Half barrels (ABOVE) are planted with pink and purple rhododendrons, to complement the spectacular backdrop of irises.

QUEEN OF THE NIGHT
A plain, wooden, half barrel (LEFT) filled with the beautiful, almost black tulip 'Queen of Night' looks dramatic against the lime-green bracts of spurge.

out. If this is the case, give the barrel a thorough soaking before you plant it. If you get barrels from a brewery, you may have to drill 1/2in- (1cm-) diameter drainage holes in the base.

To help preserve the wood of barrels, you can prime and paint them. Choose a color that suits the barrel's intended site. While white, black, and green fit most situations, the more adventurous colors can work well if they pick up the paint on the exterior woodwork of the house, or enhance the plantings. Yellow sets off golden-leaved plants, and gray goes well with silver foliage.

PLANT CHOICE

Because of their size, tubs and barrels are especially useful for growing shrubs and small trees with large root systems. Spring bulbs, especially the taller growing narcissi and tulips, look effective too, their bare upright stems echoing the straight sides of a tub. I like using just one species or variety. A group of a single variety of ivy plants looks particularly good, covering and tumbling over a large barrel, and will maintain interest all through the year. In summer, a mass of petunias or low-growing roses looks magnificent.

WATER GARDEN

If the barrel or tub is watertight, you can fill it with water and grow some aquatic plants, perhaps miniature water lilies and some small floating species (SEE PAGE 112). Make sure that you support the water-lily roots at exactly the correct depth below the water surface. If necessary, prop up the container in which the roots are held with a couple of bricks. Keep the surface of the water clean, and top it off with more water whenever it is necessary.

BLUE CONIFER

GIVEN THE CORRECT SOIL CONDITIONS, good drainage, and enough water to prevent them becoming very dry, most conifers grow well in containers. Lack of water is the most frequent cause of dying back so you must check the potting mixture's moisture content throughout the winter, as well as the rest of the year. Remember, though, never to water plants during freezing conditions.

※ Many conifers, especially pines, spruces, and junipers, tolerate exposed positions. The low-growing species make attractive and long-lived specimens and have interestingly colored foliage, ranging from the brightest lime-greens to intense silver-blues. Of the larger and faster-growing conifers, *Picea* 'Albertiana Conica' makes a wonderful specimen tree in a big container, forming a vivid green, closely packed pyramid – keep it out of strong winds or it will become scorched. *Pinus mugo* and *Pinus wallichiana* are other striking specimen trees. They also form an excellent windbreak for an exposed site.

PRACTICAL MATTERS

SOIL
Plant in a neutral or acid potting mixture with sharp sand added (proportions 5:1).
SITE
Place in a sunny or exposed site.
WATERING
Keep the potting mixture moist.
PLANTS
Grow two spruces and four ivies in a 19in- (48cm-) diameter, frost-proof ceramic tub.

∽ PLANTING A CONIFER ∽

1 *Place a layer of clean pebbles or pottery chips in the base of a frost-proof ceramic tub and firm in lime-free potting mixture mixed with sharp sand to the base of the plants' root level.*

2 *Soak the root balls of two flat-sided blue spruces for about one hour in a bucket of water, and then position them in the tub so that they sit comfortably together. Firm the soil around their root balls, and fill the tub, planting the ivies around the edge.*

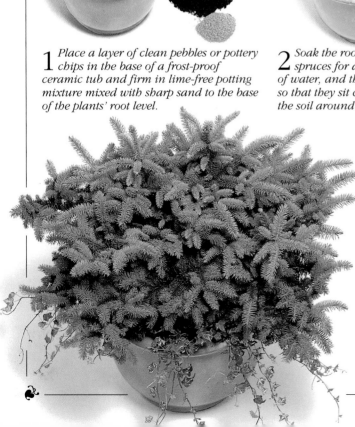

3 *Make sure that the soil is well firmed all around the arrangement and water it well. Blue spruce grows slowly so you need only prune the occasional stray shoot growing in the wrong direction to keep the shrubs in a neat shape. Do not allow the potting mixture to become too dry or too wet.*

Silver Spring Leaves
※ Three years later, this arrangement has grown so much that it is ready for repotting – late spring is a good time for planting and repotting conifers and most other evergreen shrubs. Seen here in mid spring, the new shoots are about to burst into foliage that is an even more intense silver than the old leaves.

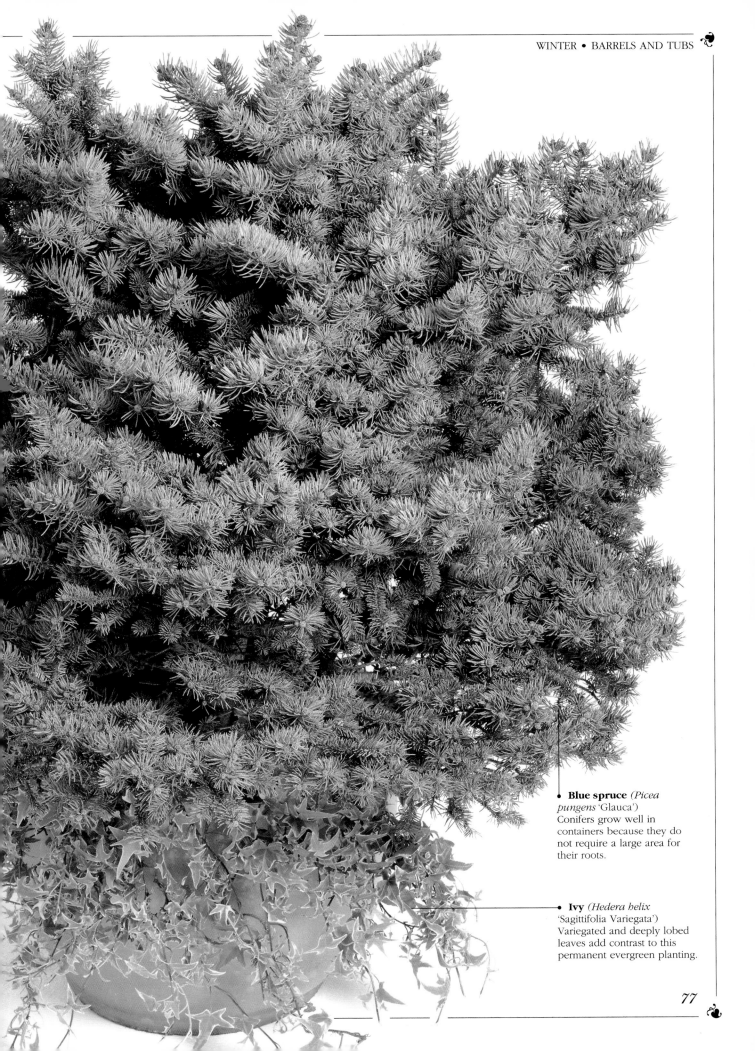

Blue spruce *(Picea pungens* 'Glauca')
Conifers grow well in containers because they do not require a large area for their roots.

Ivy *(Hedera helix* 'Sagittifolia Variegata')
Variegated and deeply lobed leaves add contrast to this permanent evergreen planting.

WINE BARREL

A NDROMEDA (OR PIERIS) IS ONE OF THOSE USEFUL SHRUBS that looks attractive throughout the year, and therefore makes an excellent basis for a permanent planting in a container. Its glossy evergreen foliage forms a marvelous backdrop for the more seasonal flowering plants, although it also has spectacular seasonal displays of its own. In spring, for example, the new leaves that unfurl are brilliant pink, before fading to pale pink and then bright yellow-green. At the same time, sprays of white flowers, reminiscent of lily-of-the-valley, come out. In this mid-spring arrangement, cinerarias have been planted among the andromeda: their vibrant heads of daisy-like flowers form a striking association with the new, pink andromeda leaves. Cinerarias are usually grown as house plants, but they do well outside in a frost-free spot, if you plant them as their flowers open.

—— YEAR-ROUND SHOW ——

In early spring, before the cinerarias are ready, plant pockets of narcissi between the andromeda. They will look stunning alongside its evergreen leaves. In summer, fill the gaps with annuals: flowering tobacco plants, impatiens, or fuchsias. Like the andromeda, all these plants enjoy shade or semi-shade; they also grow happily in the acidic potting mixture required by the andromeda.

✗ When there is no seasonal planting in the barrel, and the andromedas are growing alone, leave pots filled with soil in the position, reserved for seasonal plantings. This will prevent the shrubs' roots from invading the spaces and allow you to easily put new plants in the spaces.

PRACTICAL MATTERS

SOIL
Plant in a well-drained, acid potting mixture of high nutritional value.

SITE
Place in a semi-shady position, sheltered from wind, and protected from frost.

WATERING
Keep well watered, but not saturated, and feed once every two weeks from spring until autumn.

PLANTS
Grow three andromeda, four cinerarias, and five ivies in a wooden wine barrel.

Light padding •
Because the wine barrel is tall, I have padded out its base with a 10in- (25cm-) layer of broken polystyrene. This acts as a drainage medium and also prevents the container from becoming too heavy.

Relic from a Vineyard

✄ This antique wine barrel is planted with variegated andromeda and floriferous cinerarias. The wine barrel comes from a French vineyard where it was used to carry grapes from the fields to the press. If planting in a similar barrel, ensure that it has adequate drainage holes. Do not let the wood dry out too much, or it will shrink, loosening the iron bands that hold it together.

● **Andromeda** *(Pieris* 'Flaming Silver')
A pretty variegated form with pink new shoots in spring.

● **Cineraria** *(Senecio* x *hybridus)*
The flowers are so profuse in late winter, spring, and early summer that they conceal the leaves.

● **Ivy** *(Hedera helix* 'Pittsburgh')
A plain green ivy that does extremely well in containers.

Quick Change Over

✄ If you leave the cinerarias in their pots in the container, they are easier to remove when the flowers are over. This means that you must water them frequently to prevent the soil from drying out. Once the cinerarias finish blooming, replace them with summer-flowering annuals.

BARREL OF PETUNIAS

Most petunias are half-hardy perennials but they are best grown as annuals, as the plants tend to become leggy and less floriferous in their second year. In their first year, they flower continuously from early summer until autumn, but as with most plants that flower for a very long season, it is important to deadhead spent blooms to keep the display going. Their leaves and stems are covered with downy hairs and the leaves are also quite sticky, so grow them away from heavy pollution or they will gradually become smothered in black dust.

Petunias have been extensively hybridized and the variety of colors and flower forms now available is enormous. Colors range from deep velvety purple through violet, red, pink, and yellow, to white. Some have striped and splashed petals, and others sport a band of contrasting color around the edge of each flower. Some flowers are small, some large, some single, some double, and a few have a rich, sweet scent that is almost as heady as gardenia. The larger-flowered varieties are liable to spot in rain, but the smaller-flowered 'Resisto hybrids' are more weather-resistant.

PRACTICAL MATTERS

SOIL
Plant in a well-drained potting mixture of low nutritional value.

SITE
Place in a warm sunny site.

WATERING
Keep well watered but not soggy and feed only occasionally to promote flowers rather than leaves.

PLANTS
Grow 24 petunias in a 36in- (90cm-) diameter, half, wooden beer barrel.

Petunia
(*Petunia* x *hybrida*)
A selection of petunias, imaginatively chosen for their colors.

Color Permutations
⚘ This color mix of ice-pink, corn-yellow, and deep pink with a cream eye relates well to the old, half beer barrel. A selection of striped varieties, pale blue, cream, and white flowers, or maybe brightly mixed doubles would also make an attractive combination. Light and dark rich reds look jazzy together, too.

81

CROCK OF ROSES

IF YOU LOVE ROSES and want to grow some in containers, the smaller-growing multifloras, miniatures, and patio roses are the ones to choose. Their compact habit, tiny leaves, and small but full blossoms are neater than the larger-growing roses, so their shape looks comfortable in containers. You can try the larger-growing roses in pots, but, as they need a deep root run, they tend not to produce as many flowers as they would in the open ground. Since they are not the most beautiful plants, they can look ungainly for long periods, but you may feel that their spectacular blooms make up for this.

❧ Miniature roses and the new patio roses (crosses between miniatures and floribundas that have been specifically developed for containers) are being bred all the time, giving you many varieties from which to choose. I always try to select ones that smell sweet, such as 'Robin Redbreast,' a cheerful variety with bright scarlet flowers with pale eyes. 'Stars 'n' Stripes' is another favorite, bred from the old rose 'Ferdinand Pichard.' It has white flowers splashed with purple and crimson, and a wonderful, old rose scent.

Rose (*Rosa* 'Robin Redbreast') A patio rose that has been specially developed for growing in containers.

Second Life
❧ A broken lid ended this crock's useful life in the kitchen. By boring two ³/₈in (1cm) holes in the base with an electric drill, I easily transformed it into a plant container. As the roses are low-growing, the tall crock lifts them up from the ground, making it easy to smell them as you walk past.

PRACTICAL MATTERS

SOIL
Plant in a rich, well-drained potting mixture.
SITE
Place in a sunny site or one that receives sun for half of the day.
WATERING
Water well but do not allow to become soggy. Feed once a week.
PLANTS
Grow three 'Robin Redbreast' roses in a 14in- (35cm-) diameter crock.

SUMMER SALAD

THERE IS SOMETHING SPECIAL about picking your own fruit, vegetables, and herbs. While it is quite easy to grow most herbs in containers, fewer fruits and vegetables do well enough in containers to warrant growing them in this way. Tomatoes are the most successful, producing heavily when grown in a rich potting mixture and fed and watered well. Zucchini grown under the same conditions also produce well. You can plant them in succession to produce fruits from mid summer until autumn. Strawberries and blueberries are other fruits that also have good yields when grown in containers.

PRACTICAL MATTERS

SOIL
Plant in a very rich, well-drained potting mixture.

SITE
Place in a sunny site.

WATERING
Water well during the growing season and feed with tomato fertilizer, according to growing instructions.

PLANTS
Grow three tomato plants and two zucchini plants in a 30in- (72cm-) square fiberglass tub.

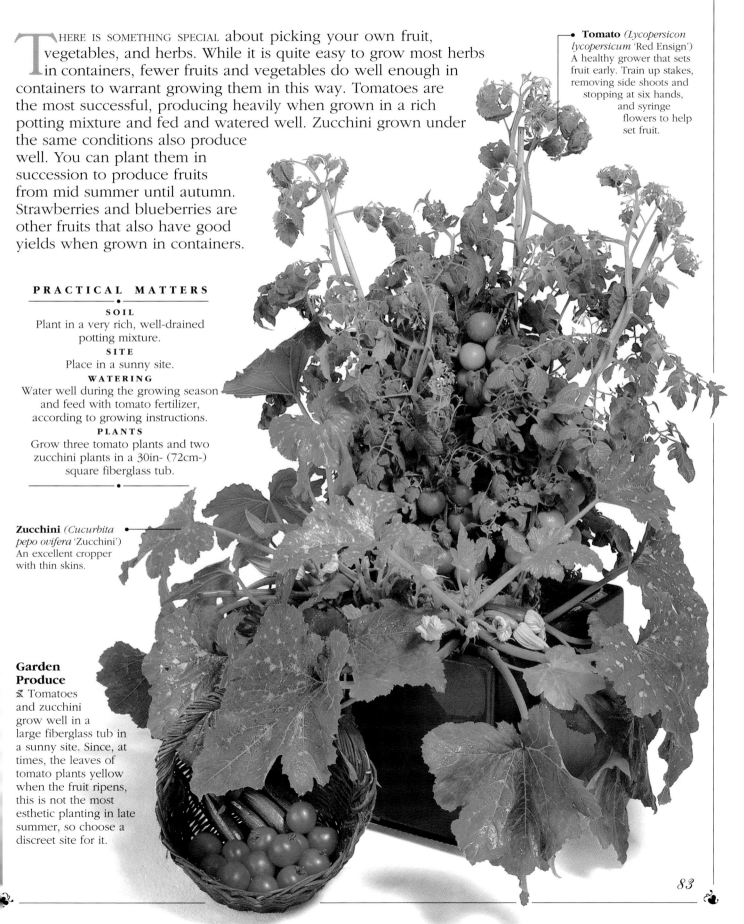

• **Tomato** (*Lycopersicon lycopersicum* 'Red Ensign')
A healthy grower that sets fruit early. Train up stakes, removing side shoots and stopping at six hands, and syringe flowers to help set fruit.

Zucchini (*Cucurbita pepo ovifera* 'Zucchini')
An excellent cropper with thin skins.

Garden Produce
Tomatoes and zucchini grow well in a large fiberglass tub in a sunny site. Since, at times, the leaves of tomato plants yellow when the fruit ripens, this is not the most esthetic planting in late summer, so choose a discreet site for it.

83

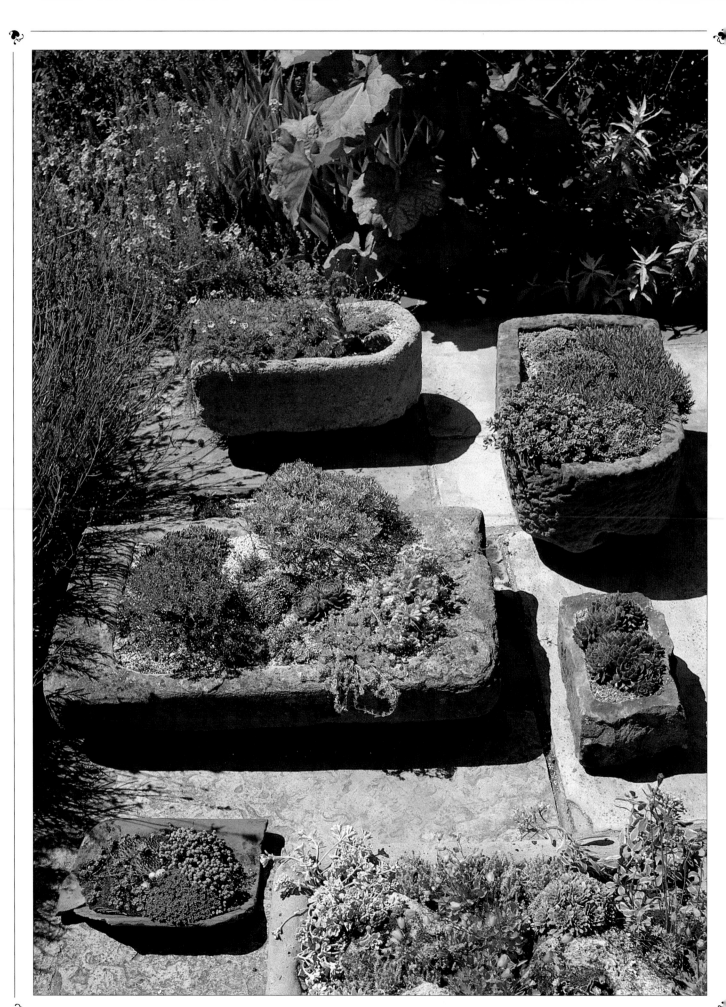

Sinks and Troughs

THE IDEA of planting a sink or a trough with garden plants is relatively new, but they both make marvelous containers. Sinks and troughs have been used in utilitarian ways for centuries, either in kitchens, or on farms for animals. The early ones were made from stone, and have the advantage of almost looking as if they are part of the landscape. The more modern sinks are more frequently made of porcelain.

� If you are lucky enough to have a stone sink, then prize it and give it a prominent place in your garden. Either set it on the ground or raise it up on legs made from stones or bricks.

WEIGHT PROBLEM

The one drawback of a stone sink is that it is very heavy. I have one that weighs substantially more than a grand piano, according to my furniture movers, but it is possible to move it on the level, solo, using a lever, and broom handles as rollers. Levering up the trough, position three broom handles at regular intervals underneath it, to act as rollers. Slowly push the trough forward, and as each roller is freed at the back, take it around to the front and position it to take the weight of the trough as it rolls forward again. It is a slow but relatively effortless process.

CONTEMPORARY ALTERNATIVES

Porcelain sinks are not as heavy as their stone counterparts, but if you cover them with a stone mix (SEE PAGES 158-9), they become almost as weighty. A range of troughs specifically for garden use is now available in lighter materials. The wooden ones are very attractive, but check that the wood will last. Teak or cedar troughs are the

LEAD HEIRLOOM
A handsome, eighteenth-century lead trough (ABOVE), planted with petunias, purple sage, pansies, marguerites, licorice plant, scented geraniums, and an abutilon, is set against the plain background of an evergreen hedge.

SINK GARDEN
A selection of succulents and alpines (LEFT), growing in various stone sinks and a terracotta roof tile on a hot sunny terrace. Each sink is raised slightly off the ground to ensure that water can drain out of the plug holes freely.

best – and the most expensive. To prolong the wood's life, paint the inside of the trough with a wood preservative and also line the trough with strong polyethylene, making holes to coincide with the drainage holes.

✗ Some of the fiberglass troughs are made to simulate lead or wood panels and can look quite convincing, especially when you leave them outside for a year or so to weather.

LOW PLANTINGS

As sinks and troughs are relatively low in comparison with their width, it seems natural to plant them with low plants: sinks tend to look out of proportion when they have plants that are on the tall side. In a sunny site, plants, such as alpines, that normally grow in rocky or stony places, are a good choice for sinks or troughs. They are also suitable for exposed sites, as most alpines tolerate wind, cold, and harsh sun. Make a miniature rock garden, carefully placing a group of small rocks on the surface of the potting mixture (SEE PAGES 158-9). In a shady site, sinks and troughs look beautiful when decorated with old pieces of rugged tree bark and planted with small ferns. A stone sink also makes a good home for a collection of houseleeks or small silver-leaved succulents.

✗ All alpines must be protected from winter wetness, otherwise they will rot and die. In sheltered spots, you can do this by driving a small stick into each corner of your sink and balancing a pane of glass on top. The glass must not touch the plants, so leave a 6in (15cm) gap between them and the glass. It is essential to have plenty of ventilation. Alternatively, you can secure an open-ended cloche over small sinks, driving it in with stakes.

WOODLAND GARDEN

IF YOU ARE FORTUNATE ENOUGH to have a large, old stone sink, but it is in a fairly shady place, do not feel that you have to struggle to move it to a sunnier spot in your garden. A good selection of very beautiful plants with wonderful shapes, colors, and perfumes will grow happily without that much sun.

❦ These semi-shade-loving spring bulbs and flowers growing on a bed of moss make a tranquil, enchanting semi-wild planting that is reminiscent of a woodland floor. Dogtooth violets are among my favorites with their flowers of white, cream, or pink with waxy reflexed petals. So, too, are the snake's head fritillaries. When seen close at hand, their papery pendent flowers resemble the finest china with an elaborate pattern of veining, varying from almost white, through pink to purple and plum-black.

❦ Wild primroses, pretty little yellow-flowered plants that grow naturally in England, are easy to grow from seed and have a delicious, sweet buttery scent. Lilies-of-the-valley have one of the best scents of all but they can be unpredictable. Usually they grow like rampant weeds, but occasionally they are impossible to start – I know people who have struggled for years to get them established without success. If you find that you cannot persuade lily-of-the-valley to grow in your garden, try uvularia instead. Another shade lover, it has small, pendent bell-shaped flowers.

Natural Colonizers

❦ All the plants in this stone sink will naturalize, forming larger clumps each year. As the dogtooth violets and snake's head fritillaries die down after flowering, introduce small summer and autumn interest plants over the top of the bulbs and beside them.

Lithodora
(*Lithodora diffusa* 'Heavenly Blue')
Flowers over a long period.

Lily-of-the-valley
(*Convallaria majalis*)
The delicate stems of
bellflowers have
an intense and
delicious fragrance.

PRACTICAL MATTERS

SOIL
Plant in a rich, lime-free potting mixture,
with leafmold added.

SITE
Place in a semi-shady site.

WATERING
Keep the potting mixture moist,
but not soggy.

PLANTS
Grow five dogtooth violets, twelve snake's
head fritillaries, seven wild primroses, one
lithodora, nine lilies-of-the-valley, and three
common polypody ferns in a stone sink
measuring 48x27x8in (120x67x20cm).

Alpine Selection
✄ In a stone sink that sits in a sunny
position, plant a selection of early-
flowering rockery plants for a spring
display. In late spring, phlox put on a
brilliant show of sweetly scented
blossoms and later the lewisia
produces bright pink flowers.

Snake's head fritillary
(Fritillaria meleagris)
Spring-flowering bulbs
favoring a damp position.

Wild primrose
(Primula veris)
The nodding trumpets of
sweetly scented flowers
are long-lasting.

Dogtooth violet
(Erythronium 'Pagoda')
Few flowers have such
poise and beauty of form.

**Common polypody
fern** *(Polypodium
vulgare)* Ferns prefer
to grow in crevices, so
this old piece of bark
suits them

Mossy floor
A layer of
moss helps
keep the
soil
moist.

MARINE THEME

A GIANT SEA SHELL may not be the first object that leaps to mind when you are trying to come up with an interesting container, but it makes a magnificent planter for low-growing specimens that do not need a deep root run. This one even has a hole close to its lowest point, solving all drainage problems. The only drawback is its great weight: two people can barely lift it.

✱ Foaming and flowing plants seemed appropriate, and white and silver flowers and foliage add to the marine effect. The kalanchoe introduced a little strong color, creating just the look I wanted.

✱ The shell could have been planted with alpines, if it was possible to give it protection from excessive dampness in winter. Alternatively, a single planting works effectively: a trailing mound of bellflowers *(Campanula* var. *elatines garganica)*, with their blue flowers; or a carpet of ivy such as 'Duck's Foot Ivy,' 'Ivalace,' 'Manda's Crested,' or the silver-streaked 'Eva,' for instance.

Knotweed *(Polygonum affine* 'Donald Lowndes') A mat-forming perennial with deep pink flowers that fade to pale pink.

PRACTICAL MATTERS

SOIL
Plant in a well-drained potting mixture of medium nutritional value and fine gravel (proportions 4:1).

SITE
Place in a sunny site.

WATERING
Take care not to overwater.

PLANTS
Grow two stonecrops, one chamomile, one pink, one heuchera, one knotweed, and two kalanchoes in a 30in- (75cm-) wide and 10in- (25cm-) deep sea shell.

Stonecrop *(Sedum anacampseros)* A hardy variety with purple-pink flowers in summer.

● **Pink** (*Dianthus* 'Little Jock')
In summer, this compact
variety bears clove-scented,
single, pale pink flowers with
deep pink centers.

● **Kalanchoe**
(*Kalanchoe blossfeldiana*)
Although this variety is not
hardy, it does well outside
in dry summers.

● **Chamomile** (*Anthemis
punctata cupaniana*)
Grown for the daisy-like flowers
and silver filigree foliage.

Heuchera (*Heuchera* ●
'Snowstorm')
A striking variety grown for its
pretty flowers and beautiful
white leaves edged with green.

Year-round Interest
❋ With the exception of kalanchoe,
all the plants are hardy, and indeed
evergreen, so the arrangement can be left
on constant display all through the year.
It is a planting that changes with the
seasons. Here, we see it in late summer,
when the knotweed is flowering.

WOODEN TROUGH OF EVERGREENS

LOW SHRUBS AND PERENNIALS grow as well as alpines in troughs and sinks, provided they have enough soil. In this 9in- (23cm-) deep wooden trough, evergreen and silver-leaved plants thrive. The white winter-flowering heather is less demanding than most ericas, as it tolerates neutral soil. In mild spells in late winter, its flowers may be joined by the lilac-blue ones of the rosemary. A hebe has been introduced for its wonderful evergreen foliage – later in the year it is covered with white star-shaped flowers. The curry plant also has flowers in summer, but here it is grown for its magnificent, glistening silver foliage.

✻ Although this trough has been planted for winter interest, you can replace the winter-flowering heathers with bellflowers or white ivy-leaved geraniums in summer.

Textured Foliage
✻ A winter arrangement of evergreens, relying on contrasting textures and colors for interest. The planting looks best from above, so place it at ground level, allowing free drainage.

Heather (*Erica carnea* •
'Springwood White')
A reliable winter-flowering variety with white flowers.

Hebe (*Hebe pinguifolia* 'Pagei')
Grown here for its low mound of silvery leaves, this hebe becomes smothered with white flowers in summer.

Ivy (*Hedera helix* 'Ivalace') •
Distinguished by its shiny, crinkly green leaves and prominent veining.

Rosemary *(Rosmarinus officinalis* 'Prostratus') A trailing variety with low foliage and flowers.

Sprawlers in Front
⚹ Plant the taller rosemary, hebe, and curry plant at the back of the wooden trough, and then set the heather, ivy, and juniper, which all have a more sprawling habit, toward the front.

PRACTICAL MATTERS

SOIL
Plant in a well-drained, lime-free potting mixture of low nutritional value, mixed with a little gravel (proportions 10:1).

SITE
Place the trough in sunshine.

WATERING
Keep just moist, concentrating the watering on the heathers.

PLANTS
Grow one hebe, two heathers, one ivy, one juniper, and one curry plant in a teak trough, measuring 31x23x8in (80x60x20cm).

Curry plant *(Helichrysum italicum)* Clip regularly but lightly to maintain a round-headed shape.

Creeping juniper *(Juniperus horizontalis* 'Bar Harbor') A low conifer, ideal for troughs.

Wooden and weatherproof Teak troughs are extremely weatherproof, and will last outside for many years without requiring any attention.

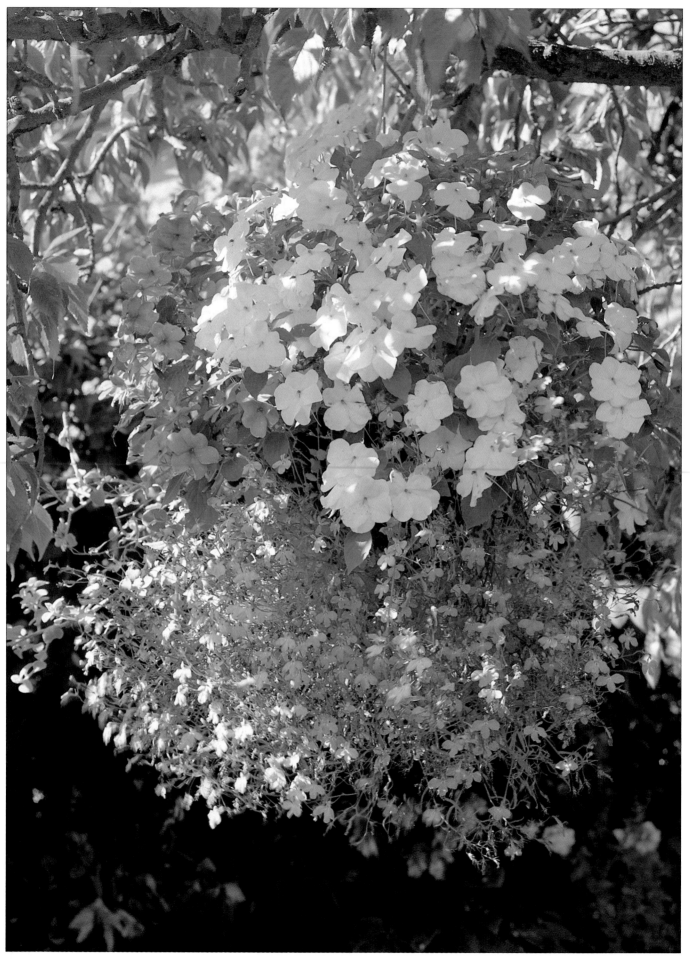

HANGING BASKETS

THE GREAT ADVANTAGE of hanging baskets is that you can grow small groups of plants in positions that it would be otherwise impossible to consider: high up on a house or on your garden walls, below the branches of a tree, or suspended from the beams of a porch, pergola, arch, or arbor.

— TYPES OF BASKET —

Most commercial hanging baskets are made from a simple, lightweight wire frame. The fact that the frame is light is important because once they are holding soil and plants they can become quite heavy (always use a lightweight potting mixture). You can improvise, using wicker baskets instead (SEE PAGES 102-3) but they must be strong and firmly attached. Bear in mind that you will not be able to grow plants out of the base of these improvised baskets, but will have plants growing out of the top and trailing down the sides.

✕ Several forms of wall container – which have one flat side so that they can be attached to a vertical surface, easily – are also available, made from terracotta, ceramic, or wire. If you are lucky enough to find one, an old hayrack made from iron and secured to a brick or stone wall can look magnificent (SEE PAGES 98-9).

✕ All baskets must be lined before planting. Commercially made liners (constructed from plastic) or fiber pots are available for standard-sized hanging baskets, but I always prefer to see a moss lining – it is less obtrusive and looks so much more natural. Kept moist, it should remain a heathy green all summer. You still need to have a plastic lining, between the moss and the soil, to help retain moisture in the potting mixture. Make sure the layer of moss is even and thick enough

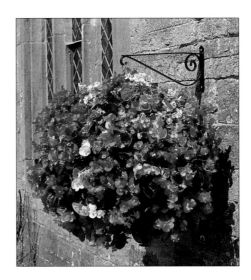

BALL OF BEGONIAS
Small-leaved, small-flowered bedding begonias, planted to grow into a compact ball of red, white, and pink flowers (ABOVE), last all summer long.

BELOW THE BRANCHES
A basket of impatiens and lobelia (LEFT), suspended from the branches of a tree. Impatiens are an excellent choice for a hanging basket in a shady site.

to hide the plastic – sphagnum or carpet moss are the best types for this purpose, and are readily available from most large garden centers.

— WHICH VIEWPOINT? —

Before choosing the plants for your hanging basket, consider the viewing height for the arrangement. It is no good planning a wonderful top display of flowers if you can only see the bottom of the basket. Choose plants that grow in a way that you will be able to see them well: the ball of flowering begonias (LEFT), for example, can be enjoyed from above, below, and from the side, but the moss baskets (SEE PAGES 102-3) are planted to be seen at about eye-level.

✕ I like to overplant hanging baskets so that they overflow with foliage and flowers. This means watering and feeding them even more frequently than usual through the growing and flowering season: in hot, sunny weather you may have to do it twice or even three times a day. The root balls of the plants can be touching each other, but avoid squashing them into place or they will not have any room to grow.

— HANGING ATTACHMENTS —

When hanging baskets are wet, they can be very heavy, so their fittings need to be extremely strong and secure. Usually, specially designed, metal brackets for attaching to vertical surfaces are sold wherever you buy hanging baskets. Secure the brackets firmly to the wall with screws and molly bolts. If you are suspending a basket from a pergola or porch, make sure that you hang it from a sturdy and stout crossbar. Every time you hang up a basket planted with a new arrangement, check that the fittings are all safe and secure.

TRADITIONAL BASKET

ALTHOUGH HANGING BASKETS can be planted for every season of the year, it is in summer that they really come into their own. Low and trailing annuals with a profusion of flowers, such as geraniums, petunias, begonias, sweet alyssum, blue lobelia, and impatiens have become favorite plants to use in baskets – and for good reason. They all give a continuous show of color from early summer until the first frosts. Many other plants also do well, including morning glory, verbena, nasturtium, lantana, lotus, portulaca, calceolaria, and blue marguerite, but only the verbena and nasturtium have the same staying power as the first stalwart group.

PRACTICAL MATTERS
•
SOIL
Plant in a lightweight potting mixture of medium nutritional value.
SITE
Hang in a sunny site.
WATERING
Keep well watered, especially in hot weather. Feed weekly.
PLANTS
Grow six lobelias, four licorice plants, two sweet alyssum, two portulacas, three ivy-leaved geraniums, and three calceolarias in a 14in- (35cm-) diameter, moss-lined wire hanging basket.
•

⚘ PLANTING A HANGING BASKET ⚘

1 *Line the basket with sphagnum moss, so that it covers the inside of the basket completely but is not so thick that it takes up valuable root space for the plants.*

2 *Place a plastic liner over the moss so that the planting will not dry out too quickly. Trim to neaten. If you are not growing plants through the base, cut five drainage holes in the plastic.*

3 *If you wish to encourage trailing plants to grow out of the bottom of the basket, carefully wrap each in a small piece of plastic, shaped into a narrow cone. Cover the roots with the wide end of the cone and the leaves with the narrow part.*

Portulaca *(Portulaca grandiflora)*
A sun lover, available in pink, red, orange, yellow, and white.

4 *Pierce a hole in the base of the lining. From the inside, thread the narrow end of the cone through the hole. Pull through until the leafy part of the plant is outside the basket, pull the plastic cone away, leaving the plant in position. Repeat.*

5 *When you have a ring of plants around the base, fill the basket with 3in (7.5cm) of potting mixture. Thread through more trailing plants and firm soil around the roots. Complete another ring before you reach the top.*

Licorice plant
(Helichrysum petiolare)
A useful, trailing foliage plant for hanging baskets.

6 *Plant the top of the basket with a mixture of trailing and bushy plants, and then fill with potting mixture, making sure that the final level of the soil is just below the top, to allow for watering. Hang the basket in its permanent position and water well.*

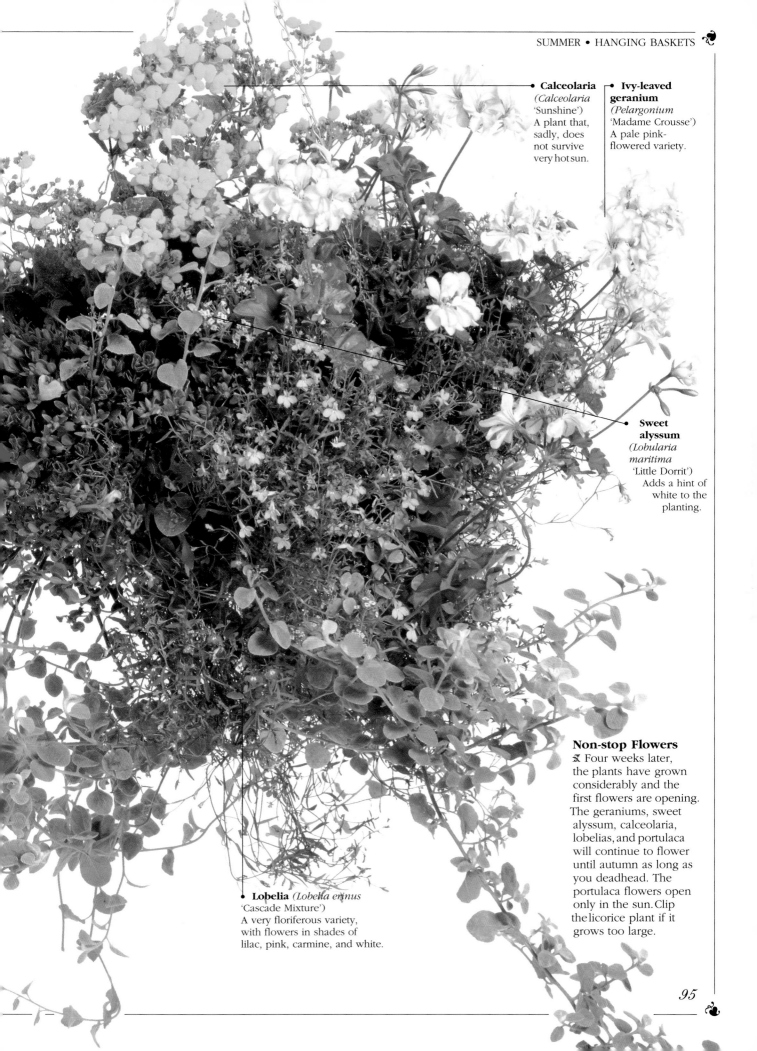

Calceolaria
(*Calceolaria*
'Sunshine')
A plant that,
sadly, does
not survive
very hot sun.

**Ivy-leaved
geranium**
(*Pelargonium*
'Madame Crousse')
A pale pink-
flowered variety.

**Sweet
alyssum**
(*Lobularia
maritima*
'Little Dorrit')
Adds a hint of
white to the
planting.

Non-stop Flowers
Four weeks later,
the plants have grown
considerably and the
first flowers are opening.
The geraniums, sweet
alyssum, calceolaria,
lobelias, and portulaca
will continue to flower
until autumn as long as
you deadhead. The
portulaca flowers open
only in the sun. Clip
the licorice plant if it
grows too large.

Lobelia (*Lobelia erinus*
'Cascade Mixture')
A very floriferous variety,
with flowers in shades of
lilac, pink, carmine, and white.

GOLD SUMMER BASKET

A BASKET OF GOLDEN FLOWERS and foliage makes a beautiful hanging feature in a semi-shady spot that needs cheering up. I find that loose, less considered plantings usually work best in hanging baskets, but, occasionally, a calculated close color scheme looks just right. The informality of the licorice plant, mixed with yellow and gold pansies, golden ivy, and yellow snapdragons creates a natural wild-looking arrangement.

PRACTICAL MATTERS

SOIL
Plant in a rich, lightweight potting mixture.

SITE
Place in a sheltered, semi-shady or sunny site.

WATERING
Keep well watered and feed twice a week.

PLANTS
Grow three licorice plants, three golden ivies, six pansies, and four snapdragons in a 14in- (35cm-) diameter wire hanging basket lined with moss and plastic.

Pansy (*Viola* Crystal Bowl Series) The clear yellow flowers have a delicious scent.

Pansy (*Viola* x *wittrockiana* 'Rhine Gold') Do not allow the plants to become straggly or their flowering will be impaired.

Threading Trick
✂ To encourage plants to grow in all directions, I threaded some ivies and two pansies through the base of the basket. The other plants were put in the top. As a general rule, you should only thread trailing or short plants through the base.

Golden ivy
(*Hedera helix* 'Harald') The leaves are gold-edged.

Snapdragon
(*Antirrhinum* 'Sweetheart') Any low-growing, yellow-flowered variety would be suitable for this basket.

Licorice plant (*Helichrysum petiolare* 'Aureum') A very fast grower, this annual needs to be kept under control with an occasional trim.

BASKET OF RED AND SILVER

CLASHING REDS WORK TOGETHER in a fascinating way. Pink-red and orange-red intensify each other when placed close together, and set against the feathery silver foliage of the winged pea, they look wonderful. I felt a little relief was needed, and so introduced two coleus plants for the gold in their leaves.

PRACTICAL MATTERS

SOIL
Plant in a rich, lightweight potting mixture.
SITE
Place in a sunny site.
WATERING
Water well, never allowing the basket to dry out. Feed twice a week.
PLANTS
Grow two 'Yale' ivy-leaved geraniums, one 'Tavira' ivy-leaved geranium, three portulacas, four verbenas, four winged peas, and two coleus plants in an 18in-(45cm-) diameter wire hanging basket, lined with moss and plastic.

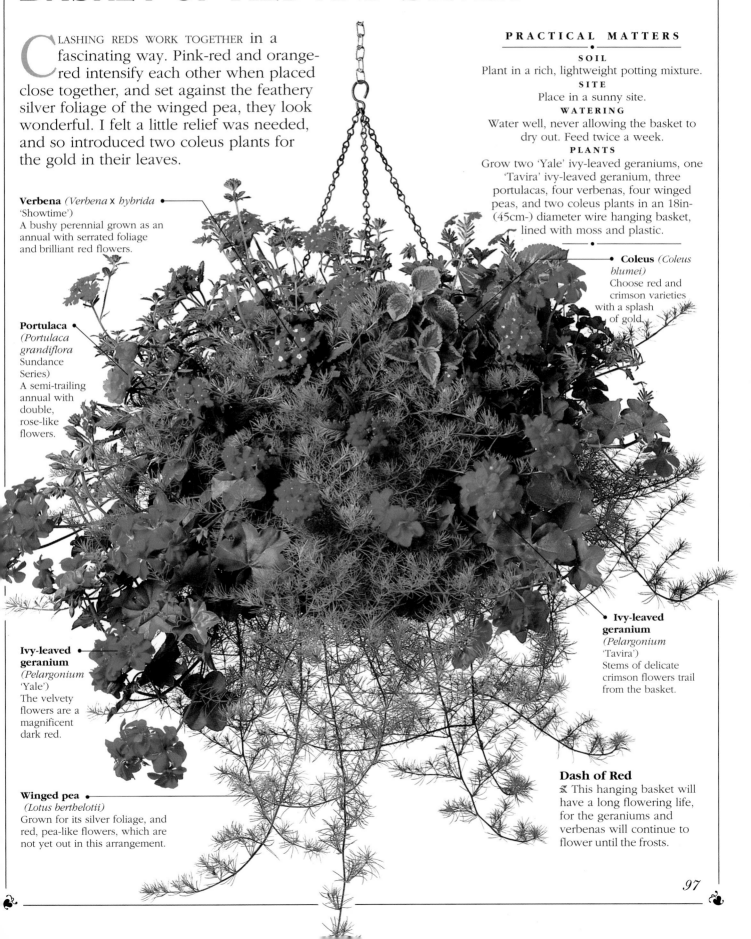

Verbena (*Verbena* x *hybrida* 'Showtime')
A bushy perennial grown as an annual with serrated foliage and brilliant red flowers.

Portulaca (*Portulaca grandiflora* Sundance Series)
A semi-trailing annual with double, rose-like flowers.

Ivy-leaved geranium (*Pelargonium* 'Yale')
The velvety flowers are a magnificent dark red.

Winged pea (*Lotus berthelotii*)
Grown for its silver foliage, and red, pea-like flowers, which are not yet out in this arrangement.

Coleus (*Coleus blumei*)
Choose red and crimson varieties with a splash of gold.

Ivy-leaved geranium (*Pelargonium* 'Tavira')
Stems of delicate crimson flowers trail from the basket.

Dash of Red
This hanging basket will have a long flowering life, for the geraniums and verbenas will continue to flower until the frosts.

HAYRACK OF FLOWERS

WALL BASKETS ARE PARTICULARLY USEFUL in tight places where a circular basket will not fit. They are only half the width of hanging baskets, with flat backs that can be attached to a wall, usually by slotting them onto two screws protruding from the wall. Originally used for holding hay in horse stables, hayracks are the same shape as a half basket, but they are larger and made with iron bars. They make excellent planters for the garden, so much so that reproductions are now sold specifically for garden plants.

The arrangement in this hayrack is designed for a position just above eye-level on a shady wall. The fuchsias and begonias will grow more and more, tumbling down the sides as summer advances and autumn arrives. To achieve this effect, when planting, slightly lean the plants in the direction that you want them to grow, and position some trailers between the bars. As with conventional hanging baskets, I have lined this hayrack with moss and plastic, so I had to make holes in the lining to thread through some plants and provide drainage.

PRACTICAL MATTERS
•
SOIL
Plant in a rich, lightweight potting mixture.
SITE
Place in a shady or semi-shady site.
WATERING
Keep well watered and feed once a week.
PLANTS
Grow three begonias, three fuchsias, and two impatiens in a 20in (50cm) hayrack.
•

• **Impatiens** *(Impatiens* 'New Guinea hybrid') White-flushed pink flowers open amid bronze leaves, veined with vibrant orange and yellow streaks.

Color Choice

�背 This rich, deep pink, dark purple, and pale pink mix would look particularly effective against a dark brick wall, where the glowing colors would brighten the shade for several months in summer. The following season use the same plants, but try different color combinations: amber begonias, orange impatiens with dark red leaves, and red fuchsias; or ice-pink begonias with gold-leaved white impatiens, and a fuchsia such as 'Pink Galore'.

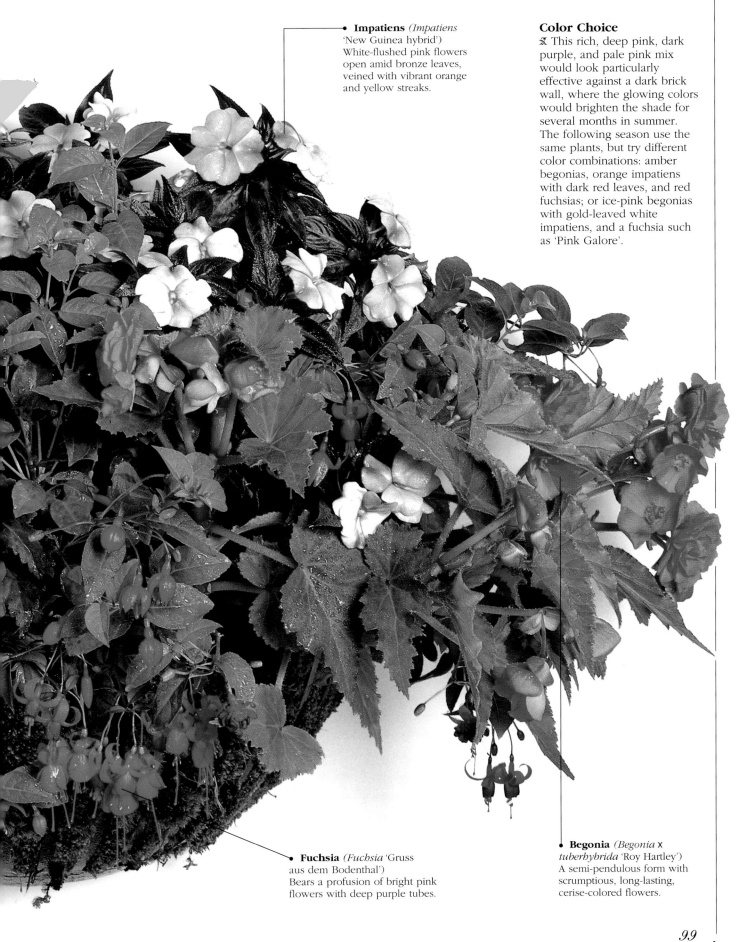

• **Fuchsia** *(Fuchsia* 'Gruss aus dem Bodenthal') Bears a profusion of bright pink flowers with deep purple tubes.

• **Begonia** *(Begonia* x *tuberhybrida* 'Roy Hartley') A semi-pendulous form with scrumptious, long-lasting, cerise-colored flowers.

99

EXCITING COLOR COMBINATIONS

HUNDREDS OF PANSY and viola varieties are available to the gardener in the most beautiful colors, providing you with enormous scope for exciting color combinations. In some areas, the summers are too hot for pansies so see if your neighbors are growing them before you try them in hot weather, or select new heat-resistant types such as 'Maxim Marina' or 'Padparadja'. After heavy flowering, cut back to promote new growth.

PRACTICAL MATTERS

SOIL
Plant in a well-drained, lightweight potting mixture of high nutritional value.
SITE
Place in a semi-shady site.
WATERING
Water and feed frequently.
PLANTS
Grow eight pansies, five alyssum, three monkey flowers, three wandering jews, and two Swedish ivies in an 18in- (45cm-) diameter, moss-lined, wire hanging basket.

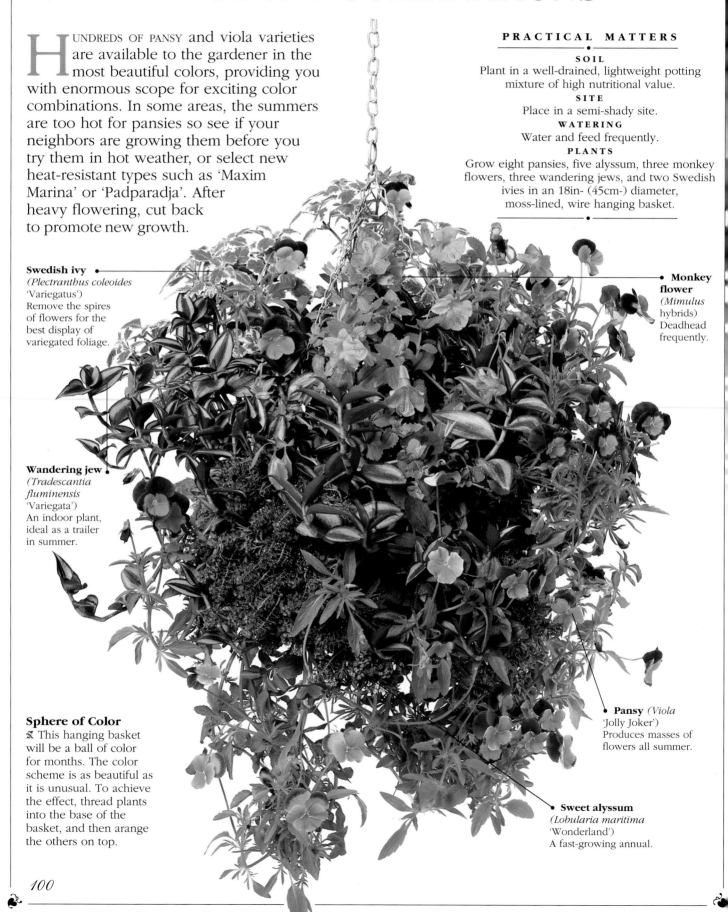

Swedish ivy
(*Plectranthus coleoides* 'Variegatus')
Remove the spires of flowers for the best display of variegated foliage.

Monkey flower
(*Mimulus* hybrids)
Deadhead frequently.

Wandering jew
(*Tradescantia fluminensis* 'Variegata')
An indoor plant, ideal as a trailer in summer.

Pansy (*Viola* 'Jolly Joker')
Produces masses of flowers all summer.

Sphere of Color
✺ This hanging basket will be a ball of color for months. The color scheme is as beautiful as it is unusual. To achieve the effect, thread plants into the base of the basket, and then arange the others on top.

Sweet alyssum
(*Lobularia maritima* 'Wonderland')
A fast-growing annual.

SPRING COLLECTION

Spring is the high point of this planting, although it will also look attractive in winter and summer. The evergreen foliage of the euonymus and spurge provides winter interest before the little English daisies start to open from mid winter onward. The daisy flowers are joined by windflowers and pasque flowers in late spring, and also the spurge. In mild areas the daisies will continue to flower in summer, against the silver spurge.

PRACTICAL MATTERS

SOIL
Plant in a lightweight potting mixture of medium nutritional value.
SITE
Place in a sunny position, sheltered from strong winds.
WATERING
Keep just moist.
PLANTS
Grow eight double daisies, three pasque flowers, twelve windflowers, three spurges, and three euonymus in a 16in- (40cm-) diameter, moss-lined, wire basket.

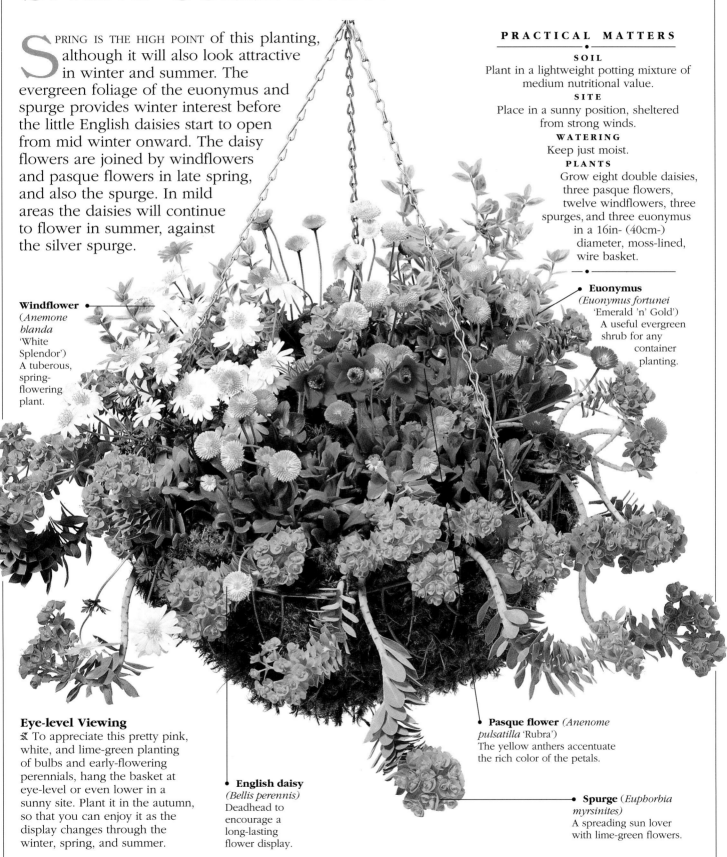

Windflower
(*Anemone blanda* 'White Splendor') A tuberous, spring-flowering plant.

Euonymus
(*Euonymus fortunei* 'Emerald 'n' Gold') A useful evergreen shrub for any container planting.

Eye-level Viewing
✂ To appreciate this pretty pink, white, and lime-green planting of bulbs and early-flowering perennials, hang the basket at eye-level or even lower in a sunny site. Plant it in the autumn, so that you can enjoy it as the display changes through the winter, spring, and summer.

English daisy
(*Bellis perennis*) Deadhead to encourage a long-lasting flower display.

Pasque flower (*Anenome pulsatilla* 'Rubra') The yellow anthers accentuate the rich color of the petals.

Spurge (*Euphorbia myrsinites*) A spreading sun lover with lime-green flowers.

MOSS BASKETS

THIS BLAZING YELLOW TRIO of favorite spring flowers grows in three moss baskets, attached to each other to make an unusual hanging container. I secured the three basket handles together in two places with garden wire: at the point where the handles join the basket, and 5in (13cm) further up the handles, just before they start to curve toward the center. I wired the chain in at the same time, securing it at both the points. Each of the baskets is lined with plastic, pricked in the bottom for drainage, and then filled with a lightweight potting mixture, which will not put too much strain on the baskets or the chain.

—— PLANTING PLAN ——

I planted both the narcissi and tulip bulbs in late autumn. The polyanthus, which are available from florists as well as garden centers, can be planted from autumn onward in very mild climates; in cold areas it is best to wait until early spring or they may be damaged by frost. All the bulbs are hardy and will need to be only lightly watered during the winter months to keep the potting mixture just moist. Do not water in frosty weather.

— LONG-LASTING FLOWERS —

If kept in semi-shade, the arrangement should remain in flower for several weeks in mid spring; in a sunny spot the daffodils and tulips might come out and finish more quickly but the polyanthus will continue flowering sporadically until late spring.

PRACTICAL MATTERS

SOIL
Plant in a well-drained, lightweight potting mixture of medium nutritional value.

SITE
Hang this arrangement in semi-shade for the best effect, although the plants will grow in a sunny or shady site.

WATERING
Keep lightly watered through the winter, so the soil does not become too dry.

PLANTS
Grow five polyanthus and twelve tulips each in two 12in- (30cm-) diameter moss baskets, and twelve narcissi in a 7in- (18cm-) diameter moss basket.

Polyanthus (*Primula* Pacific hybrids)
In mild areas these will flower during the winter as well as in the spring time.

Tulip (*Tulipa*
'Monte Carlo')
A double-flowered
variety reaching 12in
(30cm) tall.

Narcissus
(*Narcissus*
'April Tears')
A delicate pale
yellow daffodil with
a strong fragrance.

Unusual touch
Moss baskets secured
together with garden
wire and suspended
on a chain make an
unusual hanging
arrangement.

Joys of Spring
✗ The bright rich yellows
of the flowers in this
unusual hanging basket
epitomize spring. Hang it
against a house, a fence,
or a wall in semi-shade
for long-lasting flowers.

103

SUITING THE SITE

❧

A LWAYS ASSESS THE AMOUNT of sun, wind, and cold a site receives before deciding what to grow there, but also think about the esthetics: the shape, color, and texture of the proposed planting and the character and size of the container, in relation to its immediate surroundings.

UNDER THE EAVES OF A POTTING SHED
Astilbes and begonias, both summer-flowering plants, like a spot in dappled shade, away from the harsh glare of the sun.

SUNNY POSITIONS

THE MAJORITY OF PLANTS love sunshine. Good light and lots of sun makes them grow into strong specimens with healthy green leaves and an abundance of flowers. However, it can be too much of a good thing, and if plants in containers receive very hot sun all day, they dry out extremely quickly. In hot sunny spells, when plants in containers are subjected to constant sun, you may need to water them two or three times a day. Even then, it is possible that the leaves may become scorched and yellow and the flowers deformed from excess sun, so if you have a very sunny garden, choose plants renowned for their robust qualities and endurance in hot weather.

—— INTENSE HEAT ——

Cacti and succulents, aloe, dracena, yucca, and agave all thrive in baking conditions – extreme sun and little water. Conveniently, they will also put up with low temperatures, at least down to freezing in winter. They dislike a mixture of cold and damp, so if such conditions are likely, it is safest to bring them into a conservatory or greenhouse over winter. When the weather improves bring them outside for the open-air sunbathing that they so enjoy.

—— VIBRANT COLOR ——

A riot of brilliant color suits a sunny site. Flowering plants, such as zonal and Martha Washington geraniums, thrive in such conditions, as do snapdragons, petunias, marigolds, salvias, gazanias, licorice plants, hibiscus, pinks, phlox, and zinnias. All bloom over a long period, starting in early summer and continuing until the first

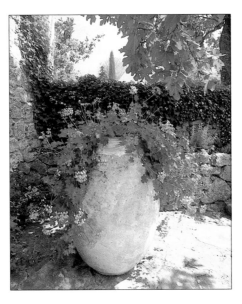

PROVENCE-STYLE
Trailing geraniums, planted in an oil jar from the south of France (ABOVE), spell out sunshine. In ideal Mediterranean conditions, geraniums reach 20ft (6m) tall, but only if grown in the open ground. A container restricts their height.

CACTUS GARDEN
A terracotta-tiled terrace (LEFT), where cereus and prickly pear grow in large clay pots, casting their dramatic shadows against a white wall. Echeverias and stonecrops grow around the base of the prickly pear.

frosts. In warm climates, geraniums, petunias, pinks, and gazanias can be grown as perennials and left outside.

Most of these flowering plants come in a wide range of colors. I like to plant a glorious mixture of them together in large containers, such as tubs and barrels, to make the most of their exuberant color. Do not overfeed them during the flowering season or they will produce too much foliage and only a few flowers.

—— HEADY FRAGRANCE ——

I always try to have plenty of containers with fragrant flowers or foliage positioned beside a doorway or garden seat. Scented flowering plants for sunny situations include pinks, lavender, some verbenas, sweet alyssum, mignonette, several varieties of petunia, and, of course, roses. Although roses thrive in sun, they need a moist root run, so plant them where it does not become too hot: halfway between sun and semi-shade is best.

Aromatic foliage plants, such as rosemary, artemisia, lemon verbena, lemon balm, chamomile, and several geraniums – all natives of the Mediterranean – also thrive in hot conditions. Plant each species in its own pot, and arrange them randomly in a group on a sunny patio where they can be enjoyed for their scented leaves.

—— FRUIT TREES ——

Many trees grow well in large containers in a sunny position. They need feeding during their growing season and copious watering in hot spells. Dwarf fruit trees, such as apples, pears, and plums, are all suitable and will produce a respectable crop.

FLOWER-FILLED PERGOLA

As the focal point at the end of a long, narrow town garden, this pergola calls out for eye-catching planting designs. It was built only three months ago, so the climbers have not yet covered the pillars and cross beams. This presented a marvelous opportunity to furnish it with pots of colorful annuals and roses for the summer.

※ Reconstituted stone baskets and terracotta pots with pink-flowered geraniums, impatiens, eustoma, and a bright patch of gold coleus rest on the stone-paved floor, providing color just above ground level. All of these plants flower non-stop and demand minimum care. With breeders always bringing out new varieties of geranium, it is impossible to tire of them.

※ The roses in the weathered, ornamental terracotta pots on either side of the steps leading to the pergola are very floriferous. 'Ballerina' starts later than other roses but makes up for this by going on non-stop until the frosts. Deadhead all the time to encourage it to throw out more sprays of flower buds.

—— HIGH-LEVEL INTEREST ——

Pergolas present excellent opportunities for using hanging baskets, brimming over with trailing, summer-flowering annuals. Suspended on the left-hand side of the pergola, red geraniums, verbenas, and winged peas burst from a traditional basket, creating a glorious red ball all summer long. (For details on planting the basket SEE PAGE 97.) More color is added at shoulder height with three standard geraniums. Although they must not be overwatered, they need a surprising amount of moisture in hot weather.

—— IN THE WINTER ——

This is very much a summer display. In autumn and winter, when the annuals are over, you could decorate the pergola with evergreen bay, box, and privet, trained and clipped into standards, neat spheres, and cones. A hanging basket of golden ivy would contrast well with their dark green foliage.

Zonal geranium •
(Pelargonium 'Yale')
The flowers are a stunning, deep, velvety blood red.

Winged pea •
(Lotus berthelotii)
Ideal for a hanging basket, with its fine, trailing silver foliage and red flowers.

Verbena *(Verbena*
x *hybrida* 'Showtime')
This comes in a range of colors, although I used only red ones here.

Portulaca *(Portulaca* •
grandiflora
Sundance Series)
Sun is essential for the pretty flowers to open.

Verbena *(Verbena*
'Silver Anne')
A pretty pink variety, chosen to echo the colors of the geraniums.

Zonal geranium •
(Pelargonium 'Rio')
A recent, pale pink variety with deep pink eyes.

Polyantha rose *(Rosa* •
'Margot Koster')
A variety that is strongly recommended for growing in containers.

PLANT CARE

Plants in a sunny site must be watered frequently. In hot summer weather this may mean up to two or three times a day. Bear in mind that hanging baskets are especially likely to dry out because they hold so little potting mixture. Although the hanging basket has a plastic liner behind the moss to conserve moisture, it still needs constant attention. Give the plants a liquid fertilizer once a week throughout the summer. In hot weather, plants in containers are more susceptible to mildew, as the soil dries out. When you see the first signs of mildew, spray with a fungicide.

Zonal geranium (*Pelargonium* 'Mauritania')
Distinguished by ice-pink flowers with deep pink centers, it is fast-growing, which makes it an excellent standard.

Zonal geranium (*Pelargonium* 'Appleblossom Rosebud')
The beautiful, two-tone flowers dislike wet weather.

Rose (*Rosa* 'The Fairy')
A pretty variety bearing dense clusters of small double flowers.

Zonal geranium (*Pelargonium* 'Ivalo')
The rich pink flowers have centers of an even deeper pink.

Rose (*Rosa* 'Ballerina')
After a late start, this variety is seldom out of flower in summer.

Coleus (*Coleus blumei*)
Clip back regularly to maintain a bushy mound of colorful foliage.

Eustoma (*Eustoma grandiflora*)
Violet- and white-flowered varieties are available, as well as the pink ones used here.

Impatiens (*Impatiens* 'New Guinea hybrid')
A striking variety with pink flowers and dark red leaves.

DESIGNS FOR SUN

MANY OF THE PLANTS THAT THRIVE in sunny sites give color for several months of the year. The most widely planted group are the summer annuals. In late spring and early summer, garden centers and nurseries are stacked with the usual and beautiful selections of petunias, geraniums, zinnias, snapdragons, salvias, lobelias, marigolds, and sweet alyssum. It is a good idea to devise a color scheme for your containers before buying the plants. Combinations that I find work well together are bluey pinks with silver-leaved plants; clear blues with pale yellows and lime-green; and the orange, red, and apricot range. Violet, lilac, and mauve also look good against silver foliage, and yellow and ice-pink make an interesting pair. Alternatively, mix many colors in just one plan.

❧ Winter calls for bright-leaved, evergreen shrubs. Gold foliage plants always look cheerful, even in gray weather, so use euonymus, aucuba, variegated fatsia, privet, elaeagnus, box, and yew. Among spring bulbs, all narcissi, tulips, hyacinths, and crocuses grow happily in sun. I favor the most heavily scented ones for containers.

Pink Splash
❧ Martha Washington geraniums excel in a sunny site (ABOVE), but their bright flowers are easily damaged in wet and windy weather. Their vibrant color is strengthened by the green background.

Pure Simplicity
❧ It is hard to beat the simple beauty of a sun-loving, white chamomile (*Anthemis punctata cupaniana*) in a plain terracotta pot (LEFT).

Water Garden
❧ A small water garden (RIGHT) holds miniature water lilies (*Nymphaea pygmaea* 'Helvola'), water lettuce (*Pistia stratiotes),* and water hyacinth (*Eichhornia acicularis).* The roots of the water lilies must be 6in (15cm) below the surface. The floaters are tender, but the lilies will survive the winter, as long as the water does not freeze solid.

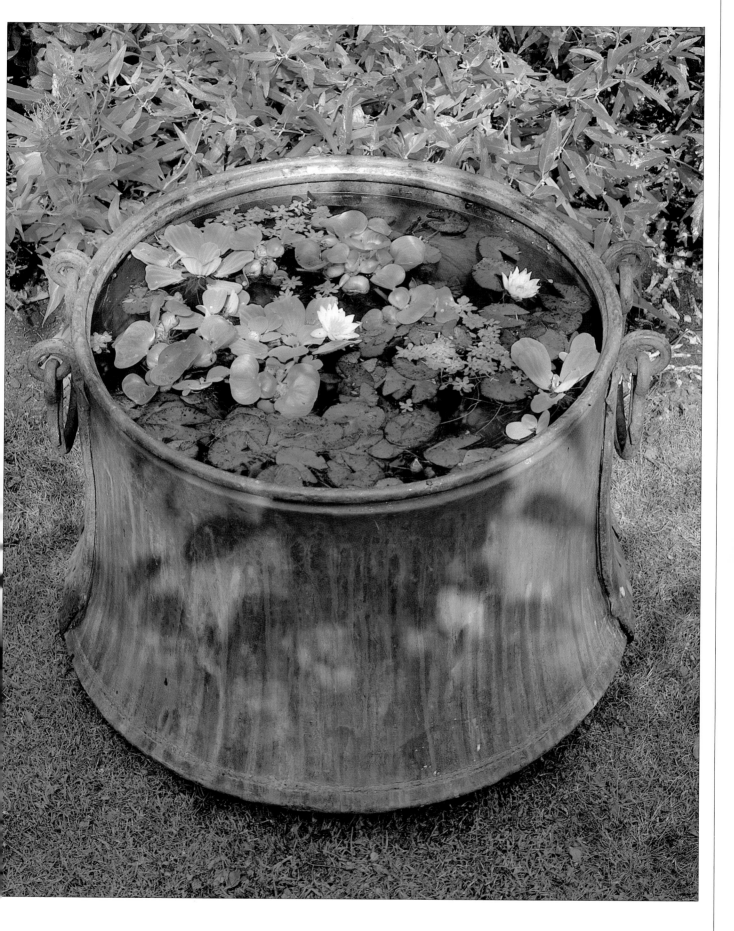

PLANTS FOR SUN

THE VAST MAJORITY OF PLANTS are sun lovers, especially those that produce a multitude of flowers. Annuals in particular like to bask in the sun, growing luxuriantly in its rays. In very hot summers, though, the heat can be too strong for even the most avid sun lovers, even scorching those that are kept well watered. If possible, move the containers to a position where they get some respite from the hottest midday sun.

ZINNIA
(*Zinnia elegans*)

DELPHINIUM
(*Delphinium elatum* 'Sungleam')

PETUNIA
(*Petunia* Ruffles Series)

EUSTOMA
(*Eustoma grandiflorum*)

∽ SPRING ∽

Auricula (*Primula auricula*)
Broom (*Cytisus*)
Cineraria (*Senecio* × *hybridus*)
Crocus (*Crocus*)
Crown imperial (*Fritillaria imperialis*)
English daisy (*Bellis perennis*)
English primrose (*Primula vulgaris* hybrids)
Flowering cherry (*Prunus*)
Forget-me-not (*Myosotis*)
Glory-of-the-snow (*Chionodoxa*)
Grape hyacinth (*Muscari*)
Hyacinth (*Hyacinthus*)
Iris (*Iris*)
Narcissus (*Narcissus*)
Pasque flower (*Anemone pulsatilla*)
Phlox (*Phlox subulata*)
Ranunculus (*Ranunculus asiaticus*)
Saxifrage (*Saxifraga*)
Spring gentian (*Gentiana verna*)
Spurge (*Euphorbia*)
Squill (*Scilla*)
Tulip (*Tulipa*)
Wallflower (*Cheiranthus*)
Weigela (*Weigela*)
Windflower (*Anemone*)

———— • ————

∽ SUMMER ∽

Abutilon (*Abutilon*)
Agapanthus (*Agapanthus*)
Ageratum (*Ageratum*)
Asparagus (*Asparagus*)
Black-eyed Susan (*Thunbergia alata*)
Calceolaria (*Calceolaria*)
Celosia (*Celosia cristata*)
Chamomile (*Anthemis*)
Chrysanthemum (*Chrysanthemum*)
Cigar flower (*Cuphea ignea*)
Coleus (*Coleus blumei*)
Common rue (*Ruta graveolens*)
Corn cockle (*Agrostemma*)
Delphinium (*Delphinium elatum*)
Diascia (*Diascia*)
Dusty miller (*Senecio maritima*)
Eustoma (*Eustoma*)
French marigold (*Tagetes*)
Gazania (*Gazania*)
Geranium (*Pelargonium*)
Godetia (*Clarkia*)
Gypsophila (*Gypsophila*)
Halimiocistus (*Halimiocistus*)
Helichrysum (*Helichrysum*)
Heliotrope (*Heliotropium*)
Houseleek (*Sempervivum*)
Kalanchoe (*Kalanchoe*)
Lantana (*Lantana*)
Lavender (*Lavandula*)
Livingstone daisy (*Dorotheanthus*)

HOUTTUYNIA
(*Houttuynia cordata* 'Chamaeleon')

VERBENA
(*Verbena* 'Sissinghurst')

ASTER
(*Aster*)

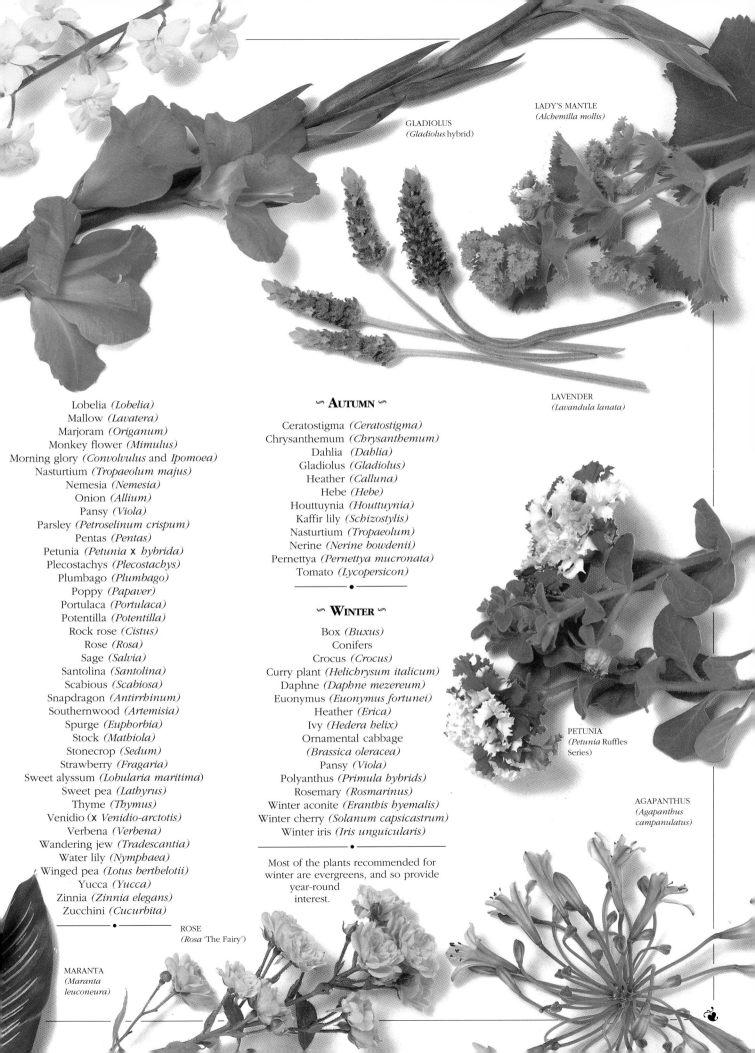

GLADIOLUS
(Gladiolus hybrid)

LADY'S MANTLE
(Alchemilla mollis)

LAVENDER
(Lavandula lanata)

Lobelia *(Lobelia)*
Mallow *(Lavatera)*
Marjoram *(Origanum)*
Monkey flower *(Mimulus)*
Morning glory *(Convolvulus* and *Ipomoea)*
Nasturtium *(Tropaeolum majus)*
Nemesia *(Nemesia)*
Onion *(Allium)*
Pansy *(Viola)*
Parsley *(Petroselinum crispum)*
Pentas *(Pentas)*
Petunia *(Petunia* x *hybrida)*
Plecostachys *(Plecostachys)*
Plumbago *(Plumbago)*
Poppy *(Papaver)*
Portulaca *(Portulaca)*
Potentilla *(Potentilla)*
Rock rose *(Cistus)*
Rose *(Rosa)*
Sage *(Salvia)*
Santolina *(Santolina)*
Scabious *(Scabiosa)*
Snapdragon *(Antirrhinum)*
Southernwood *(Artemisia)*
Spurge *(Euphorbia)*
Stock *(Mathiola)*
Stonecrop *(Sedum)*
Strawberry *(Fragaria)*
Sweet alyssum *(Lobularia maritima)*
Sweet pea *(Lathyrus)*
Thyme *(Thymus)*
Venidio *(x Venidio-arctotis)*
Verbena *(Verbena)*
Wandering jew *(Tradescantia)*
Water lily *(Nymphaea)*
Winged pea *(Lotus berthelotii)*
Yucca *(Yucca)*
Zinnia *(Zinnia elegans)*
Zucchini *(Cucurbita)*

———————— • ————————

ROSE
(Rosa 'The Fairy')

MARANTA
*(Maranta
leuconeura)*

❧ AUTUMN ❧

Ceratostigma *(Ceratostigma)*
Chrysanthemum *(Chrysanthemum)*
Dahlia *(Dahlia)*
Gladiolus *(Gladiolus)*
Heather *(Calluna)*
Hebe *(Hebe)*
Houttuynia *(Houttuynia)*
Kaffir lily *(Schizostylis)*
Nasturtium *(Tropaeolum)*
Nerine *(Nerine bowdenii)*
Pernettya *(Pernettya mucronata)*
Tomato *(Lycopersicon)*

———————— • ————————

❧ WINTER ❧

Box *(Buxus)*
Conifers
Crocus *(Crocus)*
Curry plant *(Helichrysum italicum)*
Daphne *(Daphne mezereum)*
Euonymus *(Euonymus fortunei)*
Heather *(Erica)*
Ivy *(Hedera helix)*
Ornamental cabbage
(Brassica oleracea)
Pansy *(Viola)*
Polyanthus *(Primula hybrids)*
Rosemary *(Rosmarinus)*
Winter aconite *(Eranthis hyemalis)*
Winter cherry *(Solanum capsicastrum)*
Winter iris *(Iris unguicularis)*

———————— • ————————

Most of the plants recommended for
winter are evergreens, and so provide
year-round
interest.

PETUNIA
(Petunia Ruffles
Series)

AGAPANTHUS
*(Agapanthus
campanulatus)*

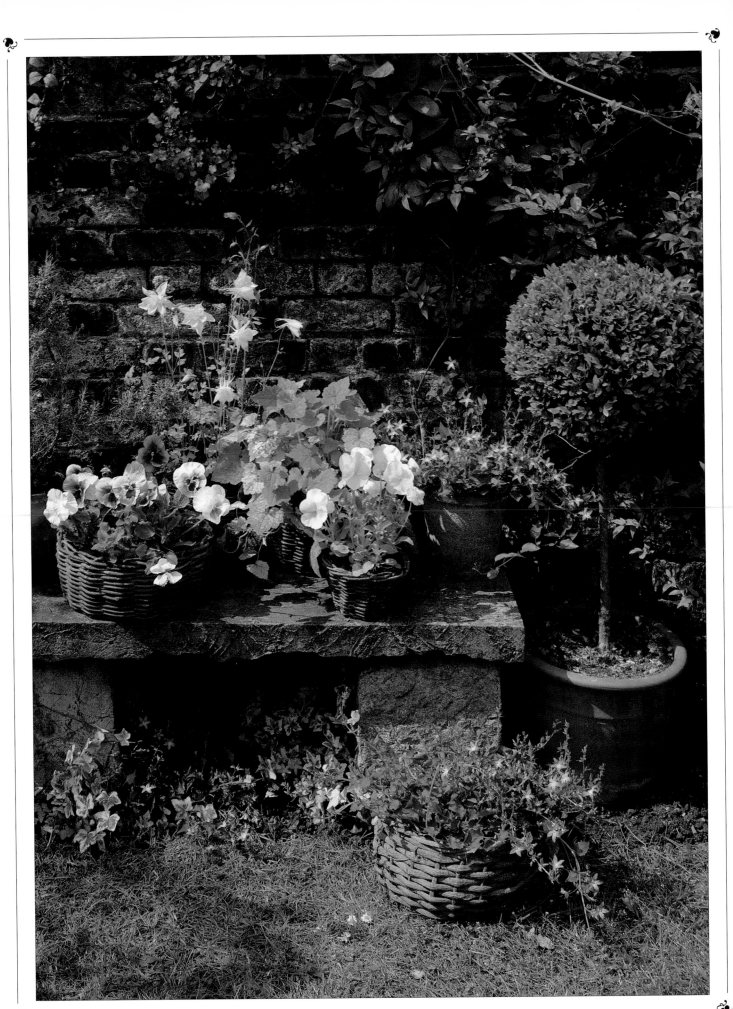

SEMI-SHADY POSITIONS

THE SEMI-SHADY garden gets the best of both worlds: it escapes the rigors of full sun beating down throughout the day, and yet does not have the rather depressing and gloomy feel of unrelieved shade. Plants love semi-shade. They receive enough sun to make them grow and flower well, and sufficient shade to prevent them from drying out too fast, or being burned and scorched by overexposure to heat.

— IDEAL SEATING AREA —

Most gardens include areas of semi-shade: if you live in a detached house you will have two or more walls that only see the sun for part of the day. If you are designing your garden, and you can choose where your paved sitting area near the house will be, allocate it a semi-shady position. You can always take a chair out into a sunny place on the lawn if you want sunlight. Preferably choose a site that receives the morning sun, because breakfast is the one meal of the day that can be enjoyed in a sunny place – by lunchtime the sun is often too strong. If you already have a sunny sitting area, you could plant a tree, placing it judiciously, so that the area is in dappled shade for at least part of the day. Some of my happiest moments have been spent sitting in the dappled, early-morning sunshine under an old apple tree, beside a path edged with pots of lavender, rosemary, and southernwood, having a breakfast of homemade breads and jams with coffee.

— CITY BENEFITS —

In the city, nearby buildings usually cast shadows on small paved gardens or roof terraces for part of the day. Unless you live in an extremely cold

WILD GARDEN
A bulbous terracotta pot (ABOVE) filled with a wild jumble of pansies, wild geraniums, bellflowers, and ferns.

FLOWER BASKETS
Placed on a sun-warmed, stone bench, baskets of pansies, columbine, a piggyback plant, bellflowers, and a small clipped mop-head of box, thrive in the dappled sun (LEFT).

area, there will be plenty of scope for having a year-round backdrop of greenery, achieved by growing evergreen shrubs in good-sized containers.

❦ Temperatures in cities are always a few degrees higher than those in the surrounding countryside, which gives you a wider choice of plants to grow in containers. Walls will become warmed by only a few hours of sunshine and they will retain the heat for several hours, so that even in winter the area at the base of the wall is substantially warmer than a site that is just a few yards away. Take advantage of this shelter and warmth to try growing some of the slightly more tender, exotic-looking, garden plants.

— PASTEL COLORS —

Furnish a semi-shady, paved terrace with containers filled with all kinds of greenery and colored flowers. Always have some perfumed plants, whether it be species with aromatic leaves or ones with fragrant flowers. They appeal to more than one of our senses and make the atmosphere much more interesting and special.

❦ While green is usually the ideal predominant color for shady sites, and a mixture of hot bright colors can be exciting for sunny places, I like semi-shady container plantings based on flowers with pastel colors. To me, they look wonderful in a site that is neither too bright nor too dark. Spring bulbs, flowering shrubs, perennials, and summer annuals and biennials all offer a range of gentle clear shades: pinks and lemons, lilacs and mauves, peach, pale orange, and sky blue. All these colors blend well with each other, either as a glorious mixture, or in a more restricted, carefully selected palette for a soothing arrangement.

CITY COURTYARD

THIS TERRACE in the heart of the city sees sun for only part of the day because of the high boundary walls and surrounding buildings. What might seem a disadvantage initially can be an asset: because the area is sheltered, tender plants survive outside all-year-round in the temperate climate.

The terrace is on view from inside the house, so I have planted a mixture of evergreen plants, such as yucca and mountain flax, to which I can add seasonal color. Seen here in early summer, the dramatic hosta by the steps has just grown its new leaves. The scented wallflowers beside it have nearly finished flowering but summer annuals are just getting underway. Against a backdrop of cool greens, impatiens, fuchsias, begonias, and pansies will produce plentiful color in summer and autumn.

Wallflower (*Cheiranthus cheiri*) •
These popular yellow, red, and pink-flowered biennials have the most glorious scent.

Hosta (*Hosta sieboldiana* 'Frances Williams') •
The magnificent gold-edged leaves of this hosta fill the dark corner next to the stone steps.

Aspidistra (*Aspidistra elatior*) •
In the wild, its flowers at the base of the leaves are pollinated by snails.

Rhododendron (*Rhododendron* 'Grumpy') •
This impressive, acid-loving plant flowers in late spring but it may also have a few autumn blooms.

Impatiens (*Impatiens walleriana* 'Tangeglow') •
The orange flowers have long spurs.

Pansy (*Viola* x *wittrockiana*) •
The rich red flowers stand out well against the pale green garden seat.

PLANT CARE

Container-grown plants in semi-shade require more attention than those grown in sun. Water to keep the potting mixture moist but not wet, remove dead leaves and flowers, and feed during the growing season.

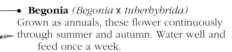

Begonia (*Begonia* x *tuberhybrida*)
Grown as annuals, these flower continuously through summer and autumn. Water well and feed once a week.

Fuchsia (*Fuchsia* 'Autumnale')
A variety combining beautiful pink-tinged, cream, and green variegated foliage, with bright pink flowers in summer and autumn.

Holly fern (*Cyrtomium falcatum*)
A slightly tender fern, best grown in a potting mixture rich in leafmold.

Mountain flax (*Phormium colensoi* 'Variegatum')
This decorative evergreen plant appreciates the sunniest spot.

Impatiens
(*Impatiens walleriana*)
These flower non-stop through summer and autumn, if watered well and given a weekly feeding.

Ivy (*Hedera helix* 'Eva')
Cascading down from the container, shade-loving ivy will live for many years.

Male fern
(*Dryopteris filix-mas*)
This semi-evergreen fern produces arching fronds over 36in (1m) long.

Yucca (*Yucca gloriosa*)
A hardy plant that lasts many years when grown in a container.

DESIGNS FOR SEMI-SHADE

NEARLY ALL THE PLANTS that are regarded as sun lovers, as well as those that prefer shade, can be grown in semi-shade, so there is no shortage of species from which to choose. It is the business of combining them that can be restrictive. Plants in one container must all like the same soil type and have similar watering requirements. Watering should not present too much of a problem as most plants like to be kept moist but not soggy. Soil demands can be more limiting, however, as certain plants only grow well, in either alkaline or acid soil conditions.

── ACID OR ALKALINE? ──

An interesting grouping of alkaline-loving plants for a large container could consist of the shrub Mexican orange – either the gold-leaved variety 'Sundance' or the fine-leaved variety 'Aztec Pearl'

– with fuchsias and evergreen ivies. Mexican orange, an attractive evergreen shrub, can grow quite large, so the container needs to be about 20in (50cm) in diameter. If your garden is not too cold, you could use hardy fuchsias, such as the variety 'Mrs Popple,' to make a permanent container planting.

Rhododendrons, azaleas, and camellias are excellent container specimens for a half-shady position, and all prefer an acid potting mixture. Rhododendrons and camellias grow quite large, so there will be little room for other plants, apart from, perhaps, some spring bulbs and small ivies around the edge of the containers. All three acid-loving shrubs flower in late spring and early summer, but the glossy leaves of most of them form an evergreen backdrop throughout the year. Camellias have the most attractive foliage, but they are the least hardy of the trio.

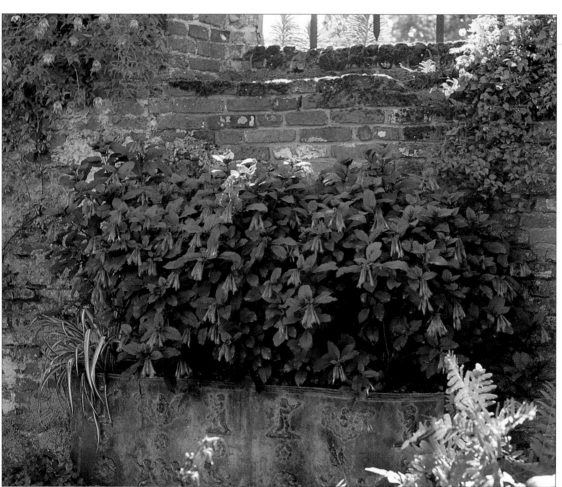

'Thalia' Fuchsias
An old lead tank makes a very special container for these small-flowered fuchsias *(Fuchsia* 'Thalia') with their dark foliage and deep orange bells (LEFT). The plants grow quickly in a partly shady place, given plenty of water and a weekly feeding. They start to flower a little later than most fuchsias but continue until the first frosts.

Evergreen Curtain
Pots and bowls of pastel-colored impatiens *(Impatiens walleriana)* and begonias *(Begonia* x *tuberhybrida),* mixed with maidenhair ferns *(Adiantum capillus-veneris)* and variegated ivy *(Hedera helix* 'Dealbata'), set against a curtain of evergreen shrubs (RIGHT). All the plants grow amazingly well on this sheltered terrace in a town garden, which receives dappled sun for much of the day.

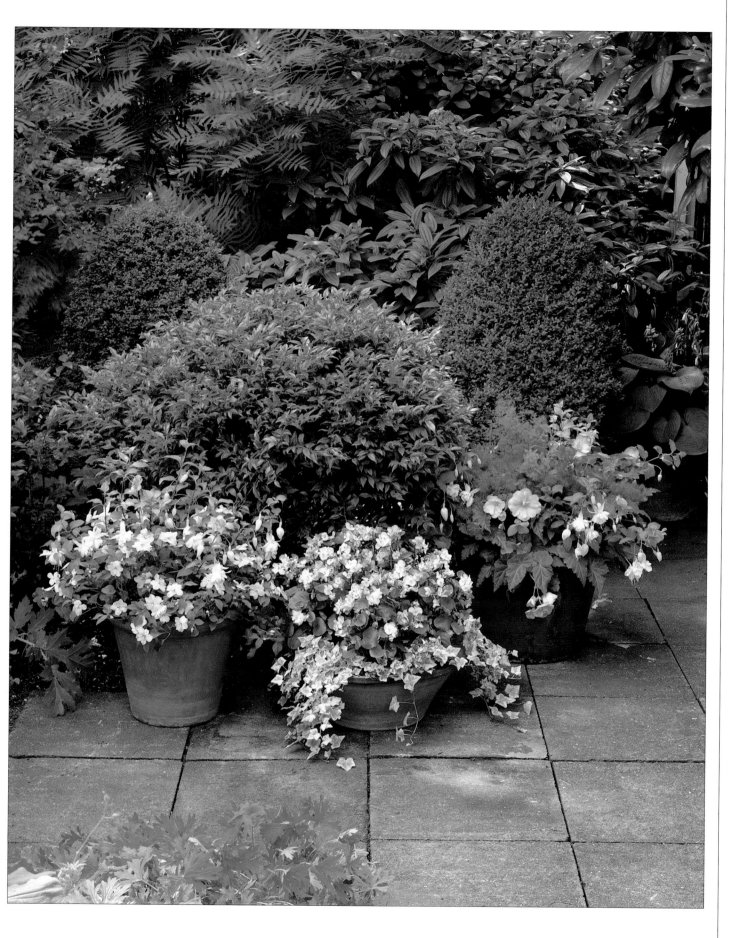

PLANTS FOR SEMI-SHADE

YOU WILL HAVE LITTLE PROBLEM finding plants that do well in a semi-shady position but you first need to establish what degree of shade you have in your garden. If the light is always bright and there is the possibility of sun for half the day, most shrubs, perennials, and annuals will thrive. If the shade is deep with a shorter period of dappled sun, then woodland plants, such as hellebores, hydrangeas, lilies, rhododendrons and azaleas, and camellias generally do best.

FUCHSIA
(*Fuchsia* 'Pink Galore')

BLEEDING HEART
(*Dicentra spectabilis*)

∽ WINTER ∽

Aucuba (*Aucuba*)
Bamboos
Bergenia (*Bergenia*)
Box (*Buxus*)
Conifers
Euonymus (*Euonymus*)
Fatsia (*Fatsia*)
Gaultheria (*Gaultheria*)
Hellebore (*Helleborus niger*)
Ivy (*Hedera helix*)
Laurustinus (*Viburnum tinus*)
Leucothoe (*Leucothoe*)
Mexican orange (*Choisya*)
Pansy (*Viola*)
Periwinkle (*Vinca*)
Skimmia (*Skimmia*)
Winter cherry (*Solanum capsicastrum*)

———————————

Most of the plants recommended for winter are evergreens, and therefore provide year-round interest.

∽ SPRING ∽

Andromeda (*Pieris*)
Auricula (*Primula auricula*)
Azalea/Rhododendron (*Rhododendron*)
Camellia (*Camellia*)
Crown imperial (*Fritillaria imperialis*)
Daffodil (*Narcissus*)
Forget-me-not (*Myosotis*)
Grape hyacinth (*Muscari*)
Hellebore (*Helleborus*)
Hyacinth (*Hyacinthus orientalis*)
Lily-of-the-valley (*Convallaria majalis*)
Narcissus (*Narcissus*)
Pansy (*Viola*)
Pasque flower (*Anemone vulgaris*)
Periwinkle (*Vinca*)
Primula (*Primula* hybrids)
Ranunculus (*Ranunculus asiaticus*)
Snake's head fritillary (*Fritillaria meleagris*)
Solomon's seal (*Polygonatum*)
Squill (*Scilla*)
Tulip (*Tulipa*)
Wild primrose (*Primula veris*)
Windflower (*Anemone*)

———————— • ————————

COLUMBINE
(*Aquilegia vulgaris*
'Nora Barlow')

ROSE
(*Rosa* 'New Dawn')

IMPATIENS
(*Impatiens* New
Guinea hybrid)

CALLA LILY
(Zantedeschia
hybrid)

MASTERWORT
(Astrantia major)

MEXICAN ORANGE
(Choisya ternata)

◦ SUMMER ◦

Asparagus *(Asparagus)*
Astilbe *(Astilbe)*
Begonia *(Begonia)*
Bellflower *(Campanula)*
Bleeding heart *(Dicentra)*
Calla lily *(Zantedeschia)*
Coleus *(Coleus blumei)*
Columbine *(Aquilegia)*
Common rue *(Ruta graveolens)*
Creeping fig *(Ficus pumila)*
Flowering tobacco plant *(Nicotiana)*
Fuchsia *(Fuchsia)*
Geranium *(Pelargonium)*
Heuchera *(Heuchera)*
Hosta *(Hosta)*
Impatiens *(Impatiens)*
Japanese maple *(Acer palmatum)*
Lewisia *(Lewisia)*
Lily *(Lilium)*
Lobelia *(Lobelia)*
Loosestrife *(Lysimachia)*
Masterwort *(Astrantia)*
Monkey flower *(Mimulus)*
Pansy *(Viola)*
Piggy-back plant *(Tolmiea menziesii)*
Potentilla *(Potentilla)*
Ranunculus *(Ranunculus asiaticus)*
Rose *(Rosa)*
Scabious *(Scabiosa)*
Swedish ivy *(Plectranthus)*
Sweet alyssum *(Lobularia maritima)*
Wandering jew *(Tradescantia)*
Yucca *(Yucca)*

◦ AUTUMN ◦

Chrysanthemum *(Chrysanthemum)*
Cotoneaster *(Cotoneaster)*
Cyclamen *(Cyclamen)*
Fuchsia *(Fuchsia)*
Heather *(Calluna)*
Houttuynia *(Houttuynia)*
Hydrangea *(Hydrangea)*
Japanese maple *(Acer palmatum)*
Knotweed *(Polygonum)*
Michaelmas daisy *(Aster)*
Pernettya *(Pernettya)*

LILY
(Lilium 'La Reve')

HELLEBORE
(Helleborus x *sternii)*

FLOWERING
TOBACCO PLANT
(Nicotiana alata
Sensation Series)

ASTILBE
(Astilbe x
arendsii)

PANSY
(Viola x *wittrockiana)*

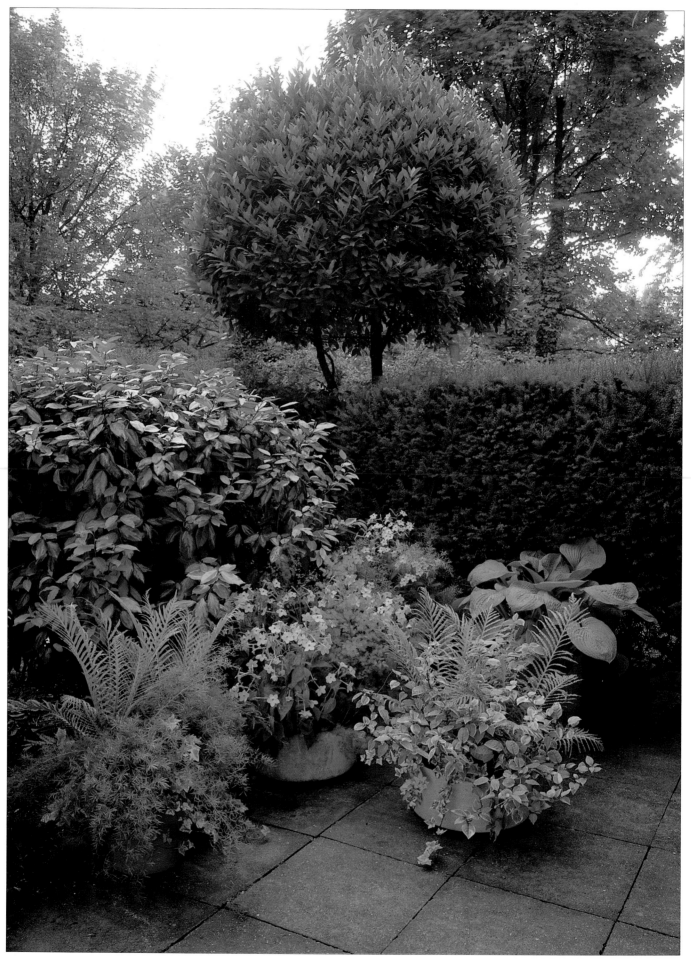

SHADY POSITIONS

SHADY SITES are the most difficult for growing plants. There are plants that like shade, but the choice is limited. Several types of shade exist. The most problematic is deep shade, created by the overhead shadows of dense trees or a roof. Shade from buildings can be a nuisance, but if the level of reflected light is high, there are many plants that will grow well there.

DEGREES OF SHADE

In deeply shaded areas between houses, or where there is a light well and little sky is visible, the overall light level is low, and this again is a problem. The plants then receive very little natural light, and soon become weak and straggly. They are also more prone to pests, diseases, and fungal infections. Painting walls in white or another light color helps considerably by increasing the amount of reflected light in the area.

✿ Several foliage plants will grow relatively happily in deep shade. Of the evergreens, try bergenia, box, elaeagnus, fatsia, gaultheria, ivy, holly, evergreen honeysuckle, mahonia, osmanthus, pachysandra, andromeda, sarcococca, skimmia, yew, periwinkle, and ferns. A number of ferns are evergreen or semi-evergreen, holding their fronds through the winter. Among summer-flowering plants, begonias and impatiens give a good show; flowering tobacco plants and fuchsias make less flowering growth and are not quite as effective in very deep shade.

✿ The choice is much wider in light shade, where there is no direct sun but the level of light is reasonably high, such as in the dappled light of a tree with delicate foliage, or in a light area that is shaded by buildings. Plants suitable for deep shade, but also most of the spring bulbs, and

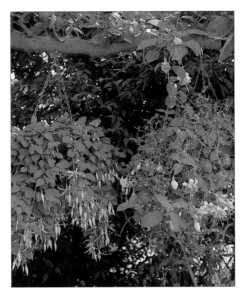

HANGING COLOR
Hanging baskets of fuchsias (ABOVE), suspended from the branches of a deciduous tree thrive in the light shade.

SERENE GREENS
A shady terrace (LEFT) furnished with bowls of ferns, asparagus, variegated-leaved fuchsia, flowering tobacco plants, ivy, hostas, and a bay tree.

certain shrubs, flowering perennials and annuals, such as bellflowers, lobelias, cranesbill, and pansies will grow in such a spot. Among the shrubs, aucuba, bamboo, camellia, Mexican orange, hydrangea, cherry laurel, and viburnum will flourish in such a position.

FOCUS ON FOLIAGE

Few flowering plants are suitable for containers in shade, so it is just as well to concentrate on foliage plantings, and add small amounts of seasonal color.

✿ The golden elaeagnus, euonymus, and Mexican orange all make a darkish area seem much brighter, almost as if the sun were shining. Sadly, the silver-leaved plants do not do well without some sunshine.

✿ There are also the plants with bold-shaped or colored foliage, such as fatsia and bamboo, and the bronze-leaved heuchera 'Palace Purple.' Ferns all do tremendously well if you give them a potting mixture with some leafmold added. Some, such as polystichum, blechnum, and phyllitis, are both hardy and evergreen. In temperate climates, holly fern, tree fern, maidenhair fern, stag horn fern, woodwardias, and the silver-leaved phlebodium all grow magnificently in pots. Aspidistras also do very well in the deepest shade, as long as the temperature does not fall much below freezing.

✿ I am always surprised by what will grow well in a shady part of my garden in London. Aspidistra, clivia, New Zealand ferns, a Chusan palm, and even an epiphyllum cactus have all lived outside for many years. I even have photographs of the cactus in full flower, surrounded and partially covered by snow in mid winter. So do not be disheartened by your shady patch. There are bound to be some treasures that will flourish there.

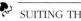

SHADY RETREAT

POSITIONED JUST OUTSIDE THE KITCHEN, this area is paved to provide an outside dining room for the warm summer months. I always believe that an eating area should be relatively shady: nothing is more unpleasant than sitting at the garden table with plates of melting butter, wilting salad, and oily cheese, blasted by the sun.

This terrace is surfaced with red brick paving and sheltered by a lush, 9ft- (2.7m-) high yew hedge, planted in a U-shape. Its only permanent plant features are six pots of box, clipped in a variety of formal shapes, and rectangular beds edged with low-growing box and filled, this year, with white impatiens. A cool green place in winter, it can be given a totally different feel in summer, with a few large pots of flowering plants in various color schemes.

The color of the brick paving prompted this choice of rich reds, with bright and pale pinks. The yellows were a happy accident – they should have been pale pink!

Box (*Buxus sempervirens*) •
A tough shrub that thrives in almost any condition, and can be clipped into interesting shapes.

Tuberous begonia •
(*Begonia* x *tuberhybrida*)
Watch out for mildew.

Terracotta pots •
A mixture of large, round, and square, handmade terracotta pots, ranging in size from 18-22in (45-55cm) in diameter.

Flowering tobacco plant •
(*Nicotiana* 'Pink Bedder')
Cut back by about 6in (15cm) after the first flush of flowers to promote side shoots and new flowering growths.

Tuberous begonia •
(*Begonia* x *tuberhybrida pendula*)
Forms a waterfall of color all summer long, and up until the first frosts.

PLANT CARE
Although plants grown in shade
need less water than those placed in
sunshine, it is still vital that you
keep the potting mixture just moist,
never soggy, and give them a
weekly dose of liquid fertilizer.
Woodland is the natural habitat of
most shade lovers, so generally they
grow best in a rich potting mixture.
Because plants growing in shade are
not as healthy as those in other
sites, they are more susceptible to
pests and diseases.

Fuchsia *(Fuchsia* 'Thalia')
A fast-growing, deciduous
variety with an upright habit
and long, slender, dark
orange flowers, accented by
bronzy green foliage.

DESIGNS FOR SHADE

OR A SHADY GARDEN, green ought to be the predominant color. Cool, but also welcoming, it feels just right for sites that the sun does not reach. Plenty of shrubs grow happily in shade, although you must take into account the degree of shade when making your choice. Hardly any plants grow in very dense shade, where the light is extremely low, but moderate shade is not a problem. Among the evergreens, box, yew, and hemlock all survive and can be clipped into dramatic shapes. Aucuba, bamboo, Mexican orange, holly, privet, and mahonia, also evergreens, will grow into good-sized specimens in large containers. For bright shade, where there is plenty of reflected light, rhododendrons and camellias can produce a display of showy flowers. Most of these shrubs look best planted as single specimens, surrounded by trailing plants, such as small-leaved ivies and periwinkle.

——— POOLS OF COLOR ———

Against this background of greenery, you can add containers of seasonal color. Tuberous begonias, impatiens, fuchsias, and flowering tobacco plants all combine well together, and their colors show up vibrantly against green foliage. I find that two or three of the small-flowered, pendent begonias look most effective in a low bowl or pot on the end of a low wall.

✄ For color in spring in a shady site, try planting bulbs. They will flower well in containers in a shady place for at least one season. In winter, plantings of box, euonymus, and ivy thrive in shady positions. If your garden is not too cold, you could also try growing winter cherry, which has orange-red fruit, with evergreen skimmia or leucothoe.

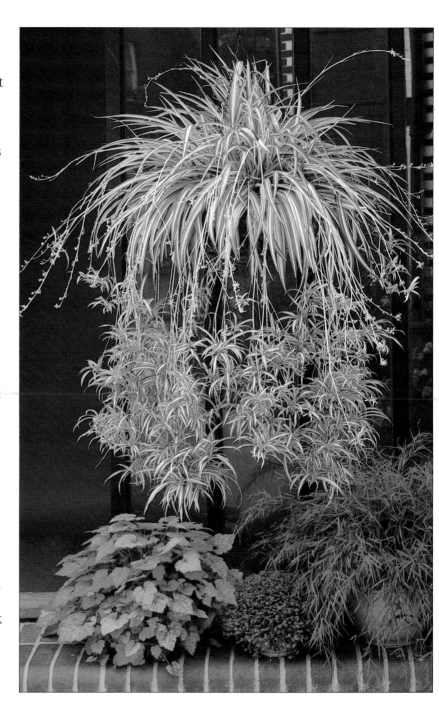

Indoor Plants
✄ An evergreen planting for a shady doorway (ABOVE), consisting mainly of plants traditionally grown in the house. In the summer months, spider plant (*Chlorophytum comosum*), piggy-back plant (*Tolmiea menziesii*), and the grass *Pogonatherum paniceum* all grow well outdoors.

Victorian Plant Stand
✄ A wrought-iron plant stand (RIGHT) holds pots of shade-loving maidenhair ferns (*Adiantum capillus-veneris*), impatiens (*Impatiens*), creeping fig (*Ficus pumila*), and begonias (*Begonia* 'Elatior hybrid'). Asters prefer semi-shade, but once they have buds, you can move them into shade for blooming.

PLANTS FOR SHADE

A MULTITUDE OF SHADE-LOVING, evergreen shrubs and perennials grow extremely well in containers. Their main attraction is their foliage, which comes in a wide range of shapes and colors and which is particularly welcome in winter, when deciduous plants are bare. But you are by no means limited to foliage-only plants for containers in the shade. In spring there are bulbs, most of which grow well in a shady but light position, for at least one season. Other possibilities include sweet-scented lily-of-the-valley, pansies, and primroses.

Come summer, some of the most brilliantly colored flowers – begonias, fuchsias, flowering tobacco plants, and impatiens – as well as lilies and bellflowers, are happiest in shade with a reasonable light level. All of these flowers look stunning next to ferns and hostas. Nearly every house plant also thrives in a bright but shaded position outdoors in summer.

HONEYSUCKLE
(Lonicera japonica 'Halliana')

BEGONIA
(Begonia x *tuberhybrida*)

FERN
(Osmunda regalis)

∽ WINTER ∽

Aucuba *(Aucuba)*
Bamboos
Bergenia *(Bergenia)*
Box *(Buxus)*
Conifers
Evergreen ferns
Fatsia *(Fatsia)*
Gaultheria *(Gaultheria)*
Hellebore *(Helleborus niger)*
Ivy *(Hedera helix)*
Leucothoe *(Leucothoe)*
Mahonia *(Mahonia)*
Pachysandra *(Pachysandra)*
Pansy *(Viola)*
Skimmia *(Skimmia)*

Most of the plants recommended
for winter are evergreens,
and therefore provide
year-round interest.

∽ SPRING ∽

Andromeda *(Pieris)*
Azalea/rhododendron *(Rhododendron)*
Bergenia *(Bergenia)*
Camellia *(Camellia)*
Dogtooth violet *(Erythronium)*
Hellebore *(Helleborus)*
Lily-of-the-valley *(Convallaria majalis)*
Narcissus *(Narcissus)*
Pansy *(Viola)*
Periwinkle *(Vinca)*
Primrose *(Primula)*
Snake's head fritillary *(Fritillaria meleagris)*
Solomon's seal *(Polygonatum* x *hybridum)*
Tulip *(Tulipa)*

RHODODENDRON
(Rhododendron 'Nobleanum')

HOSTA
(Hosta sieboldiana)

BEGONIA
(Begonia x *tuberhybrida)*

PACHYSANDRA
(Pachysandra terminalis)

BEGONIA
*(Begonia x
tuberhybrida)*

PHILODENDRON
(Philodendron)

JAPANESE SHIELD
FERN
*(Dryopteris
erythrosora)*

IVY
*(Hedera helix
'Duck's Foot')*

❧ SUMMER ❧

Begonia *(Begonia)*
Bellflower *(Campanula)*
Creeping fig *(Ficus pumila)*
Ferns
Flowering tobacco plant *(Nicotiana)*
Fuchsia *(Fuchsia)*
Honeysuckle *(Lonicera)*
Hosta *(Hosta)*
Impatiens *(Impatiens)*
Jasmine *(Jasminum)*
Monkey flower *(Mimulus)*
Pansy *(Viola)*
Philodendron *(Philodendron)*
Piggy-back plant *(Tolmiea menziesii)*

——————— • ———————

❧ AUTUMN ❧

Begonia *(Begonia)*
Cyclamen *(Cyclamen)*
Elaeagnus *(Elaeagnus ebbingei)*
Fuchsia *(Fuchsia)*
Hydrangea *(Hydrangea)*
Japanese anemone *(Anemone x hybrida)*
Kirengeshoma *(Kirengeshoma palmata)*
Maple *(Acer)*
Pyracantha *(Pyracantha)*
St John's wort *(Hypericum)*

——————— • ———————

MAHONIA
*(Mahonia
lomariifolia)*

LILY-OF-THE-VALLEY
(Convallaria majalis)

HYDRANGEA
(Hydrangea macrophylla)

IA
*ia
nica)*

EXPOSED POSITIONS

AN EXPOSED GARDEN is one that is subjected to extremes of weather: strong winds, harsh sun, and cold, either separately or in combination. Roof terraces, often blasted by both wind and sun, are perfect examples of exposed sites, so too are gardens on unsheltered hillsides, flat open expanses, or city plots at the end of a man-made wind tunnel.

✄ Growing any plants in containers under such conditions is not easy. Indeed a combination of wind, sun, and extreme cold can be pretty lethal. Plants in pots dry out extremely quickly, and their leaves and flowers may become wind-browned, even if they have been well watered. It pays to give them a reasonable depth of potting mixture: the shallower the container, the quicker the soil dries out. And if using small containers, choose ones made from non-porous materials, such as plastic or fiberglass, that retain as much moisture as possible.

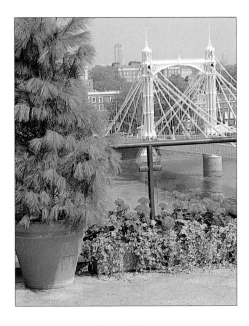

PRIME VIEW
To preserve this magnificent riverside view (ABOVE), the plantings of zonal geraniums, French marigolds, ivy, and coleus are kept low.

BULBS ON A BALCONY
Spring bulbs, pansies, box, and ivy (LEFT) are a good choice for adding color to a wind-swept balcony.

good-sized tubs, pots, and troughs when filled with potting mixture, especially after a thorough watering.

TOUGH CHOICE

If you have an exposed garden, it is essential that you choose very tough plants for growing in your containers.

✄ Long-stemmed plants hate being battered and whipped about by wind and rain. If you want to position containers in an area that is in a wind tunnel, perhaps between buildings, or somewhere that is affected by coastal winds, choose strong, tough, or wiry-stemmed plants and trim any straggly growth.

✄ It is worth remembering that low-growing plants either miss the worst of high winds or they are strong enough to withstand them. Plant them in a sink or a low trough to give year-round interest (SEE PAGES 90-1). Although alpines tolerate both sun and wind exposure in summer, they dislike a combination of cold icy winds and dampness in winter, so it may be necessary to give them some form of overhead shelter, such as a sheet of glass.

PROTECTION

It makes sense to take advantage of any protection that is available on the site. Position your tubs beside walls, ballustrading, or the sides of balconies and fences – all these features help to break up the force of the wind and provide shelter from strong sun or rain.

✄ Many of the taller, large-leaved plants or shrubs and trees, such as bamboo, with very flexible stems (SEE PAGES 132-3), tolerate both sun and wind, and are useful for giving protection to more delicate specimens. When using these larger plants on a roof terrace or balcony, make sure that the structure is strong enough to hold them. Do not underestimate the weight of large plants in

SEASONAL COLOR

All of the popular spring bulbs, especially the low-growing species and varieties, flower in exposed sites. If you are growing groups of them in a windy position, stake them well when they are only a few inches high to prevent the leaves and flower stems from breaking in strong winds. Once they have finished flowering, and all possibility of frost has passed, you can replace the bulbs with summer-flowering annuals, many of which will tolerate lots of sun at a time of year when high winds are not usually such a problem.

ROOF TOP OF TREES

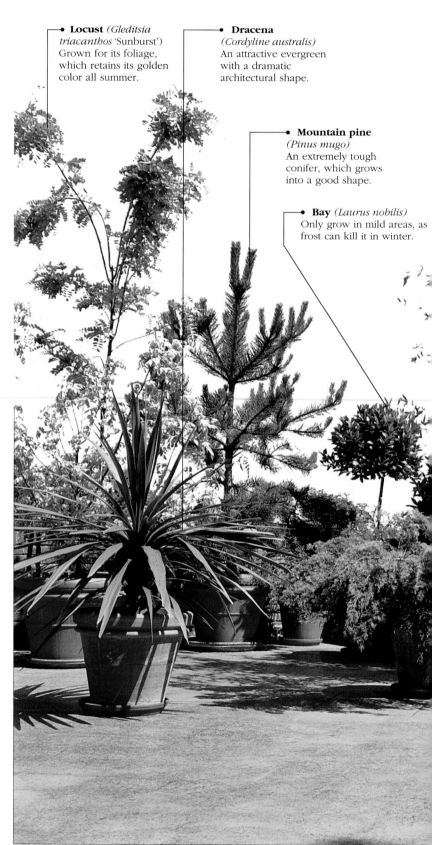

Locust *(Gleditsia triacanthos* 'Sunburst') Grown for its foliage, which retains its golden color all summer.

Dracena *(Cordyline australis)* An attractive evergreen with a dramatic architectural shape.

Mountain pine *(Pinus mugo)* An extremely tough conifer, which grows into a good shape.

Bay *(Laurus nobilis)* Only grow in mild areas, as frost can kill it in winter.

BLASTED BY THE SUN and battered by the wind, roof gardens are prime examples of exposed sites. They are not the best places to grow garden plants, but if you live in a city apartment, a roof terrace can make a useful extra room, bringing greenery closer to the urban home and providing a pleasant and relaxing place to sit, with the sky as a ceiling.

— WEIGHT CONSIDERATIONS —

The large size and sturdy structure of this roof terrace, at the top of an apartment block, makes it possible to grow a selection of heavy specimen trees in pots. The owners checked with an architect how much weight the roof could take, as large containers can be very heavy, especially when they are wet. Usually, it is best to place heavy containers near load-bearing walls, rather than arrange them in the middle of the terrace where the roof is unlikely to be supported.

—— POTTED TREES ——

Provided they are watered and fed well, trees and large shrubs grow well in good-sized containers, even in exposed positions. Generally, pots measuring 36in (1m) across will take a 12ft- (3.6m-) high tree, although in exposed sites it is best to choose species that are not higher than 10ft (3m). Unless they are well anchored, they may blow over in high winds.

When it comes to selecting trees, it is best not to consider fast-growing species, such as eucalyptus and ailanthus – they will soon grow too big for their tubs. Conifers do well, if they are watered frequently, although just a short spell without sufficient moisture kills them. For exposed spots, however, pines and junipers are the most suitable conifers – high winds will brown the foliage of other species.

PLANT CARE

In an exposed site, plants in pots need frequent watering because of the drying effects of the wind and sun. Even in winter, you should water them, except when the temperature is below freezing. Spray the leaves of large, newly planted specimens frequently, but avoid doing so in hot sunlight. After their first year, underwater rather than overwater them.

Spruce (*Picea glauca* 'Conica')
Grows into a perfect pyramid of dense, bright green foliage.

Variegated maple
(*Acer negundo* 'Variegatum')
Distinguished by its pretty pinky-cream and green-striped leaves.

Sacred bamboo
(*Nandina domestica*)
Also called heavenly bamboo, this species needs a sunny position, and wind protection from other plants.

Black bamboo
(*Phyllostachys nigra*)
A frost-hardy variety with beautiful evergreen leaves. In their second season, the stems turn black.

Juniper (*Juniperus sabina* 'Tamariscifolia')
A tough conifer, with a low spreading habit.

Mountain flax
(*Phormium colensoi* 'Variegatum')
Grown for its decorative, strap-like evergreen leaves.

DESIGNS FOR EXPOSED POSITIONS

I N GARDENS subjected to strong wind, sun, and cold, only certain types of plants will grow well. Generally, it is advisable to choose low-growing plants, as they miss the worst of high winds. Plan a permanent planting based on tough-stemmed shrubs, such as cotoneasters, spreading conifers, elaeagnus, euonymus, and potentillas. To this you can then add summer color with annuals, such as zonal geraniums, snapdragons, marigolds, nasturtiums, zinnias, and verbenas, all of which cope in windy situations and also thrive in strong sun, provided you do not allow the soil to become too dry. In hot summer weather on a sunny roof garden or terrace, this probably means watering twice or maybe even three times a day.

✠ In a cold, windy site, check which plants are hardy in your neighbors' gardens before buying winter evergreens. Most spring bulbs are fairly tough and look good planted around shrubs. Plant low-growing, summer annuals outdoors once the risk of frost has passed.

Drought Resistance

✠ Rock plants and succulents do not mind being baked by the sun or lashed by the wind, although they do object to too much wetness, especially in winter. Many of them have evergreen foliage so they remain decorative throughout the year. A single planting of stonecrop *(Sedum obtusatum)* grows informally in a low stone bowl (LEFT). The rough-hewn pedestal that supports the stone bowl rises from a bright clump of lavender *(Lavandula angustifolia)*. Low-growing lavenders, with their tight mounds of foliage, covered with a haze of flowers for many weeks in summer, are ideal for exposed gardens.

For Sun and Wind

✠ Low-growing and prostrate plants (RIGHT) – licorice plant, lobelia, ageratum, verbena, scabious, bellflower, and monkey flower – survive exposure to hot sun well. They need to be watered, but they will not require as much attention as the more delicate and taller plants. Bear in mind that the types of plants that grow on rocky hillsides around the Mediterranean, such as thymes, sages, and many silver-leaved species, suit sunny exposed sites.

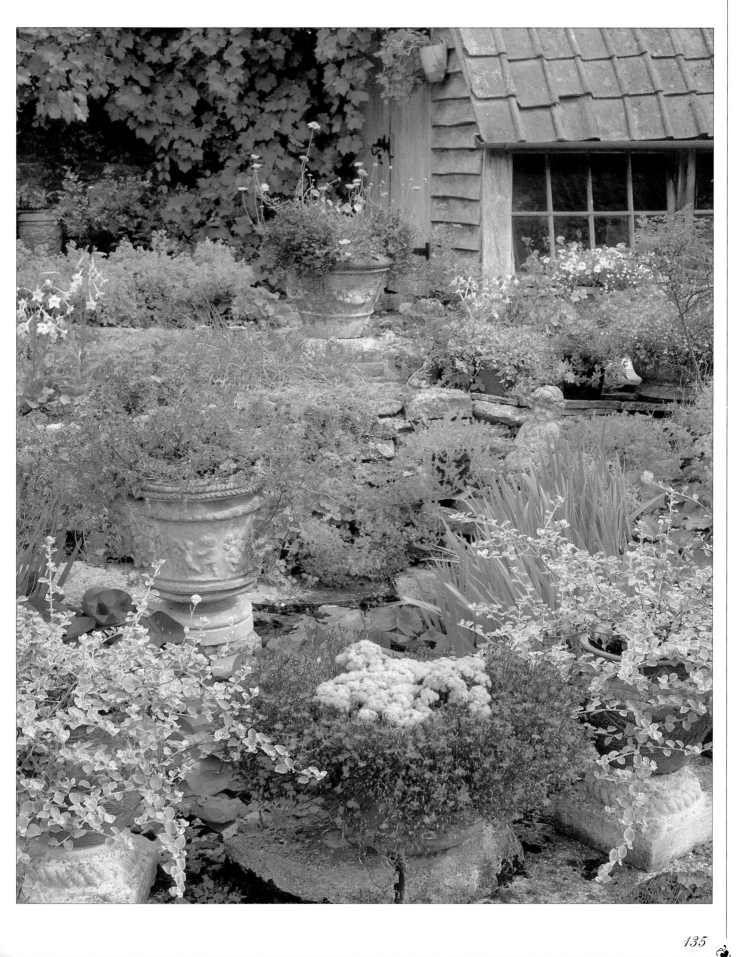

PLANTS FOR EXPOSED SITES

ZONAL GERANIUM
(*Pelargonium* 'Rio')

A N EXPOSED SITE is not the easiest place to grow plants in containers. While gardening in such a site is a challenge, there are a sufficient number of plants you can use that can make this type of container garden look attractive for most, if not all, of the year. Remember that plants which are closely related to wildflowers growing in difficult situations are the most likely to succeed in exposed sites. A large number of tough aromatic plants – especially those with silver foliage – succulents, and strap-leaved plants, such as dracenas and yuccas, will also grow well.

BEDDING DAHLIA
(*Dahlia* 'Fascination')

ZONAL GERANIUM
(*Pelargonium* 'Yale')

✑ WINTER ✑

Andromeda (*Pieris floribunda*) w
Bay (*Laurus*) s
Bayberry (*Myrica pensylvanica*) wsc
Blueberry (*Vaccinium*) wc
Box (*Buxus*) wsd
Cotoneaster (*Cotoneaster*) wsc
Cypress (*Cupressus arizonica* and
C. *macrocarpa*) ws
Elaeagnus (*Elaeagnus*) ws
Euonymus (*Euonymus fortunei*) wcd
Euonymus (*Euonymus japonicus*) wd
Gorse (*Ulex*) ws
Holly (*Ilex*) ws
Juniper (*Juniperus*) wsc
Lavender (*Lavandula*) ws
Pachysandra (*Pachysandra*) wc
Pine (*Pinus*) wsc
Rosemary (*Rosmarinus*) ws
Sage (*Salvia officinalis*) ws
Southernwood (*Artemisia*) ws

———— • ————

Most of the plants recommended for winter are evergreens, and therefore provide year-round interest.

✑ SPRING ✑

Aubretia (*Aubretia*) wsc
Bugleweed (*Ajuga*) wc
Crocus (*Crocus*) wsc
Gorse (*Ulex*) ws
Grape hyacinth (*Muscari*) wscd
Hyacinth (*Hyacinthus*) wsc
Iberis (*Iberis*) sd
Iris (*Iris*) wsc
Lower-growing daffodils (*Narcissus*) wsc
Lower-growing narcissi (*Narcissus*) wsc
Lower-growing tulips (*Tulipa*) wsc
Pansy (*Viola*) ws
Puschkinia (*Puschkinia*) wscd
Saxifrage (*Saxifraga*) ws
Spurge (*Euphorbia*) ws
Squill (*Scilla*) wsc
Wallflower (*Cheiranthus*) wsc

———— • ————

✑ KEY ✑

W tolerates wind
S tolerates sun
C tolerates cold to –33˚C (–20˚F)
D tolerates drought

WALLFLOWER
(*Cheiranthus* 'Rufus')

AMARANTHUS
(*Amaranthus caudatus*)

ACHILLEA (*Achillea millefolium*)

NASTURTIUM (*Tropaeolum majus* 'Alaska')

SCABIOUS (*Scabiosa atropurpurea* 'Cockade')

EUONYMUS
(*Euonymus
fortunei*
'Sunspot')

STATICE
(*Limonium sinuatum*)

PHLOMIS
(*Phlomis italica*)

TULIP (*Tulipa*
'Garden Party')

ECHEVERIA
(*Echeveria*)

⋰ SUMMER ⋱

Achillea (*Achillea*) WSC
Agave (*Agave*) WS
Aloe (*Aloe*) WD
Bergamot (*Monarda*) WS
Cornflower (*Centaurea*) WS
Dracena (*Cordyline*) S
Echeveria (*Echeveria*) WS
Geranium (*Pelargonium*) WS
Houseleek (*Sempervivum*) WSC
Livingstone daisy (*Dorotheanus*) WSD
Locust (*Gleditsia*) WSD
Maple (*Acer*) WC
Marigold (*Calendula/Tagetes*) WS
Mountain flax (*Phormium*) WS
Nasturtium (*Tropaeolum*) WS
Petunia (*Petunia*) S
Phlomis (*Phlomis*) WS
Pink (*Dianthus*) WS
Portulaca (*Portulaca*) WS
Scabious (*Scabiosa*) WSC
Snapdragon (*Antirrhinum*) WS
Statice (*Limonium*) WS
Valerian (*Centranthus*) WS
Yucca (*Yucca*) WSD

———— • ————

⋰ AUTUMN ⋱

Amaranthus (*Amaranthus*) S
Autumn crocus (*Colchicum*) WSCD
Ceratostigma (*Ceratostigma*) WS
Chrysanthemum (*Chrysanthemum*) WS
Cotinus (*Cotinus*) WS
Dahlia (*Dahlia*) WS
Helenium (*Helenium*) WSC
Ice plant (*Sedum spectabile*) WSCD
Kaffir lily (*Schizostylis*) WS
Liriope (*Liriope*) WSD
Nerine (*Nerine bowdenii*) WS
Stonecrop (*Sedum*) WSCD
Sumac (*Rhus*) WSC

———— • ————

EUONYMUS
(*Euonymus fortunei*
'Silver Queen')

PINK (*Dianthus*
'Monica Wyatt')

SNAPDRAGON
(*Antirrhinum majus*)

SPECIFIC LOCATIONS

Most places in the garden are improved by a plant, or group of plants, grown in an attractive container. Often, the restricting factor is how many plants you can manage to water without it becoming too much of a chore. Give priority to sites that are constantly in view, or near the house. If the side walls of the building can be drilled safely, secure attractive wall baskets, hayracks, and hanging baskets to them, ideally near doorways, or above paths where they can be enjoyed, as well as easily watered and looked after.

—— PRIDE OF PLACE ——

Doorways are very important places, especially the front door where plants should be welcoming. The plants need not be tall or expensive specimens. Front doors often have steps leading to them, and a tiered array of plant-filled pots sitting on the steps will give an informal welcome. Elsewhere in the garden, a flight of steps, or maybe just a single step, can be brought to life with a pot overflowing with trailing plants.

 If you are fortunate enough to have a porch, deck, or veranda running along a side of your house, this makes a perfect place for some groups of containers. Use weathered terracotta, stone, or wood containers that will blend well with the walls and flooring of these structures. If you want to protect the floors, use plant-pot saucers.

—— THE UNEXPECTED ——

It is always a pleasant surprise to come across container plantings unexpectedly: to turn a corner and see a path bounded by pots of colorful annuals or more subdued, clipped box trees; to

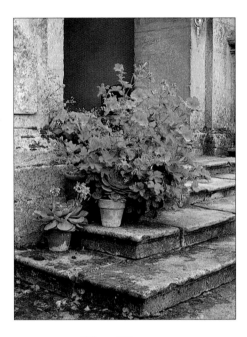

WARM WELCOME
Simple pots of Martha Washington geraniums (ABOVE) and echeverias have a cottagey look that makes this imposing house entrance homey and welcoming.

A FORMAL SETTING
Hydrangea appears simple, cool, and elegant planted in a formal planter (LEFT) against an arborvitae hedge at the end of a gravel path edged with neatly clipped, evergreen box.

walk through a dense screen of shrubs and find a comfortable seat beside a quiet pool, surrounded by pots of blue agapanthus or plumbago; to walk out of the kitchen door and find yourself among a host of pots filled with aromatic culinary herbs; to suddenly notice a small window box discreetly perched on the ledge of an old, ivy-covered brick wall, in cool shade.

—— FOCAL POINT ——

Search out the special places in your garden, where an imposing pot or urn could be used as a focal point. It might be at the end of a long straight path against a formal evergreen hedge, or opposite a door from the house, or a large window overlooking a paved patio or terrace. Like statues, containers are important garden ornaments and their plantings need to be carefully considered so that they will both stand out and relate well to the surrounding planting schemes. Sometimes a simple planting of just one type of plant, species, or variety may well be the answer, especially if the container, itself, is strongly architectural or highly decorative.

—— PRACTICAL CONSIDERATIONS ——

Make sure that a tap or source of water is never too far away from the site you choose for containers. It is all too easy to give up on plants if you have to carry a watering can a long way, particularly in hot weather when they need watering most frequently. Nothing looks sadder than a neglected pot of plants. But then nothing looks better than a group of pots, or even just a simple single urn, tub, or window box, positioned in the right place, and planted with an eye-catching scheme.

PORCHES AND PERGOLAS

PORCHES CAN BE SIMPLE, as a covered but open structure sheltering the approach to a doorway, or they can be much grander, with a roof and sides attached to the house. Being sheltered, they are useful places to grow favorite plants, which may not tolerate the cold, wet, or wind. If container plants are under the roof, you will need to water them carefully.

❦ Pergolas usually consist of a series of pillars made from stone, brick, or iron, supporting a top frame, ideally covered by climbing plants. They may be freestanding and cover an outdoor eating area, or they may form part of a paved walk. Alternatively, they can be built with one side attached to a building, like a veranda, and without an enclosed roof.

❦ As such, pergolas do not offer the same degree of protection to container plants as porches. They do, however, benefit from being furnished with pot plants, particularly around the base of the columns where climbing plants tend to become thin and woody. Some scented plants

are a must. In spring, grow plenty of scented narcissi and hyacinths for the first sorties into the garden. In summer, try marvel of Peru, or angels' trumpets, a robust but frost-tender shrub, which has hanging white trumpets, renowned for their delicious, evening fragrance in summer and autumn. Also add pots of different lilies, carefully chosen to span the summer.

PERFECT PROPORTIONS

The proportions of standards and mop-heads make them ideal for standing against the pillars of a pergola: use flowering geraniums and fuchsias in summer, and hardy evergreens in winter. Bay is a strong-growing plant which can be trained into miniature columns, pyramids, and trees. It is easy to care for, but only moderately hardy, and does not like very cold winds.

❦ If you want to cover a pergola with climbers, avoid growing them in pots, as they are unlikely to grow big enough to do a good job. It is better to plant them in beds in the ground, if possible.

Grandiose Porch
❦ An assortment of pots (LEFT), planted with the cranesbill, *Geranium palmatum*, rain daisies, verbenas, heliotropes, licorice plants, salvias, and agrostemmas, furnish an old stone porch. They give a wild and informal look to this grand entrance area making it more inviting: a place to sit and relax with a book on a hot summer's afternoon.

Pergola Planting
❦ A contemporary pergola made from cedar beams, supported by brick columns (RIGHT). As it is sheltered, this is an ideal site for growing a standard fuchsia and Martha Washington geraniums. To prevent standards from blowing over, you can secure them between the brick columns with some garden wire.

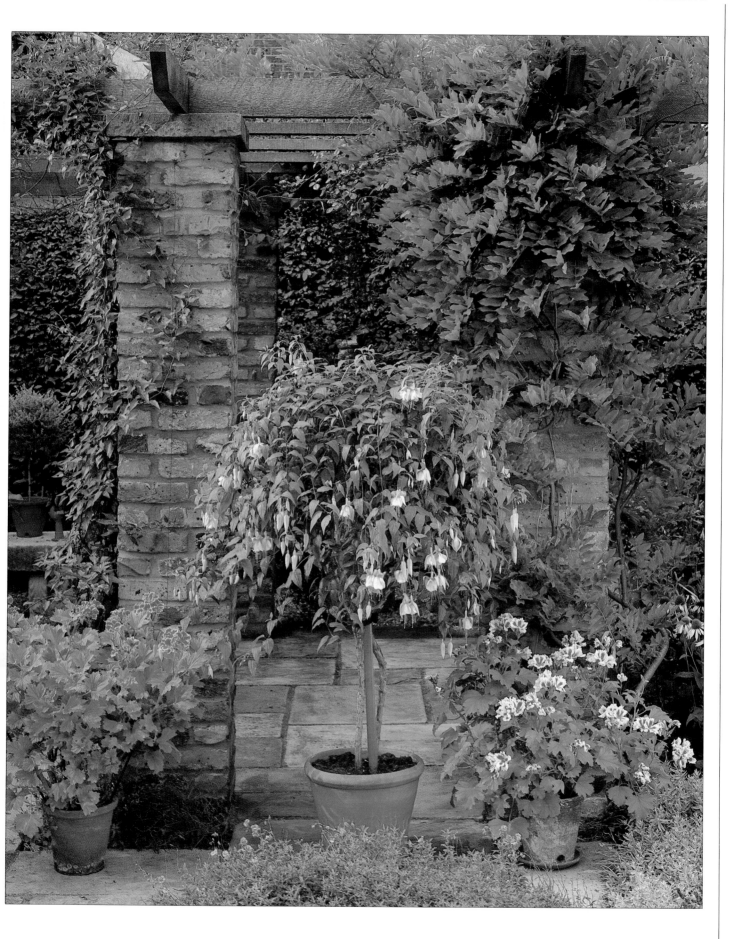

FLIGHTS OF STEPS

AKE MORE OF A FEATURE OF STEPS in your garden, and soften the edges of paving surfaces, by placing pots at the sides. Leave enough room to walk up the steps comfortably, although, if you are growing aromatic plants, it is an added bonus to brush against their foliage, releasing the fragrance as you walk past. I always grow a pot of lemon verbena at the base of some sunny steps in my garden – its leaves exude the most delicious lemon scent, which makes walking up the steps a sheer delight. Generally, I find that low sprawling plants look most effective on steps: a pot planted with ivy-leaved geraniums, trailing lobelia, some portulacas, or nasturtiums works well.

✠ Choose containers that will stand firm and steady on the treads and will complement the material of which the steps are made. Well-weathered terracotta looks attractive on almost any type of hard surface: brick, stone, concrete, metal, or wood. Glazed and colored pots need to be used with more care. They are most effective on the more hard-surfaced steps, such as those made from tile, stone, and concrete. However, there are no rules. Sometimes the most unexpected combinations work to perfection.

Scented Stairway

✠ A simple pot (RIGHT) of flowering tobacco plants *(Nicotiana alata)* sits comfortably in the curve of this shady iron stairway, leading from the house down to the garden. Planted in early summer, the plants will flower through the summer until the first frosts, exuding a delicious nutmeg-like scent from dusk till dawn. The stairs are next to a paved area – it is always a pleasure to have scented flowers where you relax.

A Complement to Old Stone

✠ The clusters of weathered terracotta pots (BELOW) on each side of this shallow flight of steps give a great sense of perspective. Situated on the sunny side of the building, the site is just right for ivy-leaved and zonal geraniums, which flower in summer and autumn, demanding only minimum attention. The pale pink flowers set off the gray stone steps and old wooden door especially well.

DOORWAYS

OORWAYS give both a first and a last impression of your house. The plants around them – often grown in containers as there is little or no soil on the site – should create a feeling of simple ease and beauty that makes visitors sense that all is well.

❧ A planting for a doorway requires careful consideration. Both containers and plants need to suit the area in scale, color, and texture. Terracotta and stone – my favorite materials – are a safe choice as they enhance most situations. Stone is expensive, but reconstituted stone soon looks as good when well weathered.

—— STANDARD WELCOME ——

Tall plants, especially standards, set off a doorway well. Mop-headed bays are great favorites, but privets and some conifers (SEE PAGE 166) can be also trained into decorative shapes. In summer, standard geraniums are ideal for a sunny doorway and standard fuchsias grow well in a semi-shady or shady porch. A pair of standards, one on each side of the door, looks formal, but where there is not enough room for two plantings, a single tub is just as striking. Bays and conifers soon take up all the root room in their containers, leaving little space for additional plantings, but around the base of other standards you can introduce trailing ivy, spring bulbs, and annuals for seasonal variation.

—— FLIGHT OF STEPS ——

When wide steps lead up to a door, arrange pots with evergreen foliage and seasonal color down the sides. If only a little space is available, a single pot of lavender is impressive in a sunny doorway, and fuchsias or hostas make a simple statement in shade. In all cases, the containers should be overflowing and opulent.

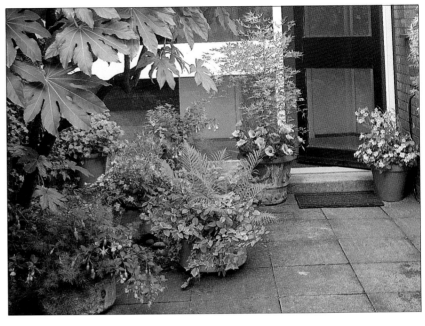

Shady Exit
❧ A shady spot beside a door (ABOVE) is ideal for eustoma *(Eustoma grandiflorum)*, impatiens *(Impatiens walleriana)*, fuchsias *(Fuchsia)*, maple *(Acer palmatum)*, ferns *(Polystichum setiferum)*, and flowering tobacco plants *(Nicotiana alata)*.

Weathered Door
❧ A simple planting (BELOW) of pale pink, daisy-like marguerites *(Chrysanthemum* 'Mary Wootton') suits this sunny corner beside a weathered door. If regularly deadheaded, the marguerites should have several flushes of their pretty flowers.

Style and Symmetry
❧ A period entrance (RIGHT) is perfect for a formal planting. Here, mop-headed privets *(Ligustrum vulgare* 'Buxifolium') grow with colorful Martha Washington geraniums *(Pelargonium* 'Braque') and ivy *(Hedera helix* 'Sagittifolia Variegata').

WALLS AND FENCES

W HEN SPACE ON THE GROUND is at a premium, you can grow plants on or up walls and fences. If the planting is above ground, the container must be firmly fixed in position, so that there is no possibility of it falling. Secure boxes on to window sills with a metal bracket or a strong wire restraint. Frequently check that the brackets and fittings remain both strong and secure.

❧ Containers standing at the base of a wall will probably be quite visible, so the material from which they are made should relate well to the background. Terracotta, stone, and painted wood are good in almost all situations; unpainted wooden containers tend to look better against rustic buildings; and the smoother finishes of fiberglass, plastic, or metal are most effective in front of contemporary structures. You can have fiberglass containers, made to order, in almost any color. Although they are quite expensive, the additional cost for a special color is not that much.

❧ Because fences are not as strong as walls, you should hang only light containers, such as wire half baskets, on them. It is easy to make your own container, using a double layer of chicken wire, cut to make a half or quarter sphere and stuffed with moss. Secure it to the fence with hooks and screws. If you have a fence crying out for foliage cover, but there is no bed at its base, use good-sized containers beside it. Tubs made from teak or cedar look extremely smart against wood. Plant them with ivy or evergreen honeysuckle.

Colored Backdrop

❧ If you are unsure what colors look good together, choose them in a closely related range. Here, I have used red-based colors: pinks, reds, and white for a window box (BELOW) against a dusky pink wall.

Climbing Geraniums

❧ In France, Germany, and Italy, geraniums are widely used in containers (RIGHT) because they grow so profusely during the warm summers. They are trained up walls, as well as left to trail.

GARDEN PATHS

PAVED AREAS CALL for container plantings, and garden paths are no exception. Frequently, a path edges a border that is filled with beautiful color for a month, but once the flowers die down it looks quite dull. It is at this point that pots come into their own, extending the flowering season of an area by a few months. There is just one obvious consideration – make sure the path is wide enough to leave room for the containers and anyone wishing to walk down it.

DELIBERATE DISTRACTIONS

Another good reason for placing containers on a path is to slow any wanderers down on their journey and make them appreciate what lies along the way. It is all too easy to use a path simply as a means of getting from one place to another. Interesting plantings will slow you down as you pause to smell some fragrant leaves, to observe the way light falls on some flowers, or to admire intricate patterning on some foliage. Interestingly, if you line a path with two rows of identical pot plantings, it will soon become a quick walkway again. If a path is very wide, line pots down one side as a border, either with a permanent planting or with plants for seasonal color.

MATCHING MATERIALS

Certain types of containers work especially well on certain surfaces. Terracotta is a natural choice for paths that are made from flagstones, bricks, or gravel. Reconstituted stone that has aged is also in keeping. Wooden containers, such as Versailles tubs, look particularly good against gravel, and the more rustic wooden barrels fit in perfectly with a bark path. In a woodland setting, try hollow trunks planted with ferns.

✤ When you position the pots, bear in mind where the light is going to fall on the path, and site them so that the sun shines through the leaves onto the containers, creating dramatic or interesting shadows.

On the Bend
✗ A group of bush mimulus *(Mimulus aurantiacus)* growing in terracotta pots (ABOVE), brighten a bend in an old stone path with their sunny orange flowers that last from late spring until summer.

Staggered Line
✗ The late afternoon light (LEFT) catches the leaves and flowers of this cheerful assortment of annual nasturtiums *(Tropaeolum)*, planted in old oil jars from the south of France, and terracotta bowls.

Topiary
✗ A formal line of pyramid-shaped clipped box *(Buxus sempervivens)* and mop-headed privet *(Ligustrum vulgare* 'Buxifolium'), divides the path from the lawn (RIGHT) and draws the eye – and the foot – to the far end of the route.

Evening Garden

After the heat of the sun has gone, the garden seems to come alive with soft sweet scents. It is a beautiful time of day to sit outside. If you have a paved eating area with chairs and a table, even if it is only a small terrace, a few pots of scented plants are a must.

✗ In dappled shade, a combination of lilies and flowering tobacco plants can perfume the evening garden from early summer until early autumn and make eating by lantern light the greatest of pleasures. Scented lilies are some of the most beautiful flowers. Their great waxy trumpets open from gracefully pointed buds to pour forth waves of sweet spicy perfume. It is impossible to judge which are the most beautiful. Madonna lilies, the earliest to open, have one of the clearest sweetest fragrances, then come the regales and auratums, with scents reminiscent of nutmeg and vanilla, and finally, in late summer and early autumn, the speciosums, with their reflexed petals and soft toffee-like perfume.

✗ Among flowering tobacco plants, the white-flowered forms have the strongest fragrance. They come into their own in the evening, when their flowers take on a new life, exuding a fragrance resembling sweet nutmeg. I favor the old-fashioned *Nicotiana alata*, easily raised from seed, as it has a better scent than most of the white bedders that you buy in trays. The taller elegant *Nicotiana sylvestris* flowers later in the summer and is also well scented.

Intoxicating Perfume

✗ An iron staircase (LEFT) leading from the living room and kitchen to the garden terrace makes a perfect platform for stepped ranks of lilies, illuminated by lanterns holding candles. The regale lilies (*Lilium regale*), seen here in high summer, are some of the easiest lilies to grow. Highly fragrant, they make ideal subjects for an evening garden, as their white petals with pink reverse sides show up in the fading light. The lilies 'Pink Perfection' and 'Golden Splendour' add just a hint of color to the group.

White Flowers

✗ Under a bower of vine leaves, and against a backdrop of cool green ivy and camellia foliage (RIGHT), transluscent lilies ('La Reve' and 'Casa Blanca') and white impatiens (*Impatiens walleriana*) grow in large terracotta pots. The heavily scented lily flowers last for several weeks. When a flower fades, remove it to encourage more buds to open. I chose pale flowers as they have a pure luminescent quality in the fading light.

MAKING AND DECORATING CONTAINERS

❧

IT IS NOT ALWAYS NECESSARY to buy expensive pots. Containers you may have around the house can be adapted, or you can make them yourself using inexpensive materials.

IDEAS FOR IMPROVISATION
Lilies and ferns grow in pieces of tree stump and a bark pot.

PLANTING A BASKET

WITH THEIR NATURAL, RUSTIC LOOK, baskets make delightful containers for arrangements of small summer-flowering annuals and trailing plants. Basketware tends to rot, especially in damp conditions, but you can increase its life span by painting it with a non-toxic, exterior wood preservative and lining the basket with a pot or a plastic bag. You must make drainage holes in the liner or the planting will drown. Use a basket with an open-weave base so that the water can drain away more freely, and the twigs will not rot so quickly.

1 *Paint the basket with two coats of an exterior matt wood preservative, covering all the wood surfaces.*

2 *When the basket is dry, line it with a black plastic bag. Trim it to size, and make drainage holes in the base.*

3 *Fill with a rich, lightweight potting mixture. Try out the positioning, and plant. Tuck any plastic out of sight.*

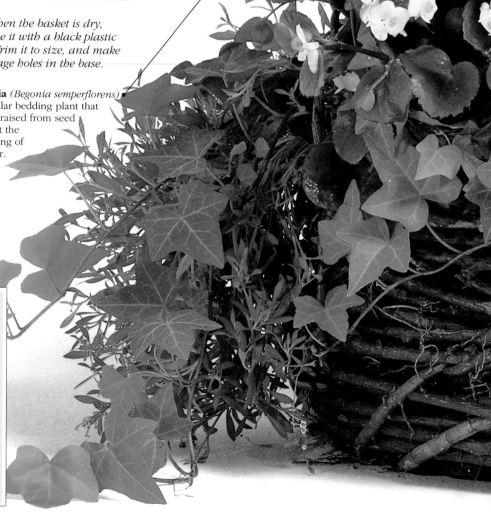

Begonia *(Begonia semperflorens)*
A popular bedding plant that can be raised from seed sown at the beginning of the year.

YOU WILL NEED
•

14in- (35cm-) long, oblong,
open-weave twig basket
Exterior matt wood preservative
Paintbrush
Tough, black plastic bag, or
plastic plant pot or low bowl
Scissors
Lightweight potting mixture of
high nutritional value
Two ivies
Three begonias
Three sweet alyssum
Two ageratum

Ivy *(Hedera helix* 'Gracilis')
Arrange to adorn the
handle of this rustic
basket.

Plant Positions

🌿 Intended for a garden table (ABOVE),
this basket is planted to be enjoyed
from all angles. The sweet alyssum and
ivy trail down the sides, while
the mounds of begonias and
ageratum fill the central area.

Summer Flowers

🌿 This arrangement (LEFT)
is best planted in early
summer. It should flower
well into the autumn and up
to the first frosts, if watered
plentifully, kept in a sunny
position, and given a weekly
liquid plant food.

Ageratum
(Ageratum
houstonianum
'Blue Mink')
Deadhead to
encourage
continuous
flowering
through
summer.

Sweet alyssum
(Lobularia maritima
'Little Dorrit')
A compact form ideal for
growing in a small basket.

CONVERTING A CHIMNEY POT

OLD CHIMNEY POTS, OR SECTIONS OF CERAMIC OR METAL PIPE, make original plant containers. As they take up less room than traditional pots and tubs, they are ideal for sites where space is limited: for example, on steps or balconies, in alleyways, or beside doorways. They are also useful for introducing height to a group of containers, as their elongated form provides the means to lift a planting well above the ground. The most effective plantings for chimney pots are those that form a mop-headed shape, or medium-height or low arrangements with foliage and flowers overflowing informally down the sides. Tall narrow plants look unbalanced and out of scale with the base.

There are two ways of planting chimney pots or pipes. The simplest technique is to fit a plastic pot exactly into the chimney pot top, so its lip is suspended on the rim of the chimney pot. As the plastic pot will need to be small, the size of the plants that you can grow is limited. The other technique is to make a base for the chimney pot so that, in effect, it becomes a very tall flowerpot.

1 *Make the base. Line a saucer with newspaper and place a bottle top or cork, ¾-1in (2-2.5cm) in diameter and at least 1in (2.5cm) tall, in the center where you want the drainage hole.*

2 *Clean the inside of the chimney pot with a mild disinfectant. Place it on the plastic saucer. Pour in enough ready-mix concrete to fill to ¾in (2cm) deep, holding the bottle top in place with a stick.*

3 *Spread the concrete evenly over the base of the chimney pot and leave, undisturbed, to set and dry. Invert the pot, remove the paper, and carefully knock out the bottle top to leave a drainage hole.*

Lobelia *(Lobelia erinus* 'White Cascade') The trailing habit of lobelia breaks and softens the strong lines of the chimney-pot rim. Lobelia flowers for one season.

4 *Stand the pot upright for planting. Place drainage pebbles or pottery chips in the base of the pot, and then firm in a potting mixture of high nutritional value, with some peat added. Plant in early summer.*

• **Fuchsia** *(Fuchsia*
x *hybrida* 'Annabel')
A tender shrub which flowers year
after year if kept in a frost-free place.

YOU WILL NEED

Plastic flowerpot saucer
Newspaper
Bottle top or cork
Old chimney pot
Mild disinfectant
Ready-mix concrete
Stick
Pebbles or pottery chips
Potting mixture of high
nutritional value
Peat
Four fuchsias
Four lobelias

Sprays of White
⚔ This fuchsia, with its
arching sprays of white
dangling flowers, makes
an excellent planting
choice for this old clay
chimney pot. Flowering
for most of the summer
and autumn, the fuchsia
is complemented by the
tiny white blooms of the
lobelia. This arrangement
is ideal for a semi-shady
or even a shady site.
Give the planting a mild
liquid plant fertilizer
once a week for a long
season of blooms.

• **Distressed chimney pot**
The outside of this old chimney pot
is deliberately not scrubbed to give
it a weathered appearance.

DISGUISING A SINK

STONE SINKS ARE DIFFICULT TO FIND, and they are expensive to buy when you do track one down, but the old porcelain models are more readily available at not such extortionate prices. It is then quite easy to convert one into a good replica of a stone sink by cleaning it, coating it with a contact bonding adhesive, and then applying a roughened layer of cement, sand, and peat, mixed together with water. The mixture should only take a few hours to dry thoroughly.

Once filled with soil and rocks, the sink will be immensely heavy, so place it in its final home while it is still empty. Even empty, it will be very heavy. (For details on how to move weighty containers, SEE PAGE 85.) If you intend to plant the sink with alpines, put it in a dry sunny position and raise it on bricks or some pieces of stone, so the plug hole is well clear of the ground. As the roots of alpines dislike the wet, cover the bottom of the sink with a very thick layer of pottery chips or pebbles, and fill it using a potting mixture which has a high gravel content. Coat the outside of the sink with live yoghurt and it should soon weather to resemble an old stone sink.

Stonecrop
(Sedum spurium 'Tricolor')
A hardy, mat-forming perennial.

Alpine poppy
(Papaver burseri)
A species that seeds itself from year to year.

Saxifrage *(Saxifraga paniculata)*
Clusters of rosettes produce spires of white flowers.

Iceland poppy
(Papaver nudicaule)
Pale yellow flowers appear all summer. This poppy dislikes wetness in winter.

1 *Thoroughly clean the outside and inside of the sink so that it is free of dirt and grease. Apply an even layer of contact adhesive to the outside surface and the top 2in (5cm) of the inside surface.*

2 *When the glue is tacky, apply a ³/8in- (1cm-) thick layer of cement mixed with sand and peat. Smooth on firmly with a trowel and roughen with a paintbrush.*

3 *Place the sink in its final position, and raise it off the ground with bricks or stones so that it can drain freely. Cover the base with a thick layer of pebbles or pottery chips for drainage. Fill with potting mixture and fine gravel.*

4 *Arrange tufa over about a quarter of the surface area of the soil, leaving sufficient room for all the plants. Using an old screwdriver, chisel out holes in the rocks for stonecrops and houseleeks.*

YOU WILL NEED
Ceramic sink
Contact bonding adhesive
Old comb
Cement, sand, and peat (proportions 8:2:1)
Trowel
Stubby old paintbrush
Pebbles or pottery chips
Potting mixture of medium nutritional value, with fine gravel (proportions 4:1)
Tufa or porous rock
Large old screwdriver

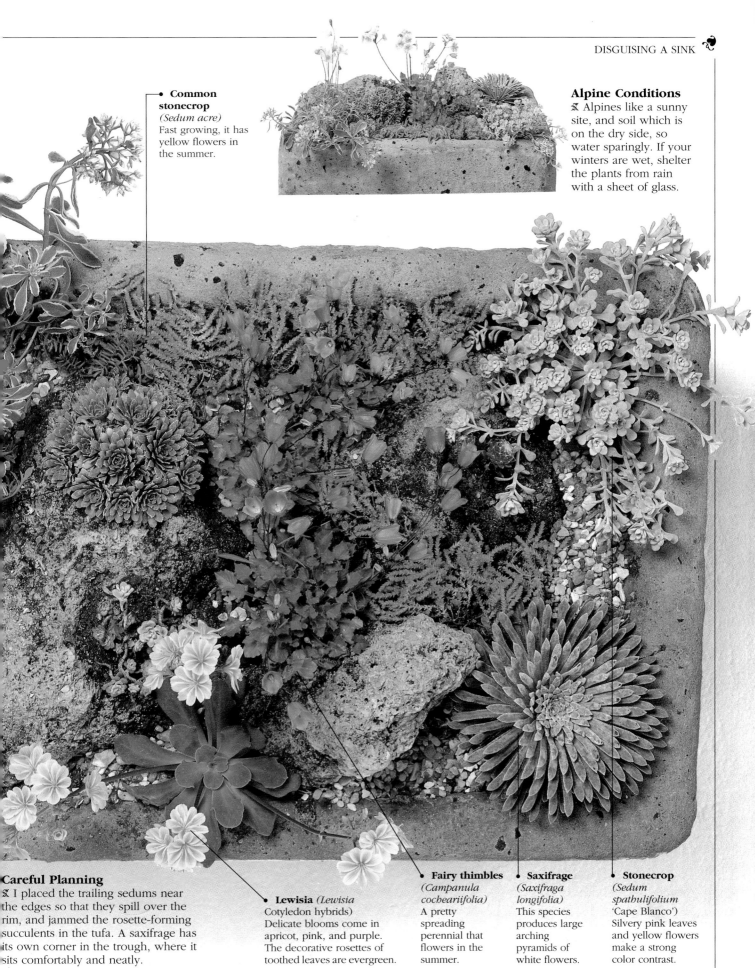

Common stonecrop
(Sedum acre)
Fast growing, it has yellow flowers in the summer.

Alpine Conditions
✿ Alpines like a sunny site, and soil which is on the dry side, so water sparingly. If your winters are wet, shelter the plants from rain with a sheet of glass.

Careful Planning
✿ I placed the trailing sedums near the edges so that they spill over the rim, and jammed the rosette-forming succulents in the tufa. A saxifrage has its own corner in the trough, where it sits comfortably and neatly.

Lewisia *(Lewisia* Cotyledon hybrids)
Delicate blooms come in apricot, pink, and purple. The decorative rosettes of toothed leaves are evergreen.

Fairy thimbles
(Campanula cocheariifolia)
A pretty spreading perennial that flowers in the summer.

Saxifrage
(Saxifraga longifolia)
This species produces large arching pyramids of white flowers.

Stonecrop
(Sedum spathulifolium 'Cape Blanco')
Silvery pink leaves and yellow flowers make a strong color contrast.

159

USING AN OLD MOP BUCKET

WHEN A METAL MOP BUCKET springs a leak, bringing to an end its value in the kitchen, give it a second life in the garden by filling it with summer-flowering plants. Annuals will happily send their roots through the colander part of the bucket, where you wring out the mop, but larger plants are not suitable. You will need to drill holes in the base to provide drainage, as leak gaps are rarely sufficient.

❦ Several other types of metal container can also be converted. Antique coppers, for example, are handsome-looking, although they are not easy to find and have become expensive to buy. Once kept outside, these soon lose their gleam, taking on a rich dark patina. They are long-lasting and unaffected by frost. Milk churns, cream pitchers, large tin cans, and even saucepans and fish kettles can all be put to use in the garden, if you drill drainage holes in the bottom. They look most effective in an informal setting, used with building materials such as wood, old brick, and stone, or try standing them among low plants in a mixed border.

1 *Make five, evenly spaced drainage holes in the bottom of each metal mop bucket, using an electric drill.*

2 *Place pebbles or pottery chips in the base for drainage, and add the potting mixture, ensuring that no air pockets are left around the colanders. Plant one bucket with one coleus toward the back, two celosia in front of it, and three French marigolds around the edge. You could fill the other bucket with strawflowers (RIGHT).*

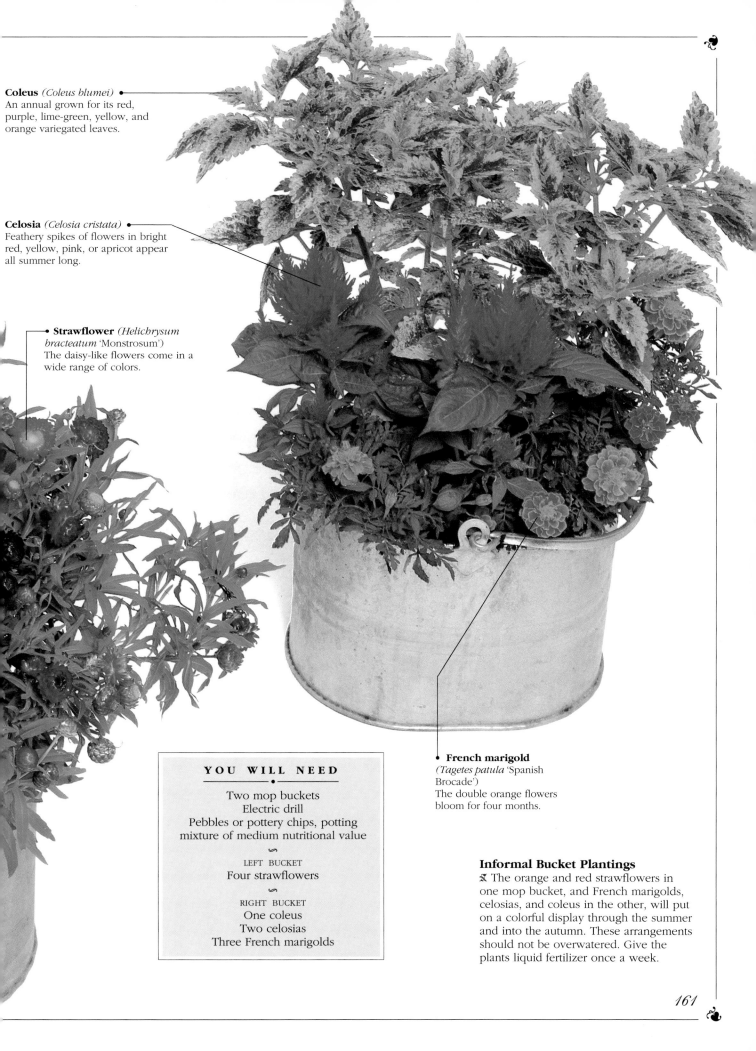

Coleus *(Coleus blumei)*
An annual grown for its red, purple, lime-green, yellow, and orange variegated leaves.

Celosia *(Celosia cristata)*
Feathery spikes of flowers in bright red, yellow, pink, or apricot appear all summer long.

• **Strawflower** *(Helichrysum bracteatum* 'Monstrosum')
The daisy-like flowers come in a wide range of colors.

• **French marigold**
(Tagetes patula 'Spanish Brocade')
The double orange flowers bloom for four months.

YOU WILL NEED
•
Two mop buckets
Electric drill
Pebbles or pottery chips, potting mixture of medium nutritional value

LEFT BUCKET
Four strawflowers

RIGHT BUCKET
One coleus
Two celosias
Three French marigolds

Informal Bucket Plantings
⚘ The orange and red strawflowers in one mop bucket, and French marigolds, celosias, and coleus in the other, will put on a colorful display through the summer and into the autumn. These arrangements should not be overwatered. Give the plants liquid fertilizer once a week.

161

MAKING A WOODEN WINDOW BOX

IT CAN BE DIFFICULT to find manufactured, wooden window boxes that exactly fit the window sills of your house. One way around this problem is to buy a simple plastic window box that approximately fits your window sill, and then make a wooden cover for it. If no plastic box is suitable for your window sill, construct your own wooden window box to the required measurements. You can use either a smooth or textured plywood, or one of the beautiful although more expensive hardwoods, such as cedar or teak.

✄ If you want a natural wood finish, paint the exterior with a non-toxic wood preservative. Alternatively, apply a primer and an exterior matt or gloss top coat in your chosen color.

∽ WOODEN FRAME FOR A PLASTIC WINDOW BOX ∽

This simple, wooden frame fits neatly over a manufactured, plastic window box. It is made from a textured plywood to give it an unusual surface and patterning that will show through paint; for a plain, more even finish and a smoother painting surface, use a hardwood, instead. Ask a lumberyard to cut the pieces of wood to your specifications. For ideas on how to paint and decorate your finished wooden window-box frame or window box with stencils, SEE PAGES 164-5.

1 *For this wooden, window-box frame you will need two sides, one front, and one back. Make the sides ½in (1.2cm) higher and ½in (1.2cm) wider than the inner plastic box. Make the front and back ½in (1.2cm) higher than the inner plastic box, and the wooden sides longer by ½in (1.2cm).*

YOU WILL NEED
Tape measure
Four pieces of textured plywood, cut to size
Eight metal brackets
Wood screws
Awl
Screwdriver
Paintbrush
Wood preservative, or primer and matt or gloss top coat

2 *Construct the frame, using two metal brackets in each corner. With an awl, mark and puncture the positions of the screws for the metal brackets. The bottom brackets should be ¾in (2cm) above the base; the top brackets should be at least 1in (2.5cm) below the rim.*

3 *Screw the brackets into position. Secure one of the short sides last of all: with the rest of the box constructed, you will find this is the least tricky part to reach with a screwdriver.*

4 *The completed frame can be treated with a wood preservative for a natural finish, or painted with a primer and matt or gloss top coat in the color of your choice.*

Dahlia *(Dahlia* 'Redskin') Grown for its deep bronze-green foliage as well as its glorious blooms.

Sage *(Salvia officinalis* 'Tricolor') The variegated leaves are delicious used as a herb.

Green Finish
✄ Painted a very dark green, this wooden window box sets off the rich flower colors and variegated foliage in this autumn planting of dahlias, ivy-leaved geraniums, sage, snapdragons, and sweet alyssum. Place the window box in a sunny position, water frequently in dry weather, and give the plants a weekly feeding.

Ivy-leaved geranium
(Pelargonium 'Elégante') A trailing ivy-leaved variety with delicate pink flowers.

∽ WOODEN WINDOW BOX ∽

To construct the sides of the window box, follow STEPS 1-3, WOODEN FRAME FOR A PLASTIC WINDOW BOX. Cut one more piece of wood for the base, to fit inside the frame. Exterior plywood gives a smooth paint finish.

YOU WILL NEED

Wood drill	Dark green undercoat
Five pieces of exterior plywood, cut to fit the window sill	Dark green matt top coat
Awl	Pebbles or pottery chips
Wood screws	Potting mixture of high nutritional value
Twelve metal brackets	Three dahlias
Screwdriver	Two sages
Tape measure	Two ivy-leaved geraniums
Paintbrush	
Waterproof paint	Two snapdragons
Primer	One sweet alyssum

1 *Attach four metal brackets to the base, positioning two on each of the long sides. Fit the frame on to the base of the box, mark the positions of the screw holes with an awl, and screw to secure.*

2 *Turn the window box upside down and, using a wood drill, make three ½in (1.2cm) holes in the base for drainage. If the box is less than 24in (60cm) long, only two drainage holes are necessary. Too many holes in the wood will hasten the rotting process.*

3 *Paint the inside of the window box with waterproof paint, and the exterior and all the edges with a primer, and then a dark green matt top coat.*

Snapdragon (*Antirrhinum majus* 'Trumpet Serenade') Flowers in a range of colors appear for three months.

Sweet alyssum (*Lobularia maritima* 'Wonderland') The flowers are honey-scented.

DECORATING WOODEN WINDOW BOXES

MOST CONTAINERS MADE from porous materials, such as wood, are easy to paint and decorate. The simplest decoration is a plain surface, painted in a shade that complements the existing colors of the site, or the plants that you are likely to be growing. White, cream, dark green, and black are safe choices as they will relate to most colors.

✖ A more adventurous design would be to paint *trompe l'oeil* paneling or, perhaps, a stenciled decoration on your window box. Beware of including painted flowers in your pattern – they tend to compete for attention with the real ones on the plants.

✖ Always prepare the surface of the container with an exterior wood primer and an exterior top coat. This should remain in good condition for a couple of years, before it needs repainting.

Rustic Effect
✖ Screw on pieces of weathered board to achieve this rustic effect (LEFT). First, glue the strips into place, and then use two screws to attach each board firmly to the inside of the frame.

***Trompe l'Oeil* Paneling**
✖ To create a paneled effect (RIGHT), mark out the panels with a pencil. Mask the edges with tape. Paint two adjacent sides of each panel a lighter shade of the background, and the other two sides a darker shade. This gives a three-dimensional appearance.

Skimmia *(Skimmia reevesiana)*
A self-pollinating variety, although it is not as hardy as other skimmias.

Cyclamen (*Cyclamen hederifolium* 'Album') Grown for its attractive, silver-marbled foliage and pure white flowers.

Stained Orange Crate

✄ A plain wooden crate (ABOVE), used for packing oranges, makes an effective container for these white autumn-flowering cyclamen. I painted this crate with a wood preservative and green stain, mixed together.

Ornamental cabbage (*Brassica oleracea*) These evergreen biennials provide warm pinks, pale greens, and creams for winter planting designs.

Design for a Winter Window Box

✄ When the top coat of paint on the window box is dry, either hand paint it, working out your pattern on paper first, or decorate it with a stencil design. Make a stencil by cutting a pattern out of an oiled stencil board with a sharp knife. For foliage, you can trace around real leaves first, then transfer the design using carbon paper on to the board.

EVERGREEN TOPIARY

THE ANCIENT ART OF TOPIARY, in which plants are encouraged to grow into formal shapes, has been practiced since early Roman times. It is not as difficult as it might appear; in a sense, it is just pruning taken to the extreme. Clipping a plant into a simple ball or pyramid design is only a question of encouraging growth within the confines of the final shape, and discouraging all other growth. With strong-growing plants, no staking or wiring is necessary. For more complicated topiary – animal shapes, for example – or plants with weaker main stems, some support, such as a stake or wire frame, should be given.

✿ Box, bay, privet, and yew all grow happily in containers and are suitable for training into special shapes. Evergreen climbers like ivy or, in frost-free climates, creeping fig, can also be used to great effect, grown from a pot and trained over a specially shaped, wire frame to make almost any architectural or animal shape.

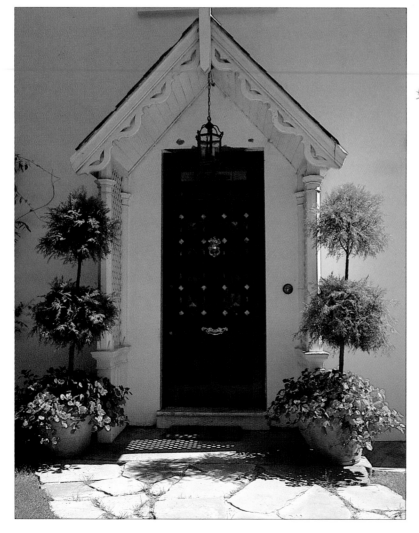

Clipped Conifers
✿ This decorative front door and porch with an ornate scalloped roof (LEFT) cries out for topiary on each side. Flanking the door are two striking conifers, *Cupressocyparis leylandii* 'Castlewellan', which have each been trained to form two spheres.

Conical Shrub
✿ To train box *(Buxus sempervirens)* into a conical shape (ABOVE), encourage the central main shoot to grow to the required height and clip the side shoots to shape as the plant develops. As the main stem of box is strong, staking is not necessary.

∽ AN IVY CONE ∽

Cover a wire frame with a climber to form a bold architectural shape. Ivy is one of the best climbers to use, as it grows quickly and thickly, and is also evergreen, providing interest throughout the year. The chicken-wire frame constructed for this ivy (BELOW) is made in two sections.

1 *For the bottom section of the frame, cut an 8ft- (2.4m-) length of chicken wire and roll it into a cylinder with a 14in (35cm) diameter. You should end up with a double layer of chicken wire, between which you can sandwich a ½in- (1.2cm-) layer of moss.*

2 *Sandwich the moss firmly between the two layers of chicken wire until you reach the end. Bind the ends of the chicken wire together and the bottom of the cylinder with garden wire to prevent any of the moss from falling out, and make the ring secure.*

3 *Mold the cylinder into shape. Form tucks towards the top so that the cylinder begins to slope inwards. Make a second smaller cylinder from chicken wire and moss to go on top of the first one. Fold the top to a point and wire onto the bottom cylinder. It is now ready to support the ivy.*

Glossy Green Cone
⚘ Ivy (Hedera helix 'Deltoidea') will cover the frame in three years. This variety is ideal for a shady or semi-shady site, but it will also grow in sunshine.

4 *Fill the terracotta pot with potting mixture over a bed of clean pottery chips. Thread wire through the metal pole's hole and place it in the center of the pot. Plant the ivies.*

5 *Next, place the completed chicken-wire frame in the pot, with its base sitting on the surface of the potting mixture. Use wire to attach the top of the metal rod to the top of the frame.*

YOU WILL NEED
•
12x1ft (3.5mx30cm) chicken wire
Moss
Garden wire
22in- (55cm-) diameter terracotta pot
Rich potting mixture, pottery chips
Metal rod, 39in (107cm) long, with a hole in the top
Five ivies

CONSTRUCTING A HERB TOWER

I ALWAYS LIKE TO HAVE POTS OF HERBS next to the kitchen door, so that I can take one step outside and pick a sprig or two while cooking. Most herbs are sun lovers, so a sunny site is of prime importance in order to grow a good crop. The smaller species – thyme, chives, oregano, and sage – can be grown in a group in a herb pot or, as here, in a herb tower made from chicken wire and moss. The larger-growing shrubs and trees, such as rosemary and bay, are best given a pot to themselves. Mint, also, should be grown on its own as it can be extremely invasive. Many of the smaller herbs, such as oregano, chives, parsley, and tarragon, even though they are perennials and biennials, produce the best flavor if planted in spring and grown as annuals.

Chives *(Allium schoenoprasum)*
Remove all the flowers to
encourage plentiful foliage.

1 *To make the frame, sandwich moss between two layers of chicken wire. Stitch the base and sides together with garden wire and cut holes for plants in the sides. Line the tower with plastic, and then punch to make drainage holes. Place pebbles or pottery chips in the bottom of the container.*

2 *Fill the chicken-wire and moss frame with potting mixture up to the first side hole. Thread the small and trailing plants through the side holes, building up the soil around them until the tower is filled to within 4-5in (10-13cm) of the top. Plant the larger herbs in the top of the tower.*

3 *Leave a gap of ¾in (2cm) between the top of the potting mixture and the rim of the tower to facilitate watering. The herbs should be ready for picking within a few weeks.*

Purple sage •
(Salvia officinalis 'Purpurascens')
An edible and decorative herb.

Thyme *(Thymus* •
praecox sub. *arcticus)*
The leaves have an
excellent flavor.

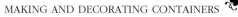

Marjoram
(Origanum vulgare)
Removing the
flowers will help
keep the plant
bushy.

Decorative Window Sill

A selection of herbs growing in small pots on
a sunny window sill can be both decorative and
practical. From left to right: purple basil, mint,
thyme, tarragon, angelica, and ruby chard.

Thyme *(Thymus vulgaris* 'Aureus')
An intensely aromatic herb.

Variegated mint *(Mentha*
x *gentilis* 'Variegata')
This variety has leaves
with a mild flavor.

Parsley *(Petroselinum crispum)*
Planted at the back, out of
sight, a useful biennial, best
picked in its first season.

Cultivation Tips

Water this herb tower frequently,
but never allow the potting mixture
to become waterlogged, and give
liquid fertilizer every two weeks.
Turn every week to give all the
plants the advantage of sun. Do
not overpick or the herbs will die.

YOU WILL NEED

7½x1ft (2.25mx30cm) chicken wire
Moss
Garden wire
Plastic for lining the tower
Pebbles or pottery chips
Potting mixture of medium
nutritional value
One chive plant
One variegated mint
One purple sage
One marjoram
Two thymes
Two parsleys

TRAINING STANDARDS

STANDARD PLANTS ARE NOT AS DIFFICULT to grow as many people assume, although it does help if you have a greenhouse. Standards are more susceptible to frost damage than low-growing plants, and therefore need to be overwintered under glass in colder climates.

You start off standards from cuttings taken in late summer and, at first, concentrate on encouraging the main growing tip. Allow the plant to grow approximately 6in (15cm) tall, then remove any side shoots as they appear. Stake the main stem well and give the plant plenty of water and fertilizer (feed twice a week during the growing season), but do not let the potting mixture become soggy. When the leader reaches 6-9in (15-23cm) below the required height of the standard, allow the side shoots to grow and bush out into a mop-head. You may need to make a spherical cage from thick wire to support the side shoots of the mop-head.

• **Zonal geranium**
(*Pelargonium*
'Deacon Bonanza')
In a sunny situation, this produces a profusion of vivid pink flowers.

∽ MOCK TREE FERN ∽

YOU WILL NEED
•
36in- (1m-) long
birch bough
10in (25cm) pot
Plaster of
Paris mix
Plant pot with
saucer, attached
with prongs
Screws
16in (40cm) pot
Medium-rich
potting mixture
Ivy, Boston fern

Make an imitation tree fern by placing a Boston fern at the end of a birch bough. In most regions, Boston ferns can only be kept outside in summer and autumn. If you want a plant that can stay outside all year, use ivy instead. Wandering jew would also look effective displayed in this way, but it, too, is only tender.

1 *Fix the tree bough into the smaller pot filled with a plaster of Paris mix. Put the pot into the larger one. Screw the saucer with pot-holding prongs to the end of the branch.*

2 *Fill the large pot with potting mixture and plant ivy around the edge. Secure a potted Boston fern onto the saucer. Place in a sheltered shady or semi-shady position, out of strong winds. Water the plants well, and occasionally clip the ivy to keep it neat and trim.*

Flowering Mop-heads

Geraniums and fuchsias make particularly good mop-heads, as they both flower profusely all summer long. The geraniums should be kept in sun, but the fuchsias and hydrangeas prefer semi-shade. Although hydrangeas are hardy, it is best to protect standards from frost, keeping them in a greenhouse over winter.

Fuchsia (*Fuchsia* 'Citation')
A strong-growing variety that is suitable for training into an attractive mop-head.

Ivy (*Hedera helix* 'Gracilis')
Planted in two of these tubs to cover the potting mixture.

Hydrangea (*Hydrangea macrophylla* 'Hamburg')
Keep in good dappled light and water plentifully. This specimen is only two years old.

Ivy (*Hedera helix* 'Deltoidea')
A variety distinguished by its heart-shaped green leaves.

SUPPORTING PLANTS IN POTS

CLIMBERS, TALL ANNUALS and perennials, and young shrubs and trees with supple stems all require support when grown in containers. As the extent of the support's base will be limited by the size of the container, traditional means used for plants growing in borders are not always possible, so you have to be a little more imaginative and inventive.

✠ The simplest form of support is a single stake or cane, driven into the potting mixture down to the base of the pot – the main stem of the plant is tied to the stake. This method is good for plants that eventually support themselves, such as young trees. For a stronger, more permanent structure, make a pyramid or fan-shaped trellis. Ensure that the stakes are long enough to reach from the bottom of the pot to above the top of the plant.

Silver Tree

✠ Licorice plant *(Helichrysum petiolare)* is a half-hardy shrub that can reach 5ft (1.5m) in just one summer season, if trained up a pyramid of four bamboo canes. Tie the main shoot to the central stake and stop side shoots at 5in (13cm) long, until the plant reaches the required height. Thereafter, clip or leave it to spread informally. Pinch off any flowers. Grow in a sunny site, feed and water regularly, and protect from frost in winter.

YOU WILL NEED

Four 5ft- (1.5m-) long
bamboo canes
Nine 14in (35cm) garden stakes
Garden wire
Pair of pliers
13in- (32cm-) diameter flowerpot
Pebbles or pottery chips
Potting mixture of high nutritional value
Garden string
One honeysuckle

❧ MAKING A TRELLIS ❧

1 *Lay out four canes and fan them out so that the bottom ends fit in your container. Lay the stakes, cut into increasing lengths, across the main canes at regular intervals. Mark the positions where they cross the canes.*

2 *Attach the bottom lateral stake to each of the canes with wire. Make a loop around the back of the cane, crossing the ends over the lateral stake and bringing them down behind.*

3 *Twist the wire tightly behind the cane on the reverse side. First, attach the base lateral stake and then the top one, to form a rigid frame, before securing the rest of the canes into position.*

Fragrant Climber

✄ The semi-evergreen Japanese honeysuckle (*Lonicera japonica* 'Halliana') produces strongly scented flowers throughout the summer and autumn; an excellent climber for a pot.

173

PLANT CARE

From seed or cutting to mature specimen, your summer annuals, spring bulbs, perennials, shrubs and trees must be looked after properly if they are to give you their best, over the longest possible period. Pruning, propagation, watering, feeding, planting, and pest and disease control are neither difficult nor complicated. Follow the few simple measures outlined here, and your plants should be healthy and happy.

ESSENTIAL GARDEN TOOLS

A watering can, trowel, clippers, garden string, and stakes are necessities for the day-to-day care of plants in containers.

PESTS AND DISEASES

PLANTS IN CONTAINERS are as susceptible to most pests and diseases as those growing in the open ground. However, slugs and snails, which crawl along the ground, may not present such a problem.

✄ A few simple measures can help to deter both pests and diseases. Start out with a container, pebbles or pottery chips, and soil that are as clean as possible. Scrub the pot and pottery chips in a solution of water and disinfectant to eradicate any fungal spores. Use a potting mixture that has been sterilized – most bagged mixes are safe – so that no diseases are carried in the soil. Re-used potting mixtures can be a source of infection. China asters, in particular, must not be planted in soil that previously has been used for them or they can get wilt.

✄ Whenever possible, try to use organic methods to control pests in the garden. Soapy household water or any natural soap spray is useful for killing aphids, and slugs and snails are attracted by grapefruit. Make a trap by cutting the fruit in half, scooping out the flesh and placing the peel, like a small igloo, on the ground. Each morning, remove all slugs or snails in the trap. A flowerpot stuffed with newspaper, and placed upside down on a stick will attract earwigs, and draw them away from dahlias. Raise your containers just slightly off the ground to deter earwigs from gathering under the pots. Keep the area around your pots free of dead leaves and debris, which might provide shelter and warm, moist living conditions for unwanted wildlife.

Leaf Miner
✄ The larvae of various species of moths and flies burrow into the fabric of leaves, marking them with a patch or a fine network of trails. Remove and discard affected leaves. Infestations do not always cause much damage. Treat the plants with a spray if the problem becomes serious. Columbines are especially likely to be affected by leaf miners.

Sowbug
✄ Hard-coated pests, sowbugs live in damp shady places and feed off organic debris. Large colonies of them may congregate in the moist crannies under containers and enter pots through the drainage holes. They are night feeders and will eat most parts of a plant. Dusts and sprays are available to control them. You can repel them with ashes.

Earwig
✄ These insects are not a major pest of plants growing in containers, although they will eat dahlias and chrysanthemums at night. Place an inverted flowerpot, filled with straw, on a stake. The earwigs will congregate in the pot overnight. Remove the pot in the morning and destroy the pests.

Slug
✄ Slugs emerge from damp shady places among dead leaves or any rotting vegetation at night to eat the young stems, leaves, and buds, and also roots, bulbs, and corms below the soil. To keep slugs in check, ensure plants are clean and free of dead leaves. Slug baits and pans of beer set out as traps are effective controls.

Aphid
✗ Several different species of aphid are troublesome on garden plants. These extremely invasive insects suck the sap of young growth and the sap around flower buds, disfiguring the plant and sometimes causing the buds to rot. They also excrete a sticky honeydew that encourages sooty molds to grow and can transmit virus diseases. They thrive in warm weather and annuals, perennials, and shrubs are all suscepible. Keep a regular check for them and treat as soon as you see them. There are several organic products made from natural soaps that kill aphids, as well as a mass of chemical insecticides. Try spraying them with a homemade soap solution.

Scale Insect
✗ These insects may infest bay trees, camellias, and other garden evergreens, leaving a sticky deposit on the foliage. The female insects are protected by a very tough scale covering that adheres strongly to the leaf. Kill scale insects with an insecticide when they are hatching during the summer, or remove the scales by hand.

Whitefly
✗ Related to aphids but looking more like miniature moths, whiteflies live on the undersides of leaves and feed on plant sap. They excrete a sticky honeydew, which adheres to leaf stems and flowers and can attract sooty mold. They breed quickly in summer, but infestations can occur from late spring onward. Control with the same insecticides that kill aphids.

Mildew
✗ Flourishing on roses, begonias, and chrysanthemums, powdery and downy mildews are caused by various fungi. Contrary to what many people believe, mildews are most prevalent in dry weather. Spray plants and any fallen leaves from early spring onward.

Rust
✗ A fungal infection that causes spots and marking on leaves. Begin anti-fungal spraying in early spring. Burn all leaves that are infected, and destroy the entire plant if it is badly infected and the rust appears two years running. Snapdragons, sweet William, mahonia, and roses are most likely to be affected.

PLANTING AND REPOTTING

Gᴠᴇ ʏᴏᴜʀ ᴘʟᴀɴᴛѕ the very best possible start by planting them properly. Ensure that the container is completely clean and that the inside is free of old soil, which might harbor disease. Porous-surfaced containers, such as stone and terracotta, should be cleaned especially well. Scrub the container with a mild disinfectant. If you would like the outside of an old terracotta pot to keep its weathered appearance, just clean the inside.

—— PLANTING CONTAINERS ——

It is a good idea to soak porous-surfaced containers, such as terracotta pots, before planting them. When they are dry, containers quickly take a great deal of moisture out of the potting mixture.

✖ Next, place a layer of drainage material in the bottom of the container. Pottery chips make one of the best drainage mediums, but pebbles, stones or even pieces of polystyrene can be used. Container plants grow best when planted in a peat-based or soil-based potting mixture. The soil-based mixtures are usually neutral, although some are made with either a higher acid or alkaline content. The peat-based mixtures tend toward acidity.

✖ Both the peat-based and the soil-based potting mixtures are sold in varying degrees of nutritional value. The one with the lowest nutritional value is ideal for raising seeds and for potting seedlings. Potting mixtures of medium nutritional value are best for young plants, and the high nutrition potting mixtures are most often used for mature plants.

✖ Soil-based potting mixtures tend to be heavy and can easily become compacted and solid, making efficient watering difficult. The peat-based ones, however, dry out very quickly, and once dry are not easy to moisten again. I find that an equal mixture of the two makes one of the best mediums unless the plant requires unusual conditions.

—— REPOTTING ——

When plants become root-bound and their roots start growing out of the bottom of the drainage holes, it is time to transfer them to larger containers. Most plants will be happy if they are planted into a pot that is larger than the previous one. For visual reasons, it is best not to use a pot that is too big or it will look unbalanced.

❧ REPOTTING LARGE PLANTS ❧

If a large plant has become completely pot-bound, so that it is attached to the pot and is too heavy to turn upside down and tap to remove the root ball, use the method outlined below to remove it.

1 *This large dracena needs repotting. Its roots have started growing out of the drainage holes of the pot. Plants also need repotting when the roots start growing in a spiral around the inner edge of the pot.*

3 *If the tapping method fails, cut the pot away from the root ball. With sharp clippers, cut a straight line down the side of the pot. If necessary, cut another line down the opposite side of the pot.*

2 *Tie back the foliage with string or with one of the leaves. To release the plant, hold it by the stem, just above the potting mixture, lift and tap around the edge of the pot. It is easier if someone helps you.*

⚘ CLEANING CONTAINERS ⚘

☙ *Clean all previously used containers thoroughly before you use them. Scrub the inside, and the outside if desired, with a weak solution of disinfectant to remove any diseases or pests that might be on the container's surface. Rinse with clean water after scrubbing. Thoroughly clean any pebbles or pottery chips that you use as a drainage medium.*

⚘ REPOTTING SMALL PLANTS ⚘

Water the plant thoroughly beforehand to make sure that it is in a healthy state. Never repot when the temperature is below freezing as many plants are susceptible to frost. Transfer the plant to a container that is at least one size larger than the one it was growing in, and make sure that the soil comes up to the same level on the plant as it did in the previous pot.

1 *Firm potting mixture onto a bed of pebbles or pottery chips in the new container so that when positioned, the old soil mark on the plant comes to just below the top edge of the pot.*

2 *Water the plant well by soaking it in a bucket of water until bubbles stop forming. Place your fingers firmly across the base of the stem, and then turn the pot upside down.*

3 *Tap the pot on a firm edge, such as the top of the bucket, to free the ball of soil from the pot. If this does not work, try pushing a small stick up through one of the drainage holes.*

4 *Gently loosen the roots at the base and at the sides with your fingers. This will encourage the roots to grow outward and downward once planted, instead of in a tight spiral.*

5 *Place the plant on the firmed soil in the new pot, making sure that it stands straight, and carefully fill in the sides with potting mixture to just below the top of the pot. Firm.*

WATERING

PLANTS IN CONTAINERS require more careful watering than those grown in open ground, as the soil in pots is more likely to dry out or become waterlogged. In hot parts of the country, plants growing in containers in full sun may need watering twice or even three times a day.

THE CORRECT BALANCE

For the majority of plant species and varieties, the soil in a container needs to be kept just moist, but never soggy, during their growing and flowering seasons (spring and summer). As plants hate to have their roots sitting in water, avoid placing a saucer under the pot which traps excess water.

The leaves often cover much of the top surface of the potting mixture, so the plants in containers do not receive as much natural rainwater as plants in beds. Check for adequate moisture, therefore, even in wet weather. For plants that need feeding in the growing and flowering seasons, add a measure of liquid or soluble solid fertilizer to their water. Different plants have different requirements, but the most usual is a weekly feeding. For specific requirements, SEE PRACTICAL MATTERS with each planting design. In winter, when the temperature is above freezing, give the plants a little water, perhaps once every two weeks. However, never water during freezing weather.

Bucket of Water
✕ *Submerge the plant in its pot in a bucket, two-thirds full of water. The water should come over the top of the pot. When no more bubbles appear, the root ball is soaked. Drain.*

Hanging Baskets
✕ *Use a compression unit to water hanging baskets that are out of reach. This method squirts water from a bottle, up a tube, which has a curved end, making it possible to direct water into the potting mixture. Hanging baskets dry out more quickly than other containers because the surface is so porous – ensure that they receive plenty of water and liquid fertilizer. In heat, they may need watering two or three times a day.*

Drip Method
✕ *A commercial drip system is useful for watering plants when you go away. Capillary tubing carries water from a bucket to the potting mixture and the plants. Keep the plants in a shady place.*

Wick System
✕ *Push one end of a kerosene lamp wick into the soil surrounding the plant and trail the other end in a bucket of water. Ensure that the wick is wet and reaches the bottom of the bucket for best results.*

Packed in Peat
✕ *Plants can be kept moist by surrounding them in damp peat. Make sure that they stand on, and are surrounded by peat. In a shady site, the plants should remain in good condition for several days.*

PRUNING AND DEADHEADING

To ENCOURAGE PLANTS to grow into an attractive shape and to produce as many flowers as possible, some pruning and deadheading are required. Pruning is generally a matter of common sense: taking away dead, weak, and unsightly growths, and cutting the shrub to maintain a good visual shape. This ensures that strong healthy growth, carrying the most flowers, can develop unhindered. Some plants, such as hydrangeas and camellias, produce flowers on the previous year's growth, while others, such as rhododendrons and some of the roses, for example, flower on the new growth. This determines the time of year when you need to prune them.

Plants with long flowering seasons, such as annuals, have many more flowers if they do not spend their energy on producing seeds. Unless the seedheads are decorative, therefore, remove all the dead flowers to encourage a continuous display through the flowering period.

DEADHEADING ANNUALS

Remove dead flowers as they appear, to prolong the flowering season. Always use sharp cutting implements, such as clippers and scissors, so that scarring is kept to a minimum. This can be tedious but it certainly pays dividends.

Geraniums should be constantly deadheaded if they are to produce a display of flowers over several months. Just snap off the flower stalk at the joint.

Like these pansies, most annuals can be deadheaded with scissors. Snip off dying and dead flowers to the flower stem joint. This prevents the seedheads from forming.

PRUNING EVERGREEN SHRUBS

Like the Mexican orange (Choisya ternata) below, most evergreen shrubs require only a little pruning. After the new spring growth has hardened, prune with clippers to improve the shape and remove dead wood.

1 Encourage Mexican orange to form a well-rounded head by removing crossing growths, and cut back longer stems to just above a leaf joint.

2 Take out spindly and dead wood. The trimmed shrub still may look slightly mis-shapen but will soon grow into a bushy form. Prune after flowering.

PRUNING ROSES IN CONTAINERS

The best roses to grow in containers are low-growing, bush, hybrid tea varieties, the cluster-flowered, bush, floribunda varieties, and miniatures. These all need pruning in spring when the new flowering growths start to develop.

1 Cut out all of the dead and spindly wood from the rose bush and any of its branches that are crossing and rubbing against one another.

2 Leaving three or four buds on each stem of the bush, make a clean cut at a slight angle, immediately above a healthy-looking, outward-facing bud.

3 The pruned rose bush should form an open fan of branches to allow the new shoots to develop healthily and produce a good crop of flowers for the next season.

PROPAGATION

GROWING YOUR OWN PLANTS from scratch is extremely satisfying. There are two basic methods of producing plants. The first, sexual propagation, involves growing plants from seed, a process that can be carried out in the home without too much difficulty. Plants such as annuals and vegetables are particularly easy to raise in this way, and most will produce flowers and fruit in the first year. If you use seed you have collected yourself, it does not always come true. If you want to be absolutely sure of getting a particular plant variety, buy the seed from a reputable seed merchant.

The second method is vegetative propagation, which involves taking cuttings, layering, or dividing. This method always produces plants that are identical to the host plants. Some species are extremely easy to propagate vegetatively. They include impatiens, wandering jew, and coleus, cuttings of which root simply in water. Others, such as camellias, are much more difficult and respond better to leaf propagation. Some simple propagation techniques are shown below, but propagation is a large subject, and if you need to know about particular plants, it is best to read a book that covers the subject in more detail.

∽ DIVIDING PERENNIALS ∽

Most perennials benefit from being divided every two or three years. As their root systems expand, the centers die out, leaving healthy growth only around the edges. By dividing the roots, you can remove the dead centers, as well as increase your stock.

1 *Hardy perennials, such as hostas, can be easily propagated by division in spring. Turn the pot upside down to release the root ball. You may need to tap it out with a stick through the drainage hole if it will not come out easily.*

2 *Gently scrape away any excess potting mixture that clings around the clump of roots, taking care not to damage the main root system. Most perennials are generally pretty tough and it is difficult to do much harm when dividing them.*

3 *Where the roots seem to divide naturally, dig down with a small, sharp spade to part the clump in two. If required, you can divide it further. Plant up again immediately.*

∽ RAISING ANNUALS FROM SEED ∽

To germinate seed, all you need is a seed tray, seed starting mixture, shaded light, and a steady temperature of 64°F (18°C). Cover the seed tray with thin plastic to create humid conditions.

1 *Make shallow drills in a tray of seed starting mixture. Thinly sprinkle in seeds and cover lightly. Water and seal with thin plastic.*

2 *When the first leaf pair opens, prick the seeds out with a forked emery board. Holding by the leaves, place them ½in (1cm) apart, in pots of seed starting mixture.*

∽ TAKING CUTTINGS ∽

Tender perennials, such as geraniums, can be rooted from softwood cuttings. Semi-ripe cuttings are mostly taken from shrubs and climbers, and rooted in mid to late summer. Hardwood cuttings are taken as leafless mature shoots from shrubs and trees in autumn and winter.

1 *To take a hardwood or semi-ripe cutting, remove a firm 6-8in- (15-20cm-) shoot from the parent plant. Using a sharp pruning knife, recut the end of the cutting just below a leaf node.*

2 *Gently remove the lower leaves (and the tip if it is a semi-ripe cutting) with a sharp knife, and dip the freshly cut end in rooting hormone powder, coating about 1in (2cm) of the stem.*

3 *Insert the cutting in a pot of very well-drained, medium-rich potting mixture mixed with sand and peat. Firm well in position and, ideally, place in a cold frame or greenhouse to root.*

∽ TAKING A LEAF BUD CUTTING ∽

Taking leaf bud cuttings is a good method of propagating camellias, magnolias, and rhododendrons. It is best to take the cuttings in summer when the plants are in full growth.

1 *Cut a leaf with a leaf bud and a heel of the plant's woody stem from a section that has just been removed from the parent. Make sure that you use a sharp pruning knife to achieve a clean cut.*

2 *Dip the heel and some of the leaf base in rooting hormone powder. Insert in a prepared half sand, half peat mix. Keep moist at 64°F (18°C) until the cutting has rooted. It can take several months.*

Cuttings in Water

✄ *You can propagate some plants by placing a stem, cut just below a leaf node with the lower leaves removed, in a glass of water. Rooting is quite rapid in a light, but not sunny, position in summer. Begonias, impatiens, coleus, and wandering jew all respond well.*

PLANT LISTS

❋ *Abutilon* (ABUTILON) **10-11**
• Hardy to half-hardy, evergreen, semi-evergreen, or deciduous shrubs, perennials, and annuals
• Summer flowers
• Rich, well-drained potting mixture
• Sunny or semi-shady site
• Very floriferous container plant

❋ *Acer* (MAPLE) **5-9**
• Hardy, deciduous shrubs or trees
• Attractive foliage
• Rich, well-drained potting mixture
• Sunny or semi-shady site
• The fine-leaved varieties do not like too much sun

❋ *Adiantum* (MAIDENHAIR FERN) **3-8**
• Hardy to half-hardy, deciduous, semi-evergreen, and evergreen ferns
• Attractive foliage
• Moist, neutral to acid potting mixture
• Semi-shady site
• Remove fading fronds

❋ *Agapanthus* (AGAPANTHUS) **8-11**
• Hardy to half-hardy, clump-forming, evergreen perennials
• Clusters of blue or white, summer flowers
• Moist but well-drained potting mixture
• Sunny site
• Divide in spring

❋ *Agave* (AGAVE) **3-11**
• Half-hardy to tender, perennial succulents
• Sword-shaped, sharp-toothed leaves
• Well-drained potting mixture
• Sunny site
• Keep frost-free over winter

❋ *Ageratum* (FLOSS FLOWER) **3-11**
• Half-hardy, bushy annuals
• Clusters of feathery, summer flowers
• Rich, well-drained potting mixture
• Sunny or semi-shady site
• Deadhead regularly

❋ *Aloe* (ALOE) **9-11**
• Half-hardy to tender, evergreen, rosetted shrubs and perennials

• Succulent foliage and bell-shaped, winter or spring flowers
• Very well-drained potting mixture
• Sunny site
• Highly architectural plants

❋ *Anenome blanda* (WINDFLOWER) **3-8**
• Hardy perennials grown from tubers
• Cup-shaped, spring flowers
• Well-drained potting mixture with leafmold
• Sunny or semi-shady site
• The fragile flowers are white, blue, and pink

❋ *Anthemis* (CHAMOMILE) **4-9**
• Hardy perennials, some evergreen
• Summer flowers and fern-like foliage
• Well-drained potting mixture
• Sunny site
• The tangy-scented flowers are wonderful in pot pourri

❋ *Antirrhinum* (SNAPDRAGON) **3-11**
• Hardy to half-hardy perennials usually grown as annuals
• Spikes of spring to autumn flowers
• Rich, well-drained potting mixture
• Sunny site
• Deadhead to prolong flowering

❋ *Artemisia* (SOUTHERNWOOD) **5-9**
• Hardy, evergreen or semi-evergreen perennials and sub-shrubs
• Aromatic leaves
• Well-drained potting mixture
• Open, sunny site
• Trim back in spring

❋ *Asparagus* (ASPARAGUS) **8-11**
• Half-hardy to tender, evergreen perennials
• Fern-like foliage
• Rich, well-drained potting mixture
• Semi-shady site
• Avoid placing in direct sun

❋ *Aspidistra* (ASPIDISTRA) **8-11**
• Half-hardy evergreen perennials

• Glossy foliage
• Well-drained, acid potting mixture with leafmold
• Semi-shady or deeply shady site
• Water frequently during the growing season

❋ *Aster* (MICHAELMAS DAISY) **4-8**
• Hardy perennials
• Daisy-like, autumn flowers
• Rich, well-drained potting mixture
• Sunny or semi-shady site
• The low-growing cultivars are the best for containers

❋ *Astilbe* (ASTILBE) **5-8**
• Hardy perennials
• Plumes of feathery, summer flowers
• Rich, moist potting mixture
• Semi-shady site
• Repot infrequently as they resent disturbance

❋ *Begonia* (BEGONIA) **8-11**
• Half-hardy to tender, evergreen perennials and annuals
• Summer flowers and attractive foliage
• Rich, well-drained, preferably acid, potting mixture
• Semi-shady or shady site
• Most can be overwintered in a frost-free situation

❋ *Bellis perennis* (ENGLISH DAISY) **3-9**
• Hardy perennials grown as biennials
• Daisy-like, spring flowers
• Rich, well-drained potting mixture
• Sunny or semi-shady site
• Deadhead regularly for continuous blooms

❋ *Bergenia* (BERGENIA) **4-9**
• Hardy evergreen perennials
• Leathery leaves and purple-pink, winter to spring flowers
• Poor, well-drained potting mixture
• Sunny or shady site
• Likes cool summers

❋ *Brassica oleracea* (ORNAMENTAL CABBAGE) **3-9**
• Hardy annuals, evergreen biennials, or perennials
• Ornamental autumn and winter foliage
• Well-drained, preferably acid potting mixture
• Sunny site
• Raise from seed sown outdoors in spring

❋ *Buxus* (BOX) **5-8**
• Hardy, evergreen shrubs or trees
• Tiny foliage and neat habit

• Well-drained potting mixture
• Sunny, semi-shady, or shady site
• Excellent for clipping into architectural shapes

❋ *Calceolaria* (CALCEOLARIA) **3-9**
• Hardy to tender annuals
• Summer flowers
• Well-drained, moisture-retentive potting mixture
• Sunny or shady site
• The extraordinary flowers appear over a long period

❋ *Calendula* (MARIGOLD) **3-9**
• Hardy, bushy annuals
• Orange, cream, and yellow, spring to autumn flowers
• Any well-drained potting mixture
• Sunny site
• Deadhead to prolong flowering

❋ *Calluna* (HEATHER) **3-8**
• Hardy, evergreen shrubs
• Bell- to urn-shaped, single or double, summer to autumn flowers
• Rich, well-drained, acid potting mixture
• Open, sunny site
• Likes cool summers

❋ *Camellia* (CAMELLIA) **7-9**
• Hardy to half-hardy, evergreen shrubs and trees
• Spring flowers and glossy, green foliage
• Well-drained, neutral to acid potting mixture
• Sheltered, semi-shady site
• Propagate by leaf cuttings

❋ *Campanula* (BELLFLOWER) **3-9**
• Hardy annuals, biennials, and perennials, some evergreen
• Bell- and star-shaped, summer flowers
• Moist but well-drained potting mixture
• Sunny or shady site
• The trailing varieties flower for months

❋ *Celosia* (CELOSIA) **3-11 as annuals**
• Half-hardy, erect perennials grown as annuals
• Plumes of summer flowers
• Well-drained potting mixture
• Sheltered, sunny site
• Flowers are red, orange, pink, and salmon

❋ *Ceratostigma* (CERATOSTIGMA) **5-9**
• Hardy to half-hardy, deciduous, semi-evergreen, and evergreen shrubs

• Blue, late summer and autumn flowers, and autumn foliage
• Well-drained potting mixture
• Sunny site
• Cut out dead wood in the spring

❋ *Chamaecyparis lawsoniana* (LAWSON CYPRESS) **4-8**
• Hardy conifers with scale- or needle-like foliage
• Year-round foliage
• Well-drained potting mixture
• Sunny site
• Dwarf and low-growing varieties are best for containers

❋ *Cheiranthus cheiri* (WALLFLOWER) **5-9**
• Hardy perennials or sub-shrubs, some evergreen or semi-evergreen
• Fragrant, spring flowers
• Well-drained potting mixture
• Sunny or semi-shady site
• Plants may get weedy, but the scent is one of the best

❋ *Chlorophytum* (SPIDER PLANT) **9-11**
• Half-hardy and tender, evergreen perennials
• Glossy foliage
• Rich, well-drained potting mixture
• Any site
• Keep out of direct sun

❋ *Choisya ternata* (MEXICAN ORANGE) **9-11**
• Hardy, evergreen shrubs
• Fragrant, spring flowers and shiny foliage
• Well-drained potting mixture
• Sunny site
• Propagate by semi-ripe cuttings in late summer

❋ *Chrysanthemum* (CHRYSANTHEMUM) **3-11**
• Hardy annuals and perennials, some evergreen
• Summer to autumn flowers
• Well-drained potting mixture
• Sunny site
• All forms do well in containers

❋ *Coleus blumei* (COLEUS) **3-11 as annuals**
• Tender perennials, annuals, or evergreen sub-shrubs
• Colorful foliage
• Well-drained potting mixture
• Sunny or semi-shady site
• Remove flowers to promote bushiness and leaf color

❊ **Convallaria**
(LILY-OF-THE-VALLEY) 3-9
• Hardy perennials grown from rhizomes
• Fragrant, spring flowers
• Moist potting mixture with leafmold
• Sunny or semi-shady site
• The best-scented plant of all

❊ **Cordyline** (DRACENA) 8-11
• Hardy to half-hardy, evergreen shrubs and trees
• Strap-shaped foliage
• Rich, well-drained potting mixture
• Sunny or semi-shady site
• Hardier than generally supposed

❊ **Crocus** (CROCUS) 5-9
• Hardy perennials grown from corms
• Spring and autumn flowers
• Well-drained potting mixture
• Sunny site
• Grows well in low bowls

❊ **Cuphea ignea**
(CIGAR FLOWER) 8-11
• Half-hardy to tender, evergreen, bushy sub-shrubs
• Tubular, orange-red, summer flowers
• Rich, well-drained potting mixture
• Sunny site
• Water freely during the growing season

❊ **Cupressus** (CYPRESS) 6-9
• Hardy, evergreen shrubs and trees
• Attractive foliage and interesting form
• Any potting mixture
• Sunny site
• All have fragrant leaves

❊ **Cyclamen** (CYCLAMEN) 4-8
• Hardy to tender perennials grown from corms
• Autumn flowers
• Well-drained potting mixture with leafmold
• Sunny or semi-shady site
• Keep the corms dry after flowers and leaves die down

❊ **Cytisus** (BROOM) 6-8
• Hardy, deciduous or evergreen shrubs
• Abundant pea-like, spring flowers
• Poor, well-drained potting mixture
• Sunny site
• Transplant with care as they dislike disturbance

❊ **Dahlia** (DAHLIA)
3-11 as annuals
• Half-hardy, bushy perennials grown from tubers
• Summer and autumn flowerheads
• Well-drained potting mixture
• Sunny site
• Store tubers in dry, frost-free place over winter

❊ **Dianthus** (PINK) 3-8
• Hardy, evergreen, clump-forming perennials
• Summer flowers and attractive foliage
• Well-drained potting mixture
• Sunny site
• Choose scented varieties

❊ **Diascia** (DIASCIA) 8-10
• Hardy to half-hardy annuals and perennials, some evergreen
• Tubular, summer flowers
• Well-drained potting mixture
• Sunny site
• Likes cool summers

❊ **Dryopteris**
(MALE FERN) 5-9
• Hardy, deciduous or semi-evergreen ferns
• Shuttlecock-like crowns
• Moist potting mixture
• Semi-shady or shady site
• Remove fading fronds

❊ **Echeveria**
(ECHEVERIA) 6-11
• Tender, rosetted, perennial succulents
• Attractive foliage and summer flowers
• Very well-drained potting mixture
• Sunny site
• These succulents are well equipped to survive drought

❊ **Elaeagnus**
(ELAEAGNUS) 7-10
• Hardy, deciduous or evergreen shrubs and trees
• Attractive foliage, fruits, and fragrant, spring to autumn flowers
• Rich, well-drained potting mixture
• Evergreens in sun or shade, deciduous species in sun
• Evergreen varieties can be made into topiary specimens

❊ **Erica** (HEATHER) 4-9
• Hardy to half-hardy, evergreen, woody-stemmed shrubs
• Flowers and year-round foliage
• Poor, well-drained, acid potting mixture
• Sunny site
• Likes cool summers

❊ **Erythronium**
(DOGTOOTH VIOLET) 3-9
• Hardy perennials grown from tubers
• Pendent flowers and sometimes mottled leaves
• Well-drained potting mixture with leafmold
• Semi-shady site
• Do not allow tubers to get too hot in summer

❊ **Euonymus**
(EUONYMUS) 4-9
• Hardy, evergreen or deciduous shrubs or trees

• Foliage
• Well-drained potting mixture
• Sunny or semi-shady site
• The evergreen varieties are best for containers

❊ **Euphorbia** (SPURGE) 3-9
• Hardy shrubs, succulents, and perennials, some semi-evergreen or evergreen, and annuals
• Foliage and spring flowers
• Moist but well-drained potting mixture
• Sunny or semi-shady site
• Milky sap can irritate skin

❊ **Eustoma**
(PRAIRIE GENTIAN) 5-10
• Tender annuals and perennials
• Poppy-like, summer flowers
• Well-drained potting mixture
• Sunny site
• Purple, pink, and white flowers offset by silver foliage

❊ **Fatsia** (FATSIA) 8-10
• Hardy, evergreen shrubs
• Bold foliage
• Rich, well-drained potting mixture
• Sunny or shady site
• Propagate by semi-ripe cuttings in summer

❊ **Ficus pumila**
(CREEPING FIG) 9-11
• Tender, evergreen climbers
• Vibrant foliage
• Rich, well-drained potting mixture
• Semi-shady site
• A plant that likes growing in soggy potting mixture

❊ **Fritillaria imperialis**
(CROWN IMPERIAL) 4-9
• Hardy perennials grown from bulbs
• Pendent, mainly bell-shaped, spring flowers
• Well-drained potting mixture
• Sunny or semi-shady site
• Potting mixture must not get too dry in winter and spring

❊ **Fritillaria meleagris**
(SNAKE'S HEAD FRITILLARY) 4-9
• Hardy perennials grown from bulbs
• Pendent, bell-shaped, spring flowers
• Moisture-retentive, well-drained potting mixture
• Sunny or semi-shady site
• Allow to dry after flowering

❊ **Fuchsia** (FUCHSIA) 7-11
• Hardy to half-hardy, deciduous or evergreen shrubs, sometimes grown as annuals
• Summer and autumn flowers
• Moist but well-drained potting mixture

• Sheltered, semi-shady or shady site
• Keep half-hardy specimens out of frost in winter and cut back in late spring

❊ **Gaultheria** (CREEPING WINTERGREEN) 3-7
• Hardy, evergreen shrubs
• Attractive foliage, spring to summer flowers, and fruits
• Moist, acid potting mixture
• Semi-shady or shady site
• Likes cool summers

❊ **Gazania** (GAZANIA) 8-11
• Half-hardy perennials, often grown as annuals
• Daisy-like summer flowers
• Sandy potting mixture
• Sunny site
• Flowers open only in sun

❊ **Geranium**
(CRANESBILL) 3-8
• Half-hardy to tender perennials, some semi-evergreen
• Spring and summer flowers
• Any well-drained potting mixture
• Sunny site; some species do better in shade
• Likes cool summers

❊ **Gleditsia** (LOCUST) 5-9
• Hardy, deciduous trees
• Attractive foliage
• Rich, well-drained potting mixture
• Sunny site
• Spectacular autumn color

❊ **Gypsophila**
(BABY'S BREATH) 3-8
• Hardy annuals or perennials
• Delicate spring and summer flowers and foliage
• Well-drained potting mixture
• Sunny site
• The species that are rock plants do well in pots

❊ X **Halimiocistus**
(HALIMIOCISTUS) 8-9
• Hardy, hybrid genus of evergreen shrubs
• Saucer-shaped, summer flowers
• Well-drained potting mixture
• Sheltered, sunny site
• Plants are smothered in flowers for many weeks

❊ **Hebe** (HEBE) 7-9
• Hardy to half-hardy, evergreen shrubs
• Neat foliage and often dense spikes, panicles, or racemes of flowers
• Well-drained potting mixture
• Sunny site
• Dislikes high heat

❊ **Hedera helix** (IVY) 4-9
• Hardy, evergreen, woody-stemmed, trailing perennials or self-clinging climbers

• Lush foliage and habit
• Well-drained, alkaline potting mixture
• Any site is suitable
• A useful evergreen trailer to plant at the front of containers

❊ **Helichrysum**
(HELICHRYSUM) 5-10
• Hardy to tender annuals, perennials, or evergreen sub-shrubs and shrubs
• Summer and autumn flowers and silvery foliage
• Well-drained potting mixture
• Sunny site
• Needs plenty of sun in summer

❊ **Heliotropium**
(HELIOTROPE) 5-10
• Hardy to tender annuals
• Fragrant, summer flowers
• Rich, well-drained potting mixture
• Sunny site
• Grow for its cherry-scented perfume

❊ **Helleborus**
(HELLEBORE) 3-8
• Hardy perennials, some evergreen
• Winter and spring flowers
• Well-drained, moisture-retentive potting mixture
• Semi-shady site
• Exceedingly beautiful flowers and decorative foliage

❊ **Heuchera** (HEUCHERA) 3-9
• Hardy, evergreen perennials
• Attractive foliage and red, pink, and white flowers
• Moist but well-drained potting mixture
• Sunny or semi-shady site
• Bronze or purple foliage

❊ **Hosta** (HOSTA) 4-9
• Hardy perennials
• Decorative foliage and spires of summer flowers
• Moist but well-drained potting mixture
• Semi-shady or shady site
• Some varieties have fragrant flowers

❊ **Houttuynia**
(HOUTTUYNIA) 5-8
• Hardy, deciduous perennials grown from rhizomes
• Aromatic leaves
• Moist potting mixture
• Semi-shady site
• Striking, colorful foliage

❊ **Hyacinthus**
(HYACINTH) 6-8
• Hardy perennials grown from bulbs
• Dense spikes of fragrant, tubular, spring flowers
• Well-drained potting mixture
• Sunny or semi-shady site
• Bring planted bowls in to perfume the house in spring

❋ *Hydrangea*
(HYDRANGEA) 3-9
• Hardy, deciduous shrubs or evergreen climbers
• Showy, summer flowers
• Rich, moist but well-drained potting mixture
• Sunny or semi-shady site
• Ideal plants for container culture

❋ *Ilex* (HOLLY) 4-9
• Hardy, deciduous or evergreen trees and shrubs
• Shiny foliage, and fruits
• Well-drained potting mixture
• Sunny or shady site
• Slow growing but can be trained as a topiary plant

❋ *Impatiens* (IMPATIENS) 3-11 as annuals
• Tender annuals and mainly evergreen perennials or sub-shrubs
• Summer flowers
• Moist but well-drained potting mixture
• Any site
• Long flowering season

❋ *Juniperus* (JUNIPER) 3-9
• Hardy conifers with scale- or needle-like foliage
• Year-round foliage, and berries
• Well-drained potting mixture
• Sunny site
• Will put up with extreme conditions

❋ *Kalanchoe*
(KALANCHOE) 8-11
• Tender, perennial succulents or shrubs
• Fleshy leaves and bell- or tubular-shaped, spring flowers
• Well-drained potting mixture
• Sunny or semi-shady site
• Keep frost free and on the dry side throughout winter

❋ *Lantana* (LANTANA) 8-11
• Tender, evergreen perennials, or shrubs or annuals
• Spring to autumn flowers
• Well-drained potting mixture
• Sunny or semi-shady site
• Prune out growing tips to promote bushy growth. Water freely during growing season

❋ *Laurus* (BAY) 8-11
• Hardy, evergreen trees
• Aromatic foliage
• Rich, well-drained potting mixture
• Sunny or semi-shady site
• Keep in sheltered position; water occasionally in winter

❋ *Lavandula* (LAVENDER) 6-9
• Hardy to half-hardy, evergreen shrubs
• Aromatic, gray-green leaves and summer flowers

• Rich, well-drained potting mixture
• Sunny site
• In milder areas, try the *Lavandula lanata*

❋ *Leucothoe*
(LEUCOTHOE) 5-8
• Hardy, evergreen, semi-evergreen, or deciduous shrubs
• White, spring to summer flowers and attractive foliage
• Moist but well-drained, acid potting mixture
• Semi-shady or shady site
• Some new varieties have multi-colored leaves

❋ *Lewisia* (LEWISIA) 4-7
• Hardy to half-hardy perennials, some evergreen
• Summer flowers and rosettes of succulent leaves
• Well-drained potting mixture
• Sunny or semi-shady site
• Likes cool summers

❋ *Ligustrum* (PRIVET) 4-9
• Hardy, deciduous, semi-evergreen, or evergreen shrubs and trees
• Glossy leaves
• Well-drained potting mixture
• Sunny or semi-shady site
• Handsome container plants

❋ *Lilium* (LILY) 4-9
• Hardy perennials grown from bulbs
• Summer flowers
• Well-drained potting mixture
• Semi-shady site
• Regale lilies are the easiest to grow

❋ *Lithodora*
(LITHODORA) 6-8
• Hardy, evergreen sub-shrubs or shrubs
• Spring to summer flowers
• Moist but well-drained, lime-free potting mixture
• Sunny or semi-shady site
• Intense blue flowers

❋ *Lobelia* (LOBELIA) 4-9
• Hardy to tender annuals, perennials, or deciduous or evergreen shrubs
• Spring to summer flowers
• Moist but well-drained potting mixture
• Sunny or semi-shady site
• Do not allow annuals to become too dry in summer

❋ *Lobularia* (ALYSSUM) 3-11
• Hardy annuals
• Tiny, summer and early autumn flowers
• Well-drained potting mixture
• Sunny site
• Deadhead regularly

❋ *Lonicera*
(HONEYSUCKLE) 3-11
• Hardy to tender, deciduous,

semi-evergreen, or evergreen shrubs and climbers
• Fragrant, summer flowers
• Any rich, well-drained potting mixture
• Sunny or shady site
• Grow climbers up trellis from large pot

❋ *Lotus berthelotii*
(WINGED PEA) 9-11
• Tender perennials, some semi-evergreen
• Silver foliage and summer flowers
• Well-drained potting mixture
• Sunny site
• A trailing plant, ideal for hanging baskets

❋ *Mimulus*
(MONKEY FLOWER) 4-8
• Hardy to half-hardy annuals and perennials
• Snapdragon-like, summer flowers
• Moist potting mixture
• Sunny site
• Does not like heat

❋ *Muscari*
(GRAPE HYACINTH) 5-8
• Hardy perennials grown from bulbs
• Spikes of small flowers
• Well-drained potting mixture
• Any site
• The blue or white flowers are buttery scented

❋ *Myosotis*
(FORGET-ME-NOT) 3-8
• Hardy annuals, biennials, or perennials
• Spring flowers
• Rich, well-drained potting mixture
• Sunny or semi-shady site
• Blue flowers fade to pink

❋ *Nandina domestica*
(SACRED BAMBOO) 7-10
• Hardy, evergreen or semi-evergreen shrubs
• Attractive foliage
• Rich, well-drained potting mixture
• Sunny site
• Young foliage is purple-red in autumn

❋ *Narcissus* (DAFFODIL) 5-9
• Hardy perennials grown from bulbs
• Spring flowers
• Well-drained potting mixture
• Sunny or semi-shady site
• Numerous varieties, mostly yellows and whites

❋ *Nerine* (NERINE) 6-9
• Hardy to half-hardy perennials grown from bulbs
• Waxy, pink, autumn flowers
• Light, sandy potting mixture
• Sunny site
• Roots dislike disturbance

❋ *Nicotiana* (FLOWERING TOBACCO PLANT) 4-11
• Hardy to tender annuals, and perennials grown as annuals
• Long-lasting, mostly scented flowers
• Rich, well-drained potting mixture
• Semi-shady or shady site
• Some varieties are more fragrant than others

❋ *Nymphaea pygmaea*
(WATER LILY) 4-11
• Hardy to tender, deciduous, perennial, floating aquatics
• Glossy leaves and striking, summer flowers
• Sunny site
• Remove fading foliage to prevent it polluting the water

❋ *Papaver* (POPPY) 3-10
• Hardy annuals, biennials, and perennials, some evergreen
• Colorful, summer flowers
• Moist, well-drained potting mixture
• Sunny or semi-shady site
• Alpine varieties do very well in sink gardens

❋ *Pelargonium* (GERANIUM) 3-11 as annuals
• Tender perennials, mostly evergreen, often cultivated as annuals
• Summer flowers and attractive leaves, sometimes scented
• Well-drained potting mixture
• Sunny site
• Take softwood cuttings in late summer

❋ *Pentas lanceolata*
(PENTAS) 9-11
• Tender, evergreen perennials and shrubs
• Summer flowers
• Rich, well-drained potting mixture
• Sunny or semi-shady site
• Some varieties have white and pink flowers

❋ *Pernettya*
(PERNETTYA) 7-9
• Hardy, evergreen shrubs
• Showy, long-lasting, autumn fruits
• Moist but well-drained, acid potting mixture
• Sunny or semi-shady site
• Most varieties require male and female plants to produce berries

❋ *Petunia* (PETUNIA) 3-11 as annuals
• Tender, bushy perennials grown as annuals
• Summer to autumn flowers
• Well-drained potting mixture
• Sheltered, sunny or semi-shady site
• Some varieties are sweetly scented

❋ *Phormium*
(NEW ZEALAND FLAX) 7-9
• Hardy, evergreen perennials
• Bold, sword-shaped leaves
• Moist but well-drained potting mixture
• Sunny or semi-shady site
• Likes cool summers

❋ *Phyllostachys nigra*
(BLACK BAMBOO) 5-9
• Hardy, evergreen, clump-forming bamboo
• Attractive stems and leaves
• Well-drained potting mixture
• Sunny or semi-shady site
• The canes turn black in their second year

❋ *Picea* (SPRUCE) 3-8
• Hardy conifers with scale- or needle-like foliage
• Year-round foliage
• Well-drained potting mixture
• Sunny site
• Many species with blue, silver, or gold foliage

❋ *Pieris* (ANDROMEDA) 5-9
• Hardy, evergreen shrubs
• Colorful foliage and small, urn-shaped, spring flowers
• Moist, acid potting mixture
• Sheltered, semi-shady site
• New foliage is pink in spring

❋ *Pinus* (PINE) 4-10
• Hardy conifers with scale- or needle-like foliage
• Year-round foliage
• Well-drained potting mixture
• Sunny site
• Several species are ideal for exposed sites, tolerating wind and cold

❋ *Plecostachys*
(PLECOSTACHYS) 9-11
• Half-hardy, evergreen sub-shrub
• Attractive silver foliage
• Well-drained potting mixture
• Sunny site
• Useful trailing foliage plant for the front of containers

❋ *Plectranthus*
(PLECTRANTHUS) 9-11
• Tender, evergreen, trailing or bushy perennials
• Attractive foliage
• Moist potting mixture
• Sunny or semi-shady site
• Cut back tips in the growing season to prevent straggly growth

❋ *Plumbago*
(PLUMBAGO) 5-11
• Half-hardy to tender annuals, evergreen or semi-evergreen shrubs, perennials, or woody-stemmed, scrambling climbers
• Primrose-shaped, summer flowers, some scented

• Well-drained potting mixture
• Sunny site
• Tie stems to supports and thin out previous year's growth in spring

✻ *Polygonatum x hybridum* (SOLOMON'S SEAL) 3-9
• Hardy perennials grown from rhizomes
• Spring or early summer flowers
• Rich, well-drained potting mixture
• Semi-shady or shady site
• Propagate by division in early spring

✻ *Polygonum* (KNOTWEED) 4-9
• Hardy annuals, perennials, some evergreen, and deciduous climbers
• Spikes of summer flowers
• Moist but well-drained potting mixture
• Sunny or shady site
• The leaves turn bronze in autumn and winter

✻ *Polypodium* (COMMON POLYPODY) 5-8
• Hardy, deciduous, semi-evergreen, or evergreen ferns
• Sculptural fronds
• Moist but well-drained potting mixture with leafmold
• Semi-shady site
• Decorative and easy to cultivate

✻ *Portulaca* (PORTULACA) 3-11
• Half-hardy, fleshy annuals and perennials
• Colorful, summer flowers
• Well-drained potting mixture
• Sunny or semi-shady site
• Flowers open only when the sun is out

✻ *Potentilla* (POTENTILLA) 3-7
• Hardy perennials and deciduous shrubs
• Saucer-shaped, summer flowers
• Well-drained potting mixture
• Sunny site
• Profuse yellow, orange, pink, and white flowers over a long period

✻ *Primula* (PRIMULA) 3-8
• Hardy to tender annuals, biennials, or perennials, some evergreen
• Attractive, spring flowers, produced in large umbels on stout stems
• Well-drained potting mixture
• Sunny or semi-shady site
• Likes cool summers

✻ *Pulsatilla vulgaris* (PASQUE FLOWER) 5-8
• Hardy perennials, some evergreen

• Upright or pendent, bell- or cup-shaped, spring flowers
• Well-drained potting mixture with leafmold
• Sunny site
• Likes cool summers

✻ *Ranunculus asiaticus* (PERSIAN BUTTERCUP) 7-9
• Hardy to half-hardy perennials grown from tubers
• Late spring flowers
• Moist but well-drained potting mixture
• Sunny or semi-shady site
• Dislikes heat

✻ *Rhododendron* (AZALEA/RHODODENDRON) 3-9
• Hardy, evergreen, semi-evergreen, or deciduous shrubs
• Showy, spring flowers, and sometimes, autumn foliage
• Rich, well-drained, acid potting mixture with leafmold
• Semi-shady or shady site
• All but the largest species do well in containers

✻ *Rosa* (ROSE) 4-9
• Hardy, deciduous or semi-evergreen shrubs and climbers
• Fragrant flowers and autumn rosehips
• Rich, moist but well-drained potting mixture
• Sunny site
• Lower-growing varieties are best for containers

✻ *Rosmarinus* (ROSEMARY) 7-11
• Hardy evergreen shrubs
• Aromatic foliage and spring flowers
• Well-drained potting mixture
• Sunny site
• Place pots where you can brush against the foliage to release the fragrance

✻ *Salvia* (SAGE) 3-11
• Hardy to tender annuals, biennials, perennials, or evergreen or semi-evergreen shrubs or sub-shrubs
• Colored foliage and spikes of summer to autumn flowers
• Well-drained potting mixture
• Sunny site
• Heat tolerant

✻ *Santolina* (SANTOLINA) 7-9
• Hardy, evergreen shrubs
• Aromatic, silver foliage and yellow, summer flowers
• Well-drained potting mixture
• Sunny site
• Good species for providing year-round interest

✻ *Saxifraga paniculata* AND *S. longifolia* (SAXIFRAGE) 6-8
• Hardy to half-hardy perennials, mostly evergreen or semi-evergreen

• Rosette form and spring to summer flowers
• Well-drained, alkaline potting mixture
• Sunny site
• Likes cool summers

✻ *Scabiosa* (SCABIOUS) 3-10
• Hardy annuals and perennials, some evergreen
• Pincushion-like, summer flowers
• Rich, well-drained, alkaline potting mixture
• Sunny site
• Some species are scented

✻ *Scilla* (SQUILL) 6-8
• Hardy to half-hardy perennials grown from bulbs
• Spikes of small, often blue, spring flowers
• Well-drained potting mixture
• Sunny or semi-shady site
• Bring pots inside to flower

✻ *Sedum* (STONECROP) 3-11
• Hardy to tender, often fleshy or succulent annuals, evergreen biennials, or mostly evergreen perennials
• Attractive foliage and summer to autumn flowers
• Well-drained potting mixture
• Sunny site
• Needs only a little potting mixture in which to grow

✻ *Sempervivum* (HOUSELEEK) 5-8
• Hardy, spreading, evergreen perennials
• Rosettes of fleshy leaves and summer flowers
• Well-drained potting mixture with fine gravel
• Sunny site
• Needs only a little potting mixture in which to grow

✻ *Senecio* (SENECIO) 4-9
• Hardy to tender annuals, succulent or non-succulent perennials, or evergreen shrubs and sub-shrubs
• Attractive foliage and, usually, daisy-like, spring to autumn flowers
• Well-drained potting mixture
• Sunny or semi-shady site
• A silver-leaved species

✻ *Skimmia* (SKIMMIA) 6-10
• Hardy, evergreen shrubs or trees
• Spring flowers, aromatic foliage, and colorful autumn fruits
• Moisture-retentive potting mixture
• Semi-shady or shady site
• Grow near the house to appreciate their sweet-scented flowers

✻ *Solanum capsicastrum* (WINTER CHERRY) 9-11
• Hardy to tender, evergreen sub-shrubs

• Glossy foliage and ornamental, winter fruits
• Well-drained potting mixture
• Sunny site
• Valuable as a winter-interest plant

✻ *Tagetes* (MARIGOLD) 3-11
• Half-hardy annuals
• Bright summer to autumn flowers
• Well-drained potting mixture
• Sunny site
• These useful flowers bloom over a long period

✻ *Taxus* (YEW) 5-8
• Hardy conifers with scale- or needle-like foliage
• Year-round, ornamental foliage
• Well-drained potting mixture
• Any site
• The decorative berries are poisonous

✻ *Thuja* (ARBORVITAE) 4-8
• Hardy conifers with scale- or needle-like foliage
• All-year ornamental foliage
• Well-drained potting mixture
• Any site
• Leaves have a fruity scent

✻ *Thunbergia alata* (BLACK-EYED SUSAN) 4-11 as annuals
• Half-hardy to tender, fast-growing, annual climbers
• Small, orange-yellow, summer flowers
• Rich, well-drained potting mixture
• Sunny or semi-shady site
• Plant out late to avoid frost

✻ *Thymus* (THYME) 5-8
• Hardy to half-hardy, evergreen shrubs and sub-shrubs
• Aromatic foliage
• Moist but well-drained potting mixture
• Sunny site
• Grow near the kitchen

✻ *Tolmiea* (PIGGY-BACK PLANT) 7-9
• Hardy perennials that are sometimes semi-evergreen
• Attractive foliage
• Well-drained, neutral to acid potting mixture
• Semi-shady or shady site
• Propagate by removing plantlets

✻ *Tradescantia* (WANDERING JEW) 3-11 as annuals
• Hardy to tender perennials, some evergreen
• Trailing habit and decorative foliage
• Rich, well-drained potting mixture
• Sunny or semi-shady site
• House plants that do well outside in summer

✻ *Tropaeolum majus* (NASTURTIUM) 3-11 as annuals
• Hardy to tender annuals, perennials, or climbers
• Bright, summer flowers
• Well-drained potting mixture
• Sunny site
• Aphids can be problem

✻ *Tulipa* (TULIP) 5-8
• Hardy perennials grown from bulbs
• Colorful, spring flowers
• Well-drained, preferably alkaline, potting mixture
• Sunny or semi-shady site
• Available in a wide range of size, colors, and forms

✻ *Verbena* (VERBENA) 3-11
• Hardy to tender perennials, and biennials grown as annuals
• Colorful, summer flowers
• Well-drained potting mixture
• Sunny or semi-shady site
• Some have scented flowers

✻ *Vinca* (PERIWINKLE) 4-11
• Hardy, evergreen, trailing sub-shrubs or perennials
• Decorative foliage and intermittent spring to autumn flowers
• Well-drained potting mixture
• Any site
• Flowers more in sunny sites

✻ *Viola* (PANSY) 4-10
• Hardy to half-hardy annuals, and perennials, some semi-evergreen
• Different varieties flower all year
• Well-drained, moisture-retentive potting mixture
• Any site
• Likes cool summers

✻ *Weigela* (WEIGELA) 4-8
• Hardy, deciduous shrubs
• Showy, spring to summer flowers and attractive foliage
• Rich potting mixture
• Sunny site
• Colored and variegated varieties are available

✻ *Yucca* (YUCCA) 4-11
• Hardy to tender, evergreen shrubs or trees
• Bold, sword-shaped leaves and showy panicles of summer flowers
• Well-drained potting mixture
• Sunny or semi-shady site
• Hardier than is supposed

✻ *Zinnia* (ZINNIA) 3-11 as annuals
• Half-hardy annuals
• Large, dahlia-like, summer flowers
• Rich, well-drained potting mixture
• Sunny site
• Striped- and splashed-flowered varieties available

INDEX

ACKNOWLEDGMENTS

The author would like to thank the following people for their help on *Container Gardening*: Charlotte Fraser, whose horticultural help throughout the book was invaluable; Jenny and Richard Raworth, Mrs. P. Franklin and Sarah Franklin, Anne Mollo, Kathleen Darby, Mr and Mrs D. Zelouf, and Mrs. B. Hervey for allowing us to photograph in their gardens; Ken Vincent of Terracotta UK of Covent Garden, who was so generous in supplying many containers; Sally Tamplin for the loan of her beautiful wire plant stand; The Garden History Museum and The Chelsea Physic Garden for the loan of their old garden tools; and Brinkman Brothers for supplying trees.

Also Quentin Roake for all his support and assistance; and especially Stephen Bennington, May Cristea, Veronica Hitchcock, Alex Starkey, and Roddy Wood; Sally Smallwood, who art directed the book until the arrival of baby Joe; and Project Editor, Mary-Clare Jerram, and Art Editor, Kevin Ryan, for being such an understanding team.

Dorling Kindersley would like to thank Hilary and Richard Bird, Damien Moore, Gillian Prince, and Betty Mackey for editorial help; Kevin Williams for design help; Steve Dobson and Greg Matanle for photographic help; and Patty Leasure of Simon and Schuster for her patience and efficiency.

All photographs by Matthew Ward, except: A.G.E. Fotostock 7; L'Ami des Jardins/J.F. Jarreau 169; Boys Syndication/Jacqui Hurst 33, 92, 107, 123, 135, 144 (bottom); Eric Crichton 85, 87 (top), 93; Geoff Dann 22-3, 24-5; English Flower Garden/John Murray 6; Fisons plc 176, 177; Garden Picture Library/Brian Carter 69, 74, 118; Garden Picture Library/Derek Fell 110 (top); Garden Picture Library/John Neubauer 130; Garden Picture Library/Ron Sutherland 11, 106, 149 (bottom), 166; Garden Picture Library/Steve Wooster 143; Derek Harris 9, 10 (top and bottom), 140; Jacqui Hurst 61, 84, 124-5, 127, 131, 132-3, 148, 150, 151;

ICI Agrochemicals 176, 177; Insight/Linda Burgess 8, 14, 32, 134, 142, 146-7; Graham Kirk 50, 67 (top), 164-5, 166; Steve Robson 139, 149 (top); Shell U.K. 176; Harry Smith 76, 177; Michael Warren 177; and Steve Wooster 115.

SOURCE LIST

W. ATLEE BURPEE & CO.
21774 Burpee Building, Warminster, PA 18974

BLUESTONE PERENNIALS, INC.
7211 Middle Rd, Madison, OH 44057

PARK SEED CO.
Cokesbury Rd, Greenwood, SC 29647-0001

SMITH & HAWKIN
25 Corte Madera, Mill Valley, CA 94941

VAN BOURGONDIEN BROS.
Box A, Babylon, NY 11702

WHITE FLOWER FARM
Route 63, Litchfield, CT 06759

THE KINSMAN CO.
River Rd, Dept. 530, Point Pleasant, PA 19590

PLANTS OF THE SOUTHWEST
1812 Second St., Santa Fe, NM 87501

THOMPSON & MORGAN, INC.
Box 1308, Jackson, NJ 08527

HARDINESS ZONES

of the United States and Canada

HAWAII

10

11

ALASKA

1

2

3

4

7

1

2

2

3

3

4

5

6

8

7

5

6

9

8

5

6

9

8

11

9

8

6

7

6

5

4